Yeats and Anglo-Irish Literature

LIVERPOOL ENGLISH TEXTS AND STUDIES

GENERAL EDITOR: KENNETH MUIR

Titles in this Series

Yeats and Anglo-Irish Literature

Critical Essays by Peter Ure

EDITED BY C. J. RAWSON
*Professor of English in the
University of Warwick*

WITH A MEMOIR BY
FRANK KERMODE

LIVERPOOL UNIVERSITY PRESS

1974

Published by
LIVERPOOL UNIVERSITY PRESS
123 Grove Street, Liverpool L7 7AF

Copyright © 1974 Liverpool University Press

Printed in Great Britain by
William Clowes & Sons, Limited
London, Beccles and Colchester

ISBN 0 85323 322 5

First published 1974

Preface

This book consists of essays and lectures, published and un-published, which Peter Ure wrote, in the last twenty years or so of his life, on Yeats and on related topics.* All were written after *Towards a Mythology* (1946), his first book, and one of the first few serious studies of Yeats in book form after the poet's death. (It still reads well, not only looking forward to later studies by Ure himself and by others, but offering in its own right illuminations that still remain vivid and fresh.)

The essays vary in character. Some, like the early 'W. B. Yeats and the growth of a poet's mind' and 'W. B. Yeats and the Irish theme', or the masterly late essay on 'The plays' (1965), stand as central, synoptic statements, which may be thought of as 'introductory' in a high sense of that term. Others are more specialized, discussing in detail particular works or particular facets of Yeats. None, however, is outside the range of the interested non-specialist reader. Equally, there is none from which a professional student of literature, or (I believe) a special-ist student of Yeats, will not derive insight and stimulus. Some of the earlier material especially will sometimes seem familiar. Inevitably, elements have been absorbed into or overtaken by subsequent scholarship (most notably, perhaps in the early general essays and in the note on 'The Statues'). But all the pieces seem to me notable for the vigour and subtlety of Ure's perceptions, for the richness of his commitment to the subject, and for that passionate yet sardonic eloquence of which he was master. And even those early pieces which in one sense might seem most dated stand not only as powerful and right for their time, but as interesting and often memorable critical statements by one of Yeats's most distinguished students.

I have made some corrections, almost exclusively of small errors and oversights. With one or two tiny special exceptions,

---

* Of the latter, Conrad falls outside the scope of this book's title, but the essay on Conrad is a good one, and clearly related to various interests and aspects of Ure's writings on Yeats and on Anglo-Irish writers. It seemed right, therefore, to include it in this volume.

I have not sought to indicate places where, in this or that detail, a passage has been overtaken by later scholarly discussion. Part of the reason is that I am not adequately equipped. But I have also thought it right to let the date of an essay speak for itself on such points. My editorial interference with what Ure wrote has therefore been kept to the minimum.

Among Ure's published articles and essays, I have omitted everything which was formally incorporated in his two later books on Yeats, *Yeats the Playwright* and the short introductory book in the Writers and Critics series (both 1963). This is not to say that what I do print does not share some themes and pre-occupations with these volumes; but the relationship is one which reflects the wholeness and coherence of Ure's thinking, and not (I hope) mere duplication.

Among unpublished papers (deposited in the School of English, University of Newcastle upon Tyne), those which I have omitted are:

1. An attractive short lecture of 1948 on 'The search for a myth in modern English literature', too sketchy and provisional for publication (for which it hardly seems to have been intended).

2. A short lecture of 1954 on Yeats's interest in the supernatural.

3. Material used in a lecture of *c.* 1957, partly concerned with the critical approaches of F. A. C. Wilson and Frank Kermode to 'Byzantium'.

4. A lecture on 'Yeats and the long poem' delivered at the Fifth International Conference of University Professors of English at Edinburgh, 1962. Ure declined an invitation to print this lecture in the proceedings of the Conference, *English Studies Today*, Third Series (ed. G. I. Duthie, 1964), perhaps because of some overlap with other writings, particularly his Writers and Critics *Yeats*, 1963. A summary is printed in the *Report* of the Conference, pp. 18–19.

5. A lecture, partly in note form, on the poetical career of Yeats, delivered in celebration of the centenary of Yeats's birth, 1965, for the University of Liverpool's Department of Adult Education and Extramural studies.

These pieces all contain some acute analysis and many eloquent formulations. They also contain good examples of Ure's vivid, sardonic wit. Thus, at the end of the paper of 1948 on

'The search for a myth in modern English literature', there is a
witty outburst about 'the many poets, imitators of Eliot, Pound,
and Joyce, who seek to make their fancies significant and rich
by again dismembering Orpheus or Adonis', which may be
compared with the jibe at bad critics twenty years later, at the
end of the lecture on 'W. B. Yeats and the musical instruments'
(p. 149).

All Peter Ure's writings contain such things. His work as a
prolific reviewer of scholarly books is particularly full of witty
and pertinent commentary on the doings of the learned. A
review of a collection of essays on *Myth and Literature*, 1966
(after remarking incidentally on a contribution by Northrop
Frye 'written very much in his best Moses-just-down-from-the-
Mountain style'), concludes:

Huge as this collection of papers is . . . it scarcely has the right to the
all-inclusive title which its editor has chosen for it; and readers may
judge whereabouts to place it on their shelves by being informed that
it has no pictures in it and very few jokes.

Reviewing, perhaps at about the same time, Kathleen Raine's
Defending Ancient Springs, 1967, Ure notes Miss Raine's 'naïve
view of the social role of the arts, and perhaps [her lack of] real
interest in it':

To transform Glasgow (see p. 164) you need something which is much
harder to get and more complicated, more civilly and artistically
human, than an image of perfection (indeed, there are several of those
in the Art Gallery).

The high-spirited sarcasm, however, modulates quickly and
characteristically to a personally felt seriousness and urgency:
'In dismal and exacting contexts of that sort, in which so many
of us live, Miss Raine's aesthetic has the power to do a lot of
harm.' At the same time the review, though severe, never
allows itself the easy pleasure of mere derision, and pays handsome and conscientious tribute to parts of the book, and 'the
passion and rectitude of its allegiances'.

It has not been possible, in the nature of the material, formally
to include in this collection examples of Ure's reviewing. He
was one of the best scholarly reviewers in the business, learned,
perceptive, and passionate. His severities were never cheap, and

his enthusiasms were always generous and intelligent. He did not regard reviewing as a vehicle for the expression of his own personality or prejudices (strong and lively as both these were). Whether or not he liked a book, he entered into it with a profoundly conscientious sense of his obligations to the book's author, and to its readers. Every book was approached with a real effort of sympathy, and discussed with the live and genuine engagement which many scholars reserve only for their own primary works, and which some scholars never show at all.

I will quote two passages here. The first is extracted from a review of *In Excited Reverie* (ed. Jeffares and Cross, 1965), in which (as in the smaller passage about Miss Raine) a sharp and delightful humour exists side by side with vividly engaged and highly acute commentary:

Most symposia are packed with articles of roughly the same size and quality, like boxes of standard eggs. Professor Jeffares and Professor Cross have devised a box which more resembles those displays of Easter eggs in shop-windows; one or two very large and splendid specimens dominating clutches of smaller ones. The Humpty-Dumpty of this collection, very finely cravatted, is Dr C. C. O'Brien's already famous piece on Yeats's politics . . .

Dr O'Brien's long, disturbing and engrossing essay . . . is written, as he says, by 'an aboriginal'. It is this, rather than any new facts or documentation, that gives it its value. Two things especially—Yeats's allegiance to the Anglo-Irish caste or class, and his siding with the Free State in 1921—are here looked at for the first time fully in print from what may be called Dr O'Brien's side of the fence, from something approximating to the postulates of what has become the Gaelic-Catholic establishment. There are several summings-up in the course of the essay, but this one is the most important:

[Yeats] defended the liberty of the artist, consistently. In politics, true to his duality, he defended the liberty of Ireland against English domination, and the liberty of his own caste—and sometimes, by extension, of others—against clerical domination. Often these liberties overlapped, and the cause of artist and aristocrat became the same; often his resistance to 'clerical' authoritarianism (his position on the Lock-out, on divorce, on censorship) makes him appear a liberal. But his objection to clerical authoritarianism is not the liberal's objection to *all* authoritarianism. On the contrary he favours 'a despotism of the educated classes' and in the search for this, is drawn towards Fascism (p. 263).

Much of this it would be hard to gainsay, though Dr O'Brien can't help his animus showing on occasion, particularly in his treatment of John O'Leary, of the Parnell funeral poem of 1891, of the failure to publish 'Easter 1916' at the time it was written, and of Kevin O'Higgins's funeral. But if there is any actual injustice to Yeats, as distinct from a marked unwillingness to give him the benefit of any doubts that may be going, it is located in the way the impression is given that the poet came out against censorship only in defence of the privileges of his own caste. His many attempts to protect literature from clerical and populist interference were steadfast and adroit and to my mind they are here greatly under-played (for a different handling of this topic, see, for example, Marion Witt's article in *College English* for 1952). It could be argued, though, that the defence of the freedom of literature is, in one sense, a different story from the one that Dr O'Brien is telling. Yeats's case for this freedom, as set out in his writings, and the varying crises which called forth those writings, form a long and complex record in which 'nationality', nationalism, and poetics are intertwined, and which is certainly not to be accounted for solely in terms of those 'defence of caste' explanations favoured by Dr O'Brien; these look a good deal more plausible and relevant when they are applied to what is (in this context) the relatively simpler matter of divorce. For, in another sense, to defend literature in the circumstances in which Yeats defended it *was* a political activity. An account of Yeats's *political* life which almost disregards those actions in which poet and politician are admittedly hardest to disjoin can be regarded as something less than complete. On Yeats's Fascism in the 1930's—publicly a flirtation, in private rather more of a commitment—the essay presents nothing that has not long been known to readers of *On the Boiler* and the Letters. It is possibly a little ungenerous of Dr O'Brien not to recognize more explicitly than he appears to that the Protestant Anglo-Irish minority, for which Yeats sometimes consciously spoke, did, even as a 'caste', have some claims for special consideration from Gaelic-Catholic Ireland. After all, rhetorical flourishes apart, they were the people of Swift and Parnell. And, for a caste, some of them seem to have educated themselves into the compassion that politicians of all parties often lacked. One notes that the couple of pages that Dr O'Brien devotes to pointing up the atrociousness of the Free State government and the implacability of Yeats consists of quotations from—Lady Gregory.

My second extract is from a long review of Torchiana's *W. B. Yeats and Georgian Ireland* (1966), a considerable work of scholarship for which Ure expressed real admiration. In this extract, where he is voicing some misgivings, the discussion extends (without departing) from the book under review, making substantive and central points about Yeats and the Anglo-Irish Myth, as well as important general points about the responsibilities of scholarship when investigating such 'myths' and the authors who live by them:

Ireland is a part of what some geographers still term the British Islands; modern Irish patriotism, in its evocation of the past, often tends to forget that the ruling classes in Ireland treated their dependents no worse than they sometimes treat the English counterparts of the Irish peasant: what are now envisioned as the peculiar mysteries of foreign oppression were often simply examples of the general callousness of the rich and privileged to the poor and socially inferior. Ireland is not the only country to have been left scarred and battered by the furious greed of an exploiting class: indeed, it could be argued that to this day industrial England carries from its past into its future altogether more severe signs of weakness and of woe. Similarly, Mr Torchiana sometimes seems to take for something peculiarly Irish or Anglo-Irish what is really simply British eighteenth-century architecture or behaviour. When he quotes Elizabeth Bowen (pp. 100–1) on the Georgian country house, on the space and the impersonal nobility and all the social connotations flowing from these, he might be describing country houses in Northumberland or Nottinghamshire which can be seen any day. No doubt when the Northumberlander groaned under his oppressors he did so without the comforting reflection that he was groaning as an oppressed patriot; but he groaned just the same. Summerson has remarked, apropos of the greatest of the Irish eighteenth-century artefacts: 'Irish Palladianism is as intimately joined to the London school as if the Irish sea were no greater an affair to negotiate than a couple of English counties.'

Despite his frequent trips to Liverpool, the city that Hawthorne discovered, England as a social and historical entity seems scarcely to have existed in Yeats's imagination; England was selected aspects of a few carefully selected writers and bits here and there of the London/Oxford literary world. Through sheer ignorance, or a kind of sentimentality, he often mistook for something specially Anglo-Irish what was really common British, of the eighteenth or some other century. The values and insights that Yeats discovered in Berkeley and the others became attached to a mystical Anglo-Irishry and this exalted and distinguished them in his mind from their contemporaries over the water. But what real substance is there in these mysterious 'Irish' qualities, such as 'solitude', that Swift had and that Pope hadn't, that Burke had and that Gibbon hadn't? Yeats, of course, hardly bothered with Pope or Gibbon —they weren't Irishmen and so couldn't be used to establish the myth.

To my mind, Mr Torchiana does not help one quite enough to distinguish between what was useful to the myth and what is historically true. Perhaps only a historian could have done so, but he is himself insufficiently sceptical about the myth; one cannot, for instance, feel very light-hearted about agreeing (p. 277) that 'despite his distortion of the historical Goldsmith, the éclat and excitement that ensue in Yeats's use of the man seem worth the damage to history'. Is the best poem in the world, let alone éclat, worth damaging history for? It is not so easy to use meaningfully the terms Irish or Anglo-Irish as their recurrence in embittered controversy (including some of Yeats's writings), and in the scholarly pages of this book, implies. Both the patriot and the mythopoeic poet are entitled to their simplicities; the scholar is not, except in so far as he is also perhaps a literary critic, and his fact is that culturally Ireland and 'Britain' are one flesh, however deplorable this may seem to Irishmen and others; to attempt to disengage from this fact is to make the attempt to live by myth. This is what Yeats chose to do—first (to put it with a crudity which it is one of the great functions of this book to dispel) by going 'Gaelic' and then by going 'Anglo-Irish'. It is most important for our general sanity that he should be very clearly seen to have lived by myths.

I owe thanks to Rolf Lass and Robert Woof for some learned answers to queries, and to Martin Wright for careful advice on some of the unpublished and unfinished papers. Ernst Honigmann, Ure's successor as Joseph Cowen Professor of English at Newcastle, gave devoted and indefatigable help of many kinds. Without his original sifting of all Ure's papers, and his invaluable inventories, the preparation of this book could not even have begun. I am also in his debt for many kindnesses during its progress. To Frank Kermode, a closer friend of Ure's than any of the rest of us was lucky enough to be, all Ure's friends owe immense gratitude for his deeply moving, and extremely attractive, memoir.

C. J. R.

Contents

Contents

A note on presentation

Ure frequently quoted from different editions of the same work. The variations in this volume are sometimes due to the fact that a particular recent edition or collection (for example, *Essays and Introductions*, 1961) had not appeared when Ure was writing his earlier articles, but was available and had perhaps become standard when he was writing his later ones. But he also continued throughout to use such earlier collections as *Plays and Controversies*, 1923, and *Essays*, 1924, and frequently went back earlier still to a work's first edition or its appearance in an early collection. I think he was sometimes merely inconsistent, but it is clear that at other times his practice had a deliberate purpose. I did not feel confident enough to make the distinction in every case, and decided that any attempt to do so would merely substitute my arbitrary mixture for Ure's. One alternative was to standardize throughout, but this would certainly have violated Ure's intentions at some points even though it might have been more convenient for readers who possess recent standard editions of Yeats. I have therefore preserved Ure's own annotation intact, with only a few small *ad hoc* exceptions, and one systematic exception. The latter was to refer all quotations from the *Autobiographies* to the enlarged edition of 1955, even in articles written before that date. This is because the earlier *Autobiographies* of 1926 is a smaller and differently paginated book which nevertheless bears the same title, and it seemed right to avoid confusion. Where there were minor textual differences between the two texts, I have altered quotations to conform with 1955.

I have also, with minor exceptions, preserved Ure's *scale* of annotation, leaving unannotated or thinly annotated those lectures or essays in which Ure did not supply page references, etc., although I have tried to track down and verify every quotation or page reference. I ought to admit that I did not succeed in every case, and that, having checked approximately ninety per cent of all quotations and references throughout, I decided to abandon the search for passages which could not be found without inordinate loss of time. (Editorial footnotes are indicated by *, †, etc.)

C. J. R.

PETER URE

1919–1969

BY FRANK KERMODE

'A man alone with a book', so Barbara Strang tells us, was Peter Ure's emblem for an English school. It would have served as well as any other for himself. Men who live so completely in a world defined by literature and given systematic meaning by little else are extremely rare. When he was swept, as most of us were, into a life of action, it was by forces he had no way of resisting; he worked in that other world with the same pertinacity and power that he brought to reading, but although he derived some satisfaction from his achievements he was never in doubt that the extraordinary events of the war constituted for him an evil interruption in the progress of the work that he was born to do. It will be clear from what follows that his dedication of himself to that work was unceasing, and also that the cost, in terms of ordinary human happiness, was high. It may even appear—and this is a question on which his closest friends will differ—that in the end—which came disastrously too soon—the cost was too high; that his achievement, remarkable though it was, fell short of the mark he set himself and which seemed within his capacity.

Much of what follows is coloured by my own feelings about Ure over the thirty-odd years of our friendship. I have tried to get the facts right, and called upon others who knew him well at times when he and I rarely met, but it seems important to intrude at the earliest moment this apology, or declaration of interest. We were close enough to survive easily those quarrels and coolnesses, the kinds of misunderstanding, that arose from deep differences of temperament and education, even from some measure of rivalry. We were of much the same age, but intellectually and professionally I was from the beginning his junior; I often envied him in a rather foolish but quite straightforward way, and was the more irritated when it appeared that he occasionally reciprocated this feeling, simply because there was no reason whatever for him to do so. What in me was perfectly natural became in him a defect of character. The absurdity of this does not mean that I ought not, in this context, to mention it.

When I first met Peter Ure in 1937 he was already a formidable figure. He was graceful and unexpectedly powerful of body, but one was at first most impressed or alarmed by that square jaw and grim mouth. Furthermore, it soon became clear that the man was already learned beyond one's own dream of learning, and that he worked as if he had never heard it suggested that one could do so too unremittingly. After months of mutual soundings-out I approached him more nearly, and began to be educated by him. He was writing a great deal of verse, much of it deriving from the Auden of the mid 1930s, much from Yeats, whom he already knew by heart. These were the last months of Yeats, and I remember our going out to get the *London Mercury* in which appeared 'The Circus Animals' Desertion' and other poems. On the day the poet's death was announced, a lecturer, happening to begin a course on the poet that morning, said with infelicitous joviality that *The Times* obituary had done some of his work for him. I doubt if I should have minded this, but Ure was in a bitter fury all day. This kind of reaction, his disgust at anything that seemed, in its foolishness or triviality, to deny the seriousness of the supreme themes of art and song, struck me as excessive but eventually altered my own behaviour. I even began to write poems that belonged, at any rate in their diction and metrics, to their modern moment. I also learned how to work. Eventually we understood each other, had private jokes, laughed a lot, so that the academic year 1939–40, which for many reasons ought to have been horrible, was in some ways the happiest of my life, and perhaps of his.

Many difficulties had to be overcome before that degree of friendship was possible, and I touch upon them in order to explain certain important matters concerning Ure's earlier life. I remember going to dine at his father's house in Meols. Probably any such occasion at a middle-class house would have been a nervous one for me; what to do in such a place could not conceivably have been part of my own domestic education in a working-class home in the remoter provinces. For all I knew everybody in the Wirral who had more than a certain income, and all schoolmasters, lived like the Ures. Anyway I had never sat at a dinner table and listened to a continuous succession of well-formed sentences about important topics; I had never eaten asparagus; and when strawberries appeared I refused sugar, not because I liked them without, but because I had simply run out of nerve and mistrusted my behaviour with the shaker. Peter remarked, in the loud clear tones he bestowed indifferently on all topics, that he had always believed sugar to be indispensable to strawberries; without it they lacked flavour. His father, in equally unambiguous tones, explained to him that this was a wholly improper remark. A brief disputation ensued; then the conversation returned, as at this time it always did, to the activities of Middleton Murry and the Peace Pledge Union, on which father and son differed, though without heat, or to the behaviour of Kingsley Martin since Munich.

What seemed to me the alarming formality of that evening suggested to me that in such a house something intervenes to replace not only the ordinary small talk but the quarrelling, and even the casual yet important expressions of affection, that I was myself more accustomed to. I still don't think this reaction can be wholly written off as due to inexperience. There was always in this man a degree of formality accompanied by some uncertainty as to when and how strong feelings (including rage) should be expressed, and this may have been related to the manner of his early life. To cultivate the mind, know the world as it is, seems in such an environment to require not only decorous speech and manners but a deliberate denial of public expressiveness. Civilization allowed no moment of riot, as educated speech permitted no aposiopesis (I doubt whether Peter ever in his life uttered an ungrammatical sentence) or slang, or even jokes that did not belong to a definable literary tradition of nonsense or fantasy.

Ure's father was first a science master, then headmaster of Birkenhead Grammar School. He was a graduate of Liverpool, and so was his wife. They were or had been Fabians; the father a man of considerable intellectual scope, though not, as I remember, especially interested in literature, which was more his wife's province. Peter was the younger of two sons, and had a clever elder brother to emulate. He was indoctrinated very early into hard intellectual labour, and developed habits which he never broke to his last day. A personal fastidiousness, a desire for order in his arrangements, operated also in his studies. He worked systematically, with file, index, and notebook; this applies as much to his poetry, which is copied in a series of notebooks in perfect chronological order, as to his journal, and to his scholarly projects throughout life.

These documents are now in the University Library at Newcastle. The manuscript material, from which this account is mainly drawn, is of three kinds: verse, fiction, and journals.

The poetry is copied into eighteen account and exercise books of various kinds, with the pages numbered consecutively up to the first page of volume 12, which is numbered 1608. The first poem was written in 1926, when Ure was 6 or 7, and that on p. 1608 is dated 15 November 1941, when he was 22. The chronological record of the poetry ceases in August 1949, after which he wrote little verse. For almost half his life Ure was certain that poetry was his vocation; but although he published some poems in the early 1940s he was always aware of his condition as aspiring apprentice. He approached his task with intense, one might say Miltonic, seriousness; but he was never to have that necessary Horton period, and in the end his poetic ambition, which was fierce enough to make Ure himself wonder at its physical manifestations, faded in the light of a commoner academic day. Reading through the poems, one sees how open he was to the voices of others—especially Yeats, but also Eliot and Auden—and with what difficulty he struggled to make his own voice heard, to achieve an athletic flexibility and touch in rhythm. A poem of 1934:

The Bird

Peace without knights and banners;
and the reedy shell clumsily blown
to make a thin song on the edge of the cliff—
that falls like a bird
with the world at its wings,
that flies to the sea.

Then on the skyline strange, unfriendly ships,
jagged and monstrous,
so that the singer ceases his song,
and far down the glades of the beeches goes running.

But only a bird in the sea and the sky,
falls, with the world at its wings.

Three years later there is total possession by the poet to whom
he gave so much of his life:

> *Chorus.* Who, when the touch of Midas
> fell on the moving child
> cried out with horror, seeing
> a still image of gold?
>
> He heard that cry last night
> when a thought rent his calm,
> and he cried out aloud
> that beauty moves like cloud
> and cannot take a form.

An example of the tougher, more individual manner of his
Greek years is given below. There is a volume of unfashionable
poetry to be quarried from the notebooks, but it would be useless to pretend that Ure came near his own mark; the only task
he set himself and failed in was the most difficult of all.

The fiction consists of two novels (one unfinished) and a number of short stories. The first novel, *Man is the Measure*, was
written in 1936, the second, *The Green Topless Tree*, finished in a
Cairo hospital, belongs to the war years and is a source of information about the period when Ure worked in Stepney, living
among co-workers who emerge as cocoa-drinking Bohemians
whose life he shared with evident reserve and gloom. He was
not under the illusion that he had great powers as a novelist,
and indeed, discussed in his journal that lack of interest in
personal relations—reflected in an indifference to the colloquial
—which prevented his carrying out what he took to be the
business of the novelist.

The journals, in five volumes, are often quoted in the sequel.

In August 1940, between an undergraduate career now over and
a future totally obscure, he began to take stock of his earlier
life. He had been, after preparatory school, a day-boy at Birken-

head School. At the age of 21 he remembers himself as 'the most unpleasant type of small boy' with a great conceit of himself because he wrote poetry. He did not get to know other boys, noting that they always went home from school in the opposite direction from him. He was bad at games, but a good sprinter—he 'broke several school records'—and later grew to like rugby, a game he continued to play at the university with a pleasure derived always from the sport and never from the company. He was teased for his 'queer name', and was 'driven once or twice into insane rages by this treatment'. He eventually enjoyed the sort of friendship—based on sex and poetry—that such a school can offer, and began to satisfy some of his ambitions: to be a prefect, to edit the school magazine, be secretary of the literary society, and captain of running. All these he achieved, except the last. Living mostly in a state described as 'nervous isolation', he cheered himself by reminders that he was a poet. On the other hand, he also recalls that he tormented a French master, who called him 'the rudest boy he had ever known'. The boys, however, thought him 'morally very exalted', and he did not join in their horseplay and public sexuality. At 14 he managed not to join the OTC, pleading 'pacifism'. At the same age he passed his Matriculation examination, coached by his father in chemistry to make up for his total inability to do mathematics.

In the sixth form, after an initial period of intense anxiety about his performance, he did most of the things he wanted, and enjoyed some power. His Higher School Certificate examinations were in classics; he speaks of the passionate enjoyment he had from these studies. He read and wrote hugely, and did well in the examination. The ordinary course would have been for him to stay on and try for an Oxford scholarship, but it was decided, because of straitened family finances, that he should not follow his brother to that place. Instead, he was, at 17, to make his living. 'Here was I, a little immature prig, let down with a bump from my power-fantasia at school.' His literary ambitions, however, remained intact. He tried several other jobs before signing on in January 1937 as a trainee manager at Selfridges.

This was an odd time, and he sometimes spoke almost with pleasure of his days at the information bureau which the shop then ran. You could telephone and ask who won the Derby in

1923 or how to get wine stains out of linen, and after a pause would be given the answer, doubtless with unambiguous force and carefully ordered detail. But Selfridges did not suit him. 'I was almost a complete failure . . . I had never before had to experience such incredible monotony, such boredom of that refined type that involves a kind of fevered nervous activity.' Although he went much to the theatre and the opera and ballet, he remembered these London days as very dull. Out of his wage of £2 a week he paid 12s. 6d. for an attic in Pimlico. 'I have always found it difficult', he remarks, 'to spend money with real abandon since.' It was, he says, a time when he thought very little, even about the coming war, but he was engrossed by the Spanish War and applied for membership of the Left Book Club, withdrawing the application when his father suggested that his employers would find out and disapprove.

In August 1937 Selfridges expressed, on quite other grounds, some dissatisfaction with his performance, and he left them in October, just in time to register as an honours student in the English department at Liverpool University. The department was by postwar standards a small one, with nine or ten honours students in each year. There was a fairly severe weeding-out process at the end of the first; one recalls the weeping girls leaving Professor Martin's office with their bad news, which he always broke to them alone, a practice followed by Ure many years later at Newcastle. Neither he nor L. C. Martin could have relished the task, but characteristically neither would delegate it. Martin, the editor of Vaughan and Crashaw, and later of Herrick, was a slight, soft-spoken man—not an impressive lecturer but an exemplar of conscientious and laborious scholarship. Since this was the essence of the career Ure had now committed himself to, he had from the first a deep respect for Martin. He always took long views of the significance of his own decisions, and had already made a projection of himself into the future as a scholar. The rest of us were for the most part bright boys with no such plans, only at best flickering anxieties about what would become of us, and much more concerned with the duties and pleasures of the moment; we were incomparably less well prepared not only as readers, but morally, and quite incapable of investing our undergraduate years with such adult significance.

The Liverpool syllabus at that time was for the first two years conventional and, I suppose, taxing; there were two subsidiary subjects, the more serious being Latin, and in the English courses there was a great deal of philology. Grattan, the Baines professor, was a great believer in 'slips', cards on which one was expected to make one's own linguistic archives, one set for loan-words, one for etymology, and so on. These had to be produced for inspection on demand, a nightmare to me, who have never had the knack of keeping three pieces of paper in the same order overnight, but a routine matter to Ure: the difference, we would say, between anal-scattering and anal-retentive types. The long hours of slow explicative plodding through Old and Middle English texts were also less trying to him, though I suppose he did not claim the same rewards from *King Horn* as from the *Hippolytus*. But there was something in the sheer dullness of all this that satisfied his need for intense and protracted concentration.

On the literary side, Liverpool was experimenting, and I remember that in the second year there were intensive courses, one on Fielding, in which we really were taught by A. R. Humphreys what it is like to study an author in depth, and one on modern poetry which, unusually for the time, included young living poets, for example Auden and Spender. In the final year, rid of 'language', we did few courses and spent far too much time on writing 'theses'. Ure's was a study, of PhD length, of Glapthorne and the Stuart court drama. It is a remark-able work on an unpromising subject, and ensured him the First that nobody had in any case ever dreamed he would not achieve. He was gratified by his successes, as the journal shows; they included the Elton Prize, won in his second year for an essay which was the basis of his later work on Yeats, and the Felicia Hemans Medal for lyrical poetry ('not necessarily in the manner of Mrs Hemans', as Martin used to say), and a scholarship, which he was unable to take up until after the war. In September 1940 he wrote an account of his undergraduate years which expresses a certain discontent with his teachers, but a footnote added later qualifies the criticism. One's own memory suggests that he rather enjoyed it all: the grinding work, the for him soli-tary pleasures of rugby, the talk over coffee punctuated with his loud sardonic laugh. One recalls the moods: Ure square-jawed and intent in the Library, lugubriously gay in the canteen. He was not witty but, in his moments, invented long ridiculous fantasies. He talked a lot about pacifism, sexual relations, religion, and there was formed a small circle of undergraduates in which he moved with relative confidence and ease, enjoying their differences from him, and also enjoying their unforced respect. They were a disparate group; Neville Newhouse, a Quaker, was closer to the religious but religionless Ure in many important respects than I was, or Miriam Allott (Marie Farris she was called then); he valued different people for different things, and with what in retrospect seems a remarkable maturity of judgement.

One had not expected him to be capable of such easy fellowship. Yet those now distant memories, perhaps by a Wordsworthian transmutation of a kind which, as the journal shows, even then absorbed him, are productive of pleasure now. Indeed, one remembers best the gaiety. We would go over to Hoylake, I remember, to swim, Ure, already in his home waters, rising from the depths with a sonorous invitation to join him before dramatically disappearing again. In the early summer of 1939 I bicycled with him in Wales, a trip I remember now, the spirit of pleasure and youth's golden gleam having supervened in the associative process, as amusing. The weather was such as only North Wales can provide; I was not well clad for it, and, perpetually soaked, suffered also a long series of punctures. Peter proceeded calmly on his admirable bicycle, totally waterproofed, to enjoy the trip. At one Youth Hostel our task was to varnish a floor which, in memory, seems to have been as large as a ballroom, and I cannot forget that it was Peter, not I, who did it with good humour and efficiency. We stayed at Dolgelly in torrents of rain and heavy mists. When we rode on, we came to a junction which indicated Snowdonia one way and home the other; I went home and he to Snowdon, a decision conveyed by gestures and accepted as sensible by both sides as we pedalled through the deluge.

Already liable to conscription, we were exempted only because of a dispensation allowing us to finish our degrees in 1940. Newhouse was, of course, registered as conscientious objector on religious grounds. Peter was faced with the need to convince the tribunal without religious arguments, and this was known to be very difficult. I myself was at first registered as a CO, but abandoned the position in the spring of 1940. I remember the annual general meeting of the Peace Pledge Union branch, which fell, unhappily, on the day of the German invasion of the Low Countries; we were quite gently roughed up by outraged students, but protected, somewhat officiously it was thought, by the Boxing Club, which held that we had a right to express our despicable opinions.

I missed Ure's tribunal, being in hospital with German measles. He failed to gain the unconditional exemption he sought; his statement was too literary, with quotations from Wilfred Owen and so forth, and did not impress the tribunal. Later his appeal also failed. These tribunals were an important part of life at the time, and I remember the consternation when Judge Burgess, Chairman of the Liverpool tribunal, was stabbed in a railway station by a disappointed pacifist. Ure was clear that he could not accept military service, and it was therefore probable that he would have to go to prison. It was a time when this, or other equally inconceivable fates, grew commonplace, without acquiring any reality in the mind; the main effort was still academic, and we all went on working quite happily.

Final examinations were taken, under conditions of the utmost absurdity, in the hot June of 1940, with Dunkirk already over and the fall of Paris occurring on the day of the last paper. For a few weeks more we were all together. In August I joined the Navy and for the next six years saw very little of Ure, though I suppose our courses, considering that they covered most of the face of the earth, crossed more often than one might have expected; we also corresponded sporadically, and for a time he acted as a very efficient 'book club', sending me, among other things, Virginia Woolf's *Between the Acts*, Auden's *New Year Letter*, and D. W. Harding's *The Impulse to Dominate*, a book he greatly admired. But most of this account of the years 1940–6 derives from his journal and from the reminiscences of people who worked with him either in England or in the Middle East.

During the summer of 1940, when he must have been thinking a good deal about prison, he wrote in the journal long speculative entries on crime and madness, on Yeats, Dostoevsky, Lawrence. He mentions at one point that Goethe did not allow a war to interrupt his researches into colour, and adds:

This is an example which we . . . should endeavour to follow, by never letting anything disturb us in the pursuit of our intellectual life . . . as our emblem and coat of arms I propose a tree mightily shaken by the wind, but still bearing its ruddy fruit on every branch; with the motto *Dum convellor mitescent* or *Conquessata sed ferax.*

Throughout the next months the journal records various intellectual enterprises which accord with that motto: reflections on the writing of poetry, on certain topics about which he needed to be clear before going to prison. The variety is remarkable: between notes on St John of the Cross and Nietzsche, a piece of fiction about a burning house. Years later, in a journal entry dated 13 June 1945, he mentions that during a twelve-mile mountain walk in the blazing summer heat of Greece he found himself recollecting in detail the crucial moment in 1942 when he was summoned to undergo his medical examination for military service.

I remember wearing my blue overcoat and being asked by a rather embarrassed doctor if I was prepared to take the examination, to which I replied with equal embarrassment, 'No, sir', and then rushed out of the room followed by the plainclothes-man (or was it a policeman in uniform?) labouring in my footsteps.

I think this was the moment of his arrest. Of his first time in prison I know nothing except that the sentence was served in Walton Gaol, Liverpool.

Ure's feelings about prison are recorded in a long entry dated 10 May 1942, on his release from Wormwood Scrubs. There he served rather under two months of a twelve-month sentence. One Saturday morning he was sewing mailbags; in the afternoon he walked round Shepherd's Bush Green, and was called 'Sir' by the bus conductor to whom he gave his penny. 'The shouting, the lining up in threes, banging of doors, the cindery exercise yard, the intolerable clothes, had gone.' He reflected that 'there are many men still in prison for conscience, more sincere and more courageous than I, who did not have the luck that I had in coming before a "good" Tribunal, or whose conscience did not allow them to offer or accept a "condition" of exemption from military service.' (He had relaxed his position on this.)

The condition imposed was 'full-time ambulance or hospital work under civilian control, full time social relief, or land work'.

No doubt the sense that invisible psychological fetters have been struck off is common to all who leave prison. 'We live life so much on the surface, our natures are so attached to that bloom which freedom of choice in little things bestows upon life, that to rob a man of that continual shifting and changing, caressing and handling . . . is indeed to punish him.' Yet there is something beautifully characteristic of Ure in his celebration of the recovery of these liberties. He walked about London and found soldiers of all nationalities enjoying the new-come spring in Trafalgar Square.

Near me on the edge of the fountain sat a girl with a great stream of auburn hair. My pleasure was enhanced when, on going up to the National Gallery, I saw posters advertising an exhibition and showing on them an Augustus John drawing of Yeats as a young man. To be again (it seemed) in a world where the truly great are given tokens of honour.

As always, he finds the right way to celebrate the 'extraordinary time-born beauty' of the city, the proper awe and elation, in art, musing over the National Gallery El Greco, *Christ and the Moneychangers*,

a cruel and clever picture . . . In a robe of acid red Christ raises the whip, with one enormous light-filled spiritual eye staring straight at the other central figure. This is a half-naked man, twisted away from Christ, with a muscular well-formed body. We cannot see his face . . . Spirit is opposed to the naked Flesh, but cruelly, the problem is as unsolved as ever. El Greco has not dared, or could not show the face of the man of flesh as he felt the impact of the Spirit, as that awful eye looked straight into his face. It is queer that the hand that raises the whip seems to be a shapeless smear, while Christ's other hand down at his side is incredibly thin and beautiful, standing clearly out.

Two days later, in a continuing mood of exaltation, he wrote one of the most remarkable of his journal entries. 'I feel myself on the verge of some important discovery, something-to-be-revealed. Premonitions of love and death along the rainy streets.' The mood attaching itself, as usual, to poetry, he speaks of those occasional perceptions great lines of poetry bear about them, at once diffused and close-packed, an aura of meaning which we cannot lay hold on, knowing only that it acts on our nerves and the backs of our eyes, yet not a nervous reaction purely, but something in which the whole being seems to take part, but without fulfilling itself, but hanging in a kind of expectant suspension that dies gradually away. I am thinking continually while writing this of Hamlet's almost final words:

> You that look pale and tremble at this chance,
> That are but mutes and audience to this act—

in which Hamlet seems to summon the whole invisible world of spectators to his aid in order that *he* may help *them*, in order that, as they hang staring at him over the gulf in which he dies, he may teach them what he has learnt—the whole mystery and secret of his life and action. But he has no time, and the right moment too passes, and his next and last speech . . . concerns itself only with that immensely trivial (and yet at the same time immensely important) question of the succession to the throne of Denmark. And the spectators draw back baffled, or scarcely realizing what was meant.

> O, I could tell you—
> But let it be . . .

says Hamlet . . . Horatio . . . can only speak of the surface of events . . . Death stops the revelation that was just about to be made.

This is the second great work of art in two days which I noticed in which such a revelation seems about to be made and yet is deliberately not made, or cannot be made. The other was the El Greco painting.

> For that which is perfect is not yet come.

Thanks be to God that I have been brought even so far.

This is surely very extraordinary criticism; the insight into El Greco reminds one of Walter Benjamin's inspired account of that painter, and there is a sense in which the whole text of *Hamlet* is illuminated by the observation that here, for the last and crucial time, it invites the spectator to a full disclosure which is then denied expression. Nor is the illumination useful for only these two works; it is strong enough in respect of all art to found a career and a method upon. And we note that the terms on which Ure accepts it are suggestive of humility and self-dedication; the experience is a liberation of the spirit corresponding to that of the body from its prison, a knowledge

learnt or re-learnt from art of the ambiguous beauty and value
of the world. Many years later Barbara Strang heard him say:
'The mistake people make is that they think literature is something apart from life. Literature *is* life; there's nothing else.'
The experience of May 1942 may suggest the true sense of this
remark, and of the vocation it implies.

Before his imprisonment Ure had worked as a volunteer in
a Friends Ambulance Unit at Stepney, and there he returned
for a while later in the year. The novel entitled *The Green Topless Tree* contains some account of his Stepney days, including
this note on the shelters:

The shelters of the East End during the air-raids of 1940–1941 (it was
now late in the 1941 period) will doubtless be the subject of social
science monographs, full of statistics and technical terms. Or perhaps
they are just forgotten? They were every variety of shape, size, comfort,
discomfort, imagined security; some were at the bottom of warehouses,
others lined the streets, or occupied odd cellars. Those which the
Searchers had under their care were built under railway arches, which
were turned into shelters by the simple expedient of building brick
walls fore and aft. In view of the fact that they were built under a railway line—and railway lines are military objectives—for we must reveal
the fact that the Germans occasionally turned their Hunnish attention
to other buildings besides hospitals and schools—their security value
could hardly be other than psychological. Before the sirens sounded,
these particular shelters—unlike the great warehouse shelters which
became permanent bedrooms for thousands of families—were usually
occupied by nervous old ladies, but when the gunfire began they were
immediately crowded with a dense mass of humanity.

There was always a lingering smell about these shelters, compounded
of the damp that trickled incessantly down the brick walls, the smell of
urine from the temporary lavatories screened off with sacking (a great
advance on original conditions), the smell of old clothes and bug-ridden
bundles, and the indigenous earthy stink of places underground. But it
would need the pen of Dickens to describe the spectacular and yet
homely nature of these extraordinary places. That atmosphere of
gloom and rot, of charged vapours and nervous cheerfulness stays in
the memory like a tune. In it sat the people of the East End 'taking
it' (for there is very little else you can do in air-raids). Things tended to
become reduced to two important personal pronouns: there was 'it'
which you took or which you gave back to Cologne and Düsseldorf, and

there was 'he' which was either the Germans as a body, or Hitler, or the Luftwaffe—Samuel was never quite sure which. 'Taking it' can perhaps be explained by a simple analogy: a very sick man is quiet, and the people of the East End at this time were very sick indeed.

It was necessary to prepare for the work that lay ahead. Professor Peter Strevens, a Quaker conscientious objector, met Ure at a training course in Birmingham late in 1942. They were being prepared for civilian relief work, learning how to drive and maintain heavy vehicles, acquiring the elements of auxiliary medical work, large-scale catering, and dietetics. Pursuing this last course, they went to Aldershot to work with the catering officer, and eventually met again at a hospital outside Glasgow. 'I still recall', says Strevens, 'the days when the one of us on the early shift had to fry 360 eggs, 36 at a time in vast square pans, juggled across the varied heat-bands of an Aga stove, for the nursing and medical staff breakfasts, before we got our own.'

At some time between this period and his departure Ure worked for the Forestry Commission in the Lake District; and he also took part in a medical experiment which required him to submit to attempts to infect him with scabies. I remember his sour amusement at the failure of all these attempts, and the conclusion that it was very easy to catch scabies by one method alone, and very difficult by any other.

Thus the time passed, though not to his satisfaction. In September 1942 we find him complaining that a career as a writer is incompatible with the sort of life he had to lead; he lacked the two essentials, solitude and freedom: 'books, paper, a regulated routine' is his gloss on the first of these, 'joblessness' on the second.

I get increasingly tired of the way in which I spend my days, increasingly bored with 'community life', its frittering away of time. Meanwhile

> Life slips by like a field-mouse
> Not shaking the grass . . .

The war has produced a vast slagheap of days through which we must shovel and burrow in ignorance of our task, like creatures in some sombre bureaucratic Hell. My one ambition, my one desire has been to write poetry, and I come to this important work miserably ill-equipped, my consciousness chopped into useless fragments by the demands of the day, every instrument blunted and stained.

This lament modulates into a long meditation on *Macbeth* and on Rilke, which ends, 'I pay homage to Shakespeare and all the Others, whose understanding was so fine . . .'

Late in 1942 Ure found himself for the first time in Newcastle. He liked it at once, though he lamented the neglect of the fine stretch towards the west end of Clayton Street, and the horrible shops of Northumberland Street. He particularly admired St Thomas's Church in the Haymarket—'the work of a genius'. Another genius designed the centre; there is a neat little sketch map of the streets radiating from the Monument, and the observation that this combination of order and flexibility cannot be fortuitous. He stayed for several months, and never lost his affection for the place; in 1947, when I suppose he would, like the rest of us, have taken a job anywhere, he was particularly pleased that he got the appointment at Newcastle.

During this time he was always expecting to be sent abroad, but in the middle of 1943 he was still in England. Sometimes he spoke of his talent, ever more demanding of his strength and concentration. His friends no longer interested him; a curious note of 31 July 1943 dwells on this, explaining what had become of some of them:

F. was found in the stable, wandering backwards and forwards saying the cat had not been fed, with a bowl of milk in his hand. The cats had long since been fed, but he would believe no one, and finally had to be put to bed.
H., who seemed so stolid, is staying at home, doing nothing. He has gone mad for Christ, with that terrifying single-mindedness with which he washed up, or planed doors, or served out tea.
D. is called to become an Anglo-Catholic priest. He makes jokes about the Holy Ghost, and lives in a perpetual mental clique.
Rilke, Yeats.

That autumn he was in Hampstead. I saw him there, and spent the night of a heavy raid as his guest. We simply sat around drinking tea. He was calm and cheerful, by now experienced in squalor and the handling of bloody emergencies. The Friends were equable, forgiving me my uniform. On 12 September 1943 he copied out a passage from *Le Visionnaire*, the work of Julien Green, a writer he had admired for years.

Ne sentez-vous pas tout ce que la présence de la mort détruit d'illusions autour d'elle? Nous sommes ses enfants qu'elle dérobe aux mensonges. Du fond de la vie, elle nous appelle. A l'âge même où nous ne comprenons pas le langage des hommes, nous nous arrêtons quelquefois au milieu de nos jeux pour écouter sa voix . . . Et tout le long des années, elle nous fait signe.

There follows this passage on an 'incident' in Hampstead.

Dust, a building that wasn't and a crowd of Hampstead wardens in unsoiled tin hats: the incident officer with his horizontal blue lamps a little askew. The bigger Hampstead houses have too much ornamental glasswork was my conclusion as I felt the stuff underfoot cutting my shoes. People pale and distinctly shaken amid the expensive soft furnishings. One woman sits amidst bits of ceiling with the inevitable teapot: the round table is of polished rosewood, and she wears something that is vaguely suggestive of a wig. I don't really enjoy bomb stories very much (or there would be a few good ones earlier on in this book, which seem unaccountably to have slipped out). Eventually we found five old ladies in bed, their front window and its frame smashed up and a good bit of ceiling on their eiderdown quilts. They were quite still and patient (the matron had doubtless supplied them with the tea).

One was distressed about her bird (parrot or canary?), another about the upper set of her false teeth (which had doubtless disintegrated with the ceiling). Suppose, I couldn't stop myself from thinking, as we put them on the stretchers and carried the stretchers to the ambulances, suppose each old lady were an incarnate judgement—what would be her verdict on us and them, and the rest of us: all this precision and destructiveness and charting and heroism and Fatherland and Democracy —ending in five old ladies lying badly frightened in bed, in their familiar room so utterly transformed. Those beautiful shining planes, and the heavy-bellied bombs, and the runways and the godlike pilots (God bless them, with a sob), all ending in a poor old woman who has lost, irreparably, the upper set of her false teeth? (Though this particular bomb, let it be said to its credit, did kill a caretaker and his wife—there are a great many caretakers in Hampstead just at present.)

But yesterday was in some ways a rather remarkable day. All days that do not terminate until four o'clock in the morning perhaps possess that quality. In the morning, arrives in a registered packet my thesis, back from the typist—*Aspects of the Mythology in the Poetry of*

W. B. Yeats, says the title page, and I am proud. Nothing gives one's work solidity so much as seeing it neatly bound and paginated. The labour of some fifteen months is completed, rather earlier than I had hoped or expected. A slight private internal celebration (which seems to be taking this rather dull form) is perhaps inevitable. Later in the day Bumpus's yielded up my Dante, cunningly bound for the trip, and charged but a moderate fee—so well done that it seems a pity to entrust it to the rigours of this impossible journey which will *not* remove itself from my mind. In the afternoon also the last of the injections—another reminder.

The thesis, which became his first book, was done in time, and all was ready for the journey east. In the spring of 1944 he sailed through the Mediterranean, now opened by the relief of Malta, and was enrolled in a Relief and Refugees team which was to work in Greece for UNRRA. But he fell ill, and spent two months in hospital at Cairo, during which time he completed *The Green Topless Tree*. This extract from the journal describes the kind of work he did among Greek refugees in Egypt; the scene is of a kind that was to become extremely familiar to him in Greece.

12th May 1944—We are in the M.I. section watching the two Greek doctors impassively inoculating and vaccinating. Many of the children— emaciated, like the pictures in official reports on famine and malnutrition—yell and struggle as though this was the last straw. The Yugoslav interpreter beside me, in the midst of all this desperate pandemonium, turns to me and says: 'By Christ, poor bloody kids! What Hitler has done, eh?'

I am brought up to an elderly couple. Each has a ticket from the M.O. saying that they are not fit for disinfestation. Both are over seventy, large-boned and very respectable looking, but bewildered and completely exhausted. The man wears a lot of clothes, a black overcoat covering all, with a soft hat. Beneath the hat his eyes are dumb and miserable: he is so tired he can scarcely walk and understands nothing. The woman is like a Lancashire housewife, with a large hat that comes almost down to the eyebrows, and glasses. She has plainly been used to years of steady housekeeping, small economies, and responsibilities. Perhaps they were once shopkeepers. Their bundles are very small: they have nothing. While I am settling where they shall go, the man looks hither and thither as though trapped. To walk, he leans on his wife's arm and they move very slowly across the compound.

One of the Greek doctors who has been loaned to us for the day is explaining why he and his colleague turned up at 10.00 am instead of at 7.00 am (thus nearly causing a breakdown). 'They offered us an open truck without cover, and it looked as though it were going to rain.' He is young and fat, with an insolent expression. Later, he makes a fuss because no gown has been provided for him. The staff regard him with malevolence.

In the bath-house I have to compel an old man of eighty to bathe. His clothes are nothing but a bundle of haphazard rags. When first examined, he was sitting on the ground covered in flies with his head buried in a brown blanket. He stinks of excrement, and his shirt and underclothes are thick with it. He tries to convey to me that he cannot take his socks off, and paddles under the shower with these on, until at last I pull them off as gently as possible while he groans lying on the concrete floor. His eyes and eyebrows have the withered yet frosty appearance of the very old.

There is a young man with his young son. The man is supported on a crutch and a stick: his nose is pinched and thin like Falstaff's on his death-bed: his body and hands are malformed by rheumatism and with these trembling and useless hands he cannot even unbutton his shirtsleeves. Even he, however, can feel sympathy for the old man.

His son (separated from his father who has been sent to the doctor) sits on the mat floor of the dressing tent sobbing for half-an-hour: young enough to be lost, and old enough to feel the despair of the lost.

Egypt did not please him. 'In the fevers of my imagination I live anywhere but here', he wrote in October 1944, blaming himself for idleness, and admitting that he had misunderstood himself in supposing that one of the rewards of humanitarian work would be to enable him to forget the neglect of 'everything for which I really care'. He had spent six months in Egypt: two in useful work at the refugee camp at El Shatt, two in hospital, and two 'waiting about at GHQ in surroundings and an atmosphere which becomes more poisonous every day'. Gordon Cox remembers sharing pleasures—a concert at which the Mozart G-minor quintet was performed—but these are not recorded in the journal. There are, however, accounts of a visit to Palestine. Ure was also writing a good deal—stories, poems, a tragedy—and there is continuous comment on books and ideas—on Kemp's *Healing Ritual*, on E. Whane's *Modern Egyptians*, on allegory, myth, and ritual. On 3 November 'read

C. S. Lewis's *The Problem of Pain* with distaste'; on 4 November 'read *Bleak House* with a good deal of irritation'. He was ready for new experiences which would make the volume of the journals recording his life in Greece the most mature and valuable of his writing to date.

He joined his unit in Athens in January 1945.

The Mountains change their colour from grey to blue, and from slaty black to gold. In the early-morning silence there is signalling from the shore, and the pouring rumble and rattle of our dropping anchor. But Piraeus wakes to no-life along its ruined quays: the three-horned mountain has become the colour of noodle-paste fried in deep fat; Parnassus is invisible in mist. Behind us lies the Island of Sucking Spoon. Aegina-Salamis, the Acropolis in the distance, and the black jagged spur of Lika-petos, spiny and exquisite as the landscapes in Botticelli.

> All that great glory spent,
> Man shifts about like some poor Arab tribesman ... [*sic*]

but here we are back in the West and back in Europe, following the old stream of culture that flowed from Egypt to Crete or dawdled along the African coast. But walk in Athens, and realise that the Greeks of ancient Hellas came from the North and brought with them Northern forms, not the rigid disorder of Arab design but the plastic order of heroic columns, and the phallus revealed in the pure air.

Greece was involved in a disastrous civil war, and British troops had returned there to oppose the revolutionary organization ELAS. Ure records that on his arrival 'Athens has only been "cleared" of ELAS troops about ten days . . . Up the Monastery hill (where live Virgins and Saints covered in thick silver) which was formerly held by ELAS are Vickers machine-gun bands and other relics . . . This ammunition is British ammunition used by ELAS against the British.' In the museum at the Dipylon, among many untouched objects, 'a large figure-painted amphora lying drastically smashed inside its glass case'. He climbed the Areopagus, and tentatively began his successful career as a speaker of modern Greek by pointing to a goat and saying to the goatboys, ὁ τραγός. Back in the streets, a strange smell issued from buildings wrecked in the recent street-fighting. 'They say [it] emanates from corpses in the basements choked with rubble. They are putting quicklime down.'

But Athens meant work; Ure was deputed to attend to the
disinfestation, registration, and the provision of rudimentary
medical and welfare requirements at the Hostages' Reception
Centre, and in prisons and police stations. 'Athens stands
revealed as a dreary and even evil town,' he wrote on 25 January
1945, 'and the Acropolis and Parthenon a grim joke.' He greatly
disliked the police, who, having worked with the Italians and
Germans, were now gaoling ELAS anti-Fascists on behalf of the
British government.

In No. 1 Police Station there were 105 people in four cells 10' × 6': one
latrine. I did not see it at its worst when it held 240. Major A says to a
Greek police commandant: 'Don't you know that no one is supposed
to be put in prison unless they have engaged in atrocities or criminal
acts? (Aside) Personally, I think it weak. I'd shoot all the buggers
myself.'

Ure was aware, as the journal shows, that he was now working
in an area where his observations had a different value than that
of self-communing, and he urged himself to make more use of
the journal. He describes conversations with two educated
ELAS women supporters in a female prison, one a London
School of Economics graduate and a friend of Papandreou, who
had refused to allow the government to place a machine-gun
post on her balcony. He mentions the TUC delegation to Athens,
led by Sir Walter Citrine, who was shown the 'corpseyard'
where ELAS shot their hostages, but not the rebellious women
prisoners, who were got out of the way before the tour began.
Ure did not favour British withdrawal; the damage had been
done, and he was sure ELAS supporters would fare worse in the
absence of the British troops. He talked much to the 'LSE
woman': 'The more one becomes by education a citizen of the
world, the more intolerable it must be to be tied by the navel
to a country like modern Greece...'

At the end of the month he travelled, with the rest of his team,
via Taranto to Kerkira. Here, according to Mr T. J. Cadoux, he
was again ill and depressed; but the journal indicates a growing
identification with the countryside of Corfu: 'a landscape of
trees covered with white blossom, olives, terraced, cypresses
that stand in groups near and distant like the people of this
world... Rotting statues in the garden, and a broken ornamental

pillar lies on the grass of the hillside facing the sun . . .' Later he calls it the most beautiful place he has ever seen. 'Such a place must be beautiful: but others are so by accident.' He enjoyed the local food and wine. Mr Donald Swann remembers him at this time as gay and benign. He made the two-and-a-half hour journey by caique to spend Easter in Corfu with Peter. 'We attended the midnight service together and the Easter candle was lit and spread to the whole congregation in a blaze of light. He had many friends among the Greeks and was thoroughly at home in Corfu.' The truth of this is attested by a new vitality in the journal entries.

On 10 April he received a letter from L. C. Martin telling him that Liverpool University Press intended to publish his thesis, and asking him to succeed A. K. McIlwraith as lecturer in English at Istanbul. He was pleased, but correctly foresaw difficulties. Correspondence about this abortive plan went on for months. Meanwhile he went on with his job, sailing about the islands. He put together a volume of poems called *Voyage to the Mareotic Lake*; and he accepted the pleasures of Corfu. Sometimes they were not unqualified: on 13 May he wrote:

The proedros insisted on killing a sheep for us; an old man stood by my plate, tore the meat from the animal with his hands and heaped it on my plate, shook the brains out of the skull, and picked out all the other highly esteemed organs for me to eat. No sooner had I disposed of these revolting objects than he would heap more on to my plate—it was like some nightmare piece of mythology.

This experience contributed something to one of Ure's best poems, published a year later in *Friends Ambulance Unit Chronicle*, 83, 4 May 1946:

Letter from Greece

Rat's teeth bite secretly at night
In the grip of the lust of the jaw, tendentiously
Making what seems ours their right.
Some hermit might inhabit the melancholy chapel
Twenty yards up along the stony road
But only washing's hung out, and a load
Of sticks lies against the old wall: the altar
Gone for firing or taken by the priest.

In this country when they intention to feast
From throat to anus they split a sheep, and
Under the almond trees the meat turns round,
Nuts, fat and wine drop on the ground.
A country where richness lies in a gesture,
Where excitement breaking like wine gone acid
Sours the breath. A people never placid
Who accept without question that Greece is a metaphor,
Where the landscape belies the most elaborate trope,
For who could infer from the olive the metope?
Now the soldiers parade on the plataea, incapable
Of replacing the old image with a new
But continually garlanding the same statue.
They don't shave or look like important powers,
But live in a frowse. And under the trees
Establish without shame their lavatories.
Thus when we judge we bring an equipment
They may not appreciate, and certainly don't care
To change their ways, where the lucid atmosphere
All day long puts the mountains in perspective;
Horn upon horn ranged and rock upon rock
To the last shelves where the tides knock
And, impregnable, repel the Ionian Sea.
Across that voyaging when in sight of home
The hero, experienced in war, on the comb
Of the wave was carried, most lasting image,
And on the beach tossed, knew that he'd come
Through witchcraft and monsters very near to home,
Out of superabundant images to the last simulacrum,
Greece. These complex coasts where the god lives
Implacable and honest, who never gives
Straight answers to any questions, full knowing
The nature of godhead whose hollow voices deny
The impervious pattern and the simple lie.
Though the hero himself lived much by his wits
And was pure man on that naked shore;
Summoned by disaster from Troy's tower,
His personal cunning was proof against the myth.
What was it he remembered? The lines of the tents,
The trucks grinding in convoy down the desert road,
Smell of cloth and rifles, the improbable blood
From his own wounds? At any rate he knows
Now, that all images thrive in one—
The Woman-headed Sphinx that waits by the stone.

Reflecting on the news of the VE-day celebrations in London he asks 'What are the qualities that go to make up an expatriate type? . . . I am beginning to suspect that I possess some of them myself.' But love of Greece could not put an end to all depression: 'I cannot understand why I should continue to get so little enjoyment out of life, since I am in Greece and find the country beautiful and interesting. It is a "sickness set in my heart's motion".' He complains of 'book-starvation' and boredom with his colleagues. 'We are all suffering from a dreadful sense that events have stopped, although the carriage rolls on meaninglessly.' Elsewhere, he remarks that the journal gives an unduly gloomy view of his life because he writes it only when relaxed, idle, and melancholy. However, there is no doubt that 'book-starvation' was a serious and incapacitating disease of those years; I can remember the desperate scavenging one did to find something, anything, to read. Peter, with his small portable collection of *livres de chevet*, and his incessant meditations on the best, could make no concessions to the unlucky books that fell in his way.

Read a stupid book called *Wild Strawberries* by one Angela Thirkell: a dreadful piece of prewar circulating library whimsy and hollow as a rotten nut . . . Somebody produced a copy of *Lady Chatterley's Lover* in an unexpurgated Swedish edition. Nothing could be further from pornography than this work, although no doubt its chief function nowadays is to act as a stimulant for masturbation. Nevertheless, it is really rather a painful work: the scene where the miserable gamekeeper apostrophises his penis is one of the most embarrassing examples of an *idée fixe* destroying judgement and craftmanship at a blow.

In May 1945 the team established its headquarters at Ioánnina, with sub-stations in other nome-capitals. Ure was first at Arta, then, from the end of July, at Igoumenítsa, in charge of the distribution of gift clothing. During this time he saw a good deal of R. G. Cox and of T. J. Cadoux. Cox shared a room with him at Ioánnina, and recalls in particular one conversation, which Ure often recounted to me with relish, about *Wuthering Heights*, on which they had a fundamental disagreement, and another on Basic English, which they concurred in abominating. Cox was with Ure when he bought in a local antique shop the ikon of St Thomas which he later displayed in his house, remarking on the propriety of his possessing an image of this archetypal doubter. Cox remembers how he looked and comported himself:

Peter's appearance and manner were, I should say, remarkably consistent with what they became later. He always had that rather remote and solemn air with its way of relaxing into a slow smile, and the deep and resonant voice with a highly cultivated accent and something of a sarcastic drawl. I think his irony was often lost upon some of our more simple-minded members, but equally I think they came to recognize the genuine qualities underneath a somewhat formidable manner.

Cadoux recalls a chaotic moment in the distribution of relief clothing in Corfu: 'Outside a loud murmuring predominates, but voices are frequently raised and hot arguments are waged between disputants for a prior place. The stentorian yet refined tones of Peter, who controls this stage, can be heard ordering everyone downstairs at intervals.' Later he often recalled that he has somehow naïvely expected the recipients of free clothing to be orderly and grateful, but the expectation did not survive the first distribution. In ELAS villages the beneficiaries tended to be sullen and hostile; elsewhere they fought for the best of the issue. Cadoux describes the work.

Instead of the recipients coming to distribution-centres, the distributions had to take place in the villages, or rather—since the quantities at our disposal were not sufficient for all those in need—in those villages which had been hardest hit by the war-situation. While Greek volunteers sorted out and catalogued the supplies in the stores in each nome-capital, individual members of the British team visited selected villages, ascertained their relative poverty, determined the number of men, women, boys and girls who might receive a garment each, and appointed a local distribution committee. Many of the villages were situated far from roads and we had to reach them on foot or, somewhat less comfortably, by mule. Peter and I on various occasions drove together from Arta as far as possible, and then struck off on foot across the country separately. In most villages all the talking had to be done in Greek. Peter's knowledge of classical Greek gave him a good start in the acquisition of the modern tongue; he was making progress at this in March and by the time he went to Arta was quite capable of conducting an interview on his own. One of the most difficult tasks was to provide against political or other discriminations by the appointment of courageous, honest and impartial men to the distribution committees. Nevertheless, the distribution was often followed by a crop of complaints which one would try rather hopelessly to investigate. In general, the work required immense patience and understanding, tempers were easily frayed, and sympathy for the Greeks strained. To my recollection Peter bore his share with as much steadiness and equanimity as any of us, though trying situations sometimes provoked him into acid remarks.

The journal speaks of some of the events of these months: an alarming drive in a three-tonner with Cox, solitary walks, rage with people who tore the whole of *Samson Agonistes* and *Paradise Regained* out of a copy of Milton which he left in the lavatory. An entry for 1 August is particularly vivid:

I write this under rather peculiar circumstances in the village of Frosini, surrounded in fact by a circle of villagers to whom I try to give the impression that I am making notes in a case-book about their village. I brought the diary within me and without me on this journey as a precautionary introspective measure, and as I now have several hours to wait before the weather is likely to become cool enough for me to set out for the next village, I must spend it somehow in introspective observations. I left Arta to my great regret on Saturday last and am not likely to return, but have transferred myself to Igoumenítsa on the West coast opposite Kerkyra. The Two Repulsions are regrettably there but unfortunately I have to go where there is work to do without bothering too much about the company. Igoumenítsa is in an extremely beautiful situation in a small, almost land-locked bay with a view of Kerkyra on the horizon, although it is not possible to see the double-horned citadel. (This account interrupted by the ceremony of lunch: I consume an enormous cheese omelette . . . watched by twenty interested spectators: however, I have got so accustomed to these ceremonies now that I no longer permit my embarrassment to destroy my appetite.) I was persuaded on Monday to visit villages in the Paramithia region and prepared myself for a Tuesday–Friday tour. Was driven in the car to Paramithia—a very steep road which we attacked with an excessive speed and no mercy on the springs. Reached Paramithia about 5.30 in the evening, and I decided, as there was still time before it grew dark, to go out to a village called Karioti about an hour's walk away from the town. Paramithia itself is a big place with a population, so the proedros told me, of 2,000: it stands in front of a great wall of mountain—the Korilla-Tsiandi range (1564 and 1358 metres high respectively). The local tailor from Karioti who has a shop in Paramithia took me out to his village which lies part of the way up the wall. It was dark when I reached the village, only to find that the proedros wasn't there. However I found his *substitude* (as an Anglo-Greek document I saw the other day so charmingly put it), and also his wife who gave me some food and had a rather nice-looking daughter with the usual slave-girl approach to existence. There were five children who slept outside the cottage on one board stretched out and covered with blankets, while I and another man, who was going to the village where I am now, slept on another. Great amusement when I produced my sleeping-bag and demonstrated how you get inside it (only a sheet sleeping-bag of course). I removed my jacket, but as the lady of the house was still bustling about, got inside the sleeping-bag before removing my shorts and slept in my pants. No mosquitoes, I think,— anyway I had no net and am well fortified by mepacrine. I think all these villages are probably too far away from the plains of Hell and too high up to be gravely affected by malaria, although the peasants who go to work in the fertile plain bring it back with them. I slept moderately well in view of the hardness of the board, though I woke up several times and saw the moon through the fig-tree (which incidentally the woman stoutly denied was a fig-tree though I could see the figs hanging on it myself—perhaps my Greek was at fault). I cannot think what the woman was doing all the night; whenever I woke up she seemed to be flitting about in her curious skirt—a kind of skirt that makes some of the peasant women look like animated dolls since it sticks out all round like a bell; at one time she appeared to be driving a flock of sheep with all their bells ringing through the little yard where we slept underneath the fig-tree; then there was a great banging about of the wooden heirloom of a cradle on the floor which they appear to consider the most efficacious method of putting a crying infant to sleep—though how the baby could sleep for the racket of its own cradle I cannot understand.

I got up at 5.15 am and had a rather summary wash and shave, and was given a very pleasing breakfast of sheep's milk, bread and honey. In view of what followed I was extremely glad of the breakfast, which was certainly much more substantial than one has any right to expect in the Greek countryside. We then started to climb up this confounded wall and a more tiring and dispiriting journey I have rarely endured, especially as we had no sooner reached the top than we climbed immediately all the way down the other side. It took nearly five hours to get from Kariote to Frosini, although as the crow flies it is only four and a half kilometres. I much dislike the prospect of having to make the return journey on Friday. Tonight I go to Kouklior.

That autumn he had to prepare for further and heavier responsibilities.

21 October 1945—Spent a quiet and peaceful afternoon visiting the island in the Lake of Ioánnina, where Ali Pasha had his retreat. There were six of us—Paul, Donald Swann, Mary and Marjorie Whittles, who has come up from Rhodes on leave. Ali Pasha's villa is still standing though in a profoundly ruined condition. Behind it stands a small church, its walls entirely covered with murals in the Byzantine style— some originally Byzantine work I believe. The villa itself is built round a courtyard, a very humble version of the grand Cairene 'palace', to use the terminology of the Thousand and One. On the way back Donald bathed from the boat. He has just joined us from Rhodes to become welfare officer in one of the homes. He is a remarkable person —the only person, with possibly one exception, in whom I have felt creative genius to be present. I think that I felt this when I first met him three and a half years ago. His conversation is at times disconcertingly crowded with rather obscure metaphors and images. He is extremely modest and courteous, entirely unselfseeking also, I should say; but his intelligence is plainly more luminous and his mind more wide-ranging than that of anyone else in this company.

I have been feeling rather depressed all week and suffer from a shocking cold. I felt suddenly the conviction this afternoon . . . that I must try more profoundly to appreciate and enjoy the passing days. It is a mistake to have expectations in the future. But I feel now more than ever a dreadful isolation pressing upon me which can only increase with the years. I was astounded to hear the other day that L. H. Myers, the author of *The Root and the Flower,* had committed suicide. It seems remarkable that the author of that particular book should destroy himself. Our sanity is terribly threatened, and the longer and the further away the mountain happiness seems, the more fearful becomes the prospect. Occasionally I see with clarity the hellish dilemma and what its results are likely to be.

This week I have started on a definite programme of trying to improve my Greek in preparation for my departure to Kerkira; and have also been making a study of the welfare files. Time will show whether I can do the job there to my own or anyone else's satisfaction; and also whether I am to stay in Greece until I can go home or visit another country.

There is no doubt that in these days, as throughout his life, Ure was conscious of a difficulty in simply treating other people as genuinely having the kind of interest they promised. He regarded this as a serious defect in himself. He found the task of describing new people and new experiences a tedious one, and blamed 'a kind of timid arrogance' in himself which prevented him 'from being interested, writer-like, in the nature and relation-ships of other people'. This observation, recorded in the journal for 8 December, when he was enjoying an enforced solitude, is interesting not least for that word *writer-like*. It was hard for him to conceive that there are other ways of relating to people. Cadoux remarks that Ure joined in all the fun—swimming, excursions, and so on—but was less expansive than the others. He could sometimes seem almost inhumanly cut off from the lives of his companions. One member of the team remembered arriving in Ioánnina after the long and tiring drive from Athens, and finding, when he entered the house after midnight, that everybody had gone to bed except Peter, who was sitting with his feet up, smoking a large pipe, and reading, through heavy-rimmed spectacles, something by Eliot. He looked up, spoke a word of greeting, and returned to his book. Cadoux also remem-bers what looks in retrospect like a pure wartime farce, but must have been disturbing at the time. Ure drove a truck past the Prefecture in Kerkira just as the ceremonial lowering of the flag was in progress; instead of stopping he tried to squeeze between the band and some parked cars, and had the bad luck to damage the one that belonged to the Governor. In the official report on this accident he explained the accident thus: 'As I passed, the rear offside wing of the Governor's car caught the front nearside wing of my vehicle.' This endowment of a stationary vehicle with dynamic force and malicious motive will be treated sympathetically by anyone who has ever written, or even read, a report on a traffic collision. Such adventures are anyway the stuff of campaigning; at least they force one into some rough practical relationship with other and perhaps less sensitive people. In a way they must have provided some relief from the growing absorption of his own thought.

The practice of poetry merely exploits the deficiencies and defects already in my personality—because out of them the poetry is made. I know no other subject, fundamentally, so perhaps I shall fail or grow peculiar in the end . . . Into poetry I flee, escaping from the varieties of people, from the indissolubly hard task of describing the relationships between people. And this cause will prove, does prove, a defect in the effect. 'Perfection of the life or of the work'—Yeats was wrong, alas. One does not choose between them—they are the same. And I at present am raging in the dark.

On 15 January 1946, after three and a half years with the FAU, Ure became an UNRRA officer, and took on a much larger and more complex organization. He found himself, near the end of the war, a person of importance, consorting, however uneasily, with the higher military. They occasionally made some routine remark about the conscientious objectors thought to be operating in Save the Children Fund or FAU; but he no longer wore the FAU flashes, and did not have to admit that he was one of the unspeakables. However, he could not help reflecting that his was a strange war: 'I started this war being rudely treated by Walton Gaol warders and end it drinking gin with generals' (15 April 1946).

In May he was appointed Regional Welfare Officer for the Cyclades, a further promotion. When he left Corfu on 23 May he was kissed on both cheeks by the Archbishop and given handsome farewell presents. The Nomarch sent him a letter suitable for framing. In the new job he worked hard, as usual, travelling his difficult beat by caique, mule, and truck. His friends began to go home to lectureships and other jobs. A visit from the heavily protected Fiorello La Guardia resulted in a heavy cut in UNRRA funds. He made new friends, but repeated his favourite Rilke quotation: 'So badly does one live because one always comes incomplete into the present, inept and scatterbrained.'

Always conscious of any failing in a set task, he cannot but have taken pleasure in the thought that his career in Greece had been so successful. In little more than a year he rose from his humble position on a relief team to a position of administrative power in which his Greek, as well as his administrative ability, were judged of high importance in a national crisis. This satisfaction is perhaps in part reflected in his expressions of pain at the prospect of leaving Greece. He had money enough to stay on for a year or so. 'This evening', he writes on 17 August, 'I walked up to what in England would be called the "moor" and contemplated the flat stones in the dying light, the stout fig-trees and the outline of hills and rocks in the sky. I cannot bear the thought of leaving this landscape'—but he adds characteristically that this feeling might vanish if he had a job to go back to. 'In any case,' he says, 'a period is ending.' In September 1946, with the UNRRA project in great confusion, he was called

to Athens, and he concluded his Greek journal with these lines
from Pope's *Odyssey*, xiii:

> Now all the land another prospect bore,
> Another port appeared, another shore,
> And long-continued ways, and winding floods
> And unknown mountains, crowned with unknown woods . . .

But he had six more weeks to pass in the Cyclades. His departure
having been postponed by an illness, he sadly left Syros for
Athens in early November, and on the 14th sailed for Toulon.
He spent a few days in Paris en route, and ended his journal.
'On the whole I have *fait un bon voyage* and am content.'

He had no job to go back to, but he did have a graduate scholarship at Liverpool, and there he went, just after his book came
out, to work for his doctorate. I had got back a little before him,
at the beginning of 1946. Everybody who had a similar experience
will recall the low spirits and subdued dismay of the first year
of return from the wars. One was extremely glad to be out of it
after five or six years; but the loneliness, the sense, no doubt
unjustified, of neglect—of lost friends and out-of-touch teachers
—perhaps above all an unconscious reluctance to begin all over
again at 26 the life one had lost at 20—these miseries went deep
enough to remain always within the power of recall, so that to
be asked which was the unhappiest period of one's life is to have
an easy answer: 1946. It was a return to the cold, to squalor, to
what seemed an endless prospect of solitude and poverty.

I remember thinking that Ure identified himself with these
conditions with an almost unnecessary willingness. He took a
room or rooms in, I think, Princes Drive, and there we would
sit and conduct conversations of very low tone among the
remarkable furnishings—crazy leather armchairs with the
springs sticking up at prohibitive angles, unbearable brown
wallpaper and skirtings. Once when he came to dinner during
the appalling heatless winter of 1946-7 at the hall in which I
lived he was struck down, as were all the other diners, by the
diarrhoea which in those days quite often followed the consump-
tion of tainted food. I remember his lugubrious account of the
sufferings of the night, which somehow distinguished them
from one's own.

Meanwhile he applied himself, with that unmatched self-dedication, to the task of turning himself into a scholar. He had the Socratic intuition that he knew nothing, and the further intuition that scholarship was a craft that one could learn only by the most intense labour. He lived with a frugality he admitted to be excessive, and worked day and night. He had few amusements and few friends. It was undoubtedly a miserable time, and for good or ill it was the period during which he revised his life-plan, for the output of poetry now began to diminish (it virtually dried up in 1949 after two years as a teacher) and he who had through all his literate years thought of himself as a probationary poet now became a probationary scholar. The work he did on allegory during that time was never finished, though it must have nourished his later studies; so far as I know he did not go back to it after being required, by his teaching duties at Newcastle, to become expert in Elizabethan and Jacobean drama.

I had not then, and have not now, the slightest doubt that he was professionally the best-equipped man who ever sought a job in English literature; but he did not find one at once. There were jobs to be had, of course, as departments opened up a little; but there was a tendency to be half-hearted in one's applications and interviews, out of an unhappy conviction, more justified in my case than in Ure's, that the six-year break had incapacitated one from taking on immediately the routine duties of the job; and of course we were desperately trying to write theses rather than re-educating, or educating, ourselves.

After a number of depressing failures we found ourselves, in May 1947, bound for Newcastle to compete for a job. We never forgot the intelligent and sympathetic handling of those interviews by Lord Eustace Percy; he made it possible for one to forget one's disabilities, and when the ordeal was over John Butt revealed that there were two jobs, not one, and appointed us both. Thus, having arrived together at Liverpool by very different routes in 1937, we were once again, after inscribing our eccentric routes all over the globe, in company; and we started work that autumn, with a workload that would seem incredible to a new man nowadays, but with a certain contentment to mitigate our apprehensions.

Ure very efficiently found himself rooms in Archbold Terrace and settled to the task. It lasted him for the rest of his life, for

he never believed that he knew enough, and could teach what
he knew well enough, to slacken off. The anomalous conditions
of that first year tended to strengthen this feeling. We were
not only beginners, but had very unusual classes to teach, mostly
of ex-servicemen with a strenuous desire to learn and to qualify,
men of our own age almost, insatiable in class and in those
extempore discussions which were so much more common on
the narrow crowded stairs of 32 Eldon Place than they can ever
be in academic corridors. Peter worked day and night at his
lectures. (We had six a week each, and John Butt often found us
ready, if hardly willing, to stop gaps in the teaching casually
complained of by students, so that one was always hastily preparing lectures.) At the same time Ure saw it as part of his job
to publish scholarly papers, and his essay on Senecan and
Elizabethan tragedy was written in this year; of course his output broadened as the pressures of teaching diminished.

The atmosphere at Eldon Place was certainly conducive to
hard work. We owed a great deal to the challenge of the students, but also to the example of older colleagues. Ralph Elmes,
who lived in Eldon Place, was wonderfully friendly, courteous,
and hospitable, and full of useful advice; Angus Macdonald
brooded by the hour in his attic over the apparent chaos of the
Annual Bibliography; John Butt out-taught everybody, yet managed to get on with his own books and edit the *Review of English
Studies*. In this, his Thursday task, we found ourselves increasingly involved, and soon we were both launched as reviewers. So,
whether or not truth flourished, the student's lamp shone over
Eldon Place; I remember Chalmers Burns, observing it at midnight week in and week out, asking if we ever went home.

Ure's mood in those days, as nearly always, was slightly withdrawn and melancholy. I remember once, in Archbold Terrace,
his announcing that he was a poet *manqué*. He had so heavy a
cold at the time that I did not hear clearly, and asked him to say
it again; he thought he was being teased and responded with one
of his black flares of temper. Another favourite self-description:
'Time's eunuch'. Meanwhile in his study at Archbold Terrace he
built up that collection of books which has happily remained
intact; characteristically orderly and carefully chosen, it is an
image of the scholarly life he chose for himself. Sometimes he
was reluctant to leave that life, even when socially committed

to do so; I recall one extraordinary occasion, about 1949, when he had invited some people including myself to dinner; but discovered on sitting down that he could not face it, and resigned to me his duty as host. On such occasions, or on others more academic, he was not so much gloomy as a sort of representation of a Humour: his name might have been Morose. But this wasn't, of course, the normal mood, and one remembers rather from off-duty encounters a sort of resonant joking, fantasies about scholarly foolishness, giggling and making giggle.

From the beginning he interested himself in Newcastle and the region; he lectured very early at the Literary and Philosophical Society, enjoyed wandering about the city, and explored Northumberland, which supplanted Cornwall as his favourite English county. Eventually he bought a car and drove himself about in it, very fast. His interest in cars may strike some as uncharacteristic; not in that he looked after them carefully, but in that he drove them hard and changed them often. The cinema was another relaxation; here he persuaded himself to be less discriminating than when reading, and he went to large numbers of very bad pictures. Before his illness set in he enjoyed travel; I remember an early British Council visit to Germany. He went by sea with Fr Coplestone, and their conversations on the way were reported with relish. Peter had mixed feelings about Jesuits; a student subtle in argument was likely to be called 'jesuitical'. Indeed, his deep distrust of the Roman Catholic Church corresponded with his affection for the Quakers; he recognized in himself a strong religious faculty, under the control of a deep scepticism ('doubting Thomas'), but hated the power generated by institutionalized religion. Mr Frank McCombie, a student of his who went up in 1950 and thenceforth remained his friend, remembers as a Catholic that Ure's strictures on his Church, though severe, were always delivered inoffensively; the tone changed but the views did not, and were similarly expressed towards the end of Ure's life. Not that this would interfere with his valuation of a mind. He could enjoy and admire a Jesuit without changing his views on the jesuitical.

The other teachers of those early days—Butt, Macdonald, Elmes, Colin Clarke, Ruth Christian—are all either dead or long departed from Newcastle, and Barbara Strang alone remains of those who were his colleagues in the days before he took the

Chair. I left Newcastle in December 1949. As an increasingly old
friend I saw him quite often, and was, I suppose, a privileged
mark for that affectionate derision which he enjoyed dealing
out. He had a relation of special affection with my wife Maureen,
with whom he laughed more than with anybody else I knew. In
1956, after giving the matter a good deal of thought, he consented
to stand as godfather to my son, and he carried out his attenuated
and secularized duties with the customary punctilio. But as time
went on one saw less of him. This was largely due to his illness.
His last visit to us was in 1966, when we were living in the
country in Gloucestershire. He stayed for lunch but declined
further invitations, wishing to push on to Dorset. It was a soaked
West Country day. What would he do when he got there? Go
to the cinema, he supposed. He enjoyed company and children,
but not for long. In a letter of May 1967 he remarked that he
had given up the Sunday papers years before and knew nothing
of what went on in London. He liked the idea of staying with us
there; but 'I have no excuse to visit London, except sheer wan-
tonness of fancy. What on earth happens to all those publishers'
luncheons one hears about? A publisher once invited me to have
a drink in a pub—but that was in Edinburgh, and was the
highwater-mark of my relations with publishers. I don't even
belong to any metropolitan committees, as all my colleagues
seem to.' This half-joking tone conceals a genuine resentment
at the neglect and impoverishment of the regions by a greedy
metropolis; he wrote angrily to the *Guardian* about the reluctance of the national companies to tour, and, more positively,
supported and worked for the Northern Arts Association. I saw
him last a year before his death, appropriately in Newcastle.
I was bound for Edinburgh and have always been glad I broke
the journey to see him. He gave a pre-lunch sherry party for me.
Surrounded by his staff, a little unbending I thought, he must
have seemed a rather formal boss. But in private he was relaxed,
and spoke calmly of his illness. Sometimes this calm was broken;
he told my wife on the telephone, in the spring of 1969, that
'Things are closing in'.

It is not my purpose to recount in detail the history of his
Newcastle career. His books, and all his published writings were
meditated and composed in Newcastle; they include the best
study of Yeats's drama we have, the best brief account of Yeats,

and many essays on that poet. His edition of *Richard II* is standard; he also edited Ford's *Perkin Warbeck*, and a long-pondered
edition of *Two Noble Kinsmen* for the New Cambridge Shakespeare was still incomplete at his death; unhappily, the Syndics of
the Cambridge University Press did not feel that in the case of a
play so controversial they could ask another scholar to finish it.
Over the years he wrote many articles, some of great importance, on the Elizabethan and Jacobean drama; the body of work
on Chapman is particularly impressive. His inaugural lecture
was a memorable piece of Shakespearian criticism. He was an
admirable reviewer. His list of publications hints at, without in
any way equalling, the range of his reading: he wrote for example on Milton, Byron, Wordsworth, Conrad, George Moore, and
Shaw. He was reading Shaw at the time of his death; we found
some very recent notes in his study. He continued, in short, to
honour that original obligation to conduct research. In doing so
he made himself one of the acknowledged masters of academic
criticism in his time, and only those who knew the true scope
of his ambitions, and of the talents that justified them, could find
cause to lament that his whole power was not put forth.

As a teacher he naturally believed students should work
hard. In 1947 there was a student with polio, who often had to
wait in his chair for others to carry him up or down the stairs of
32 Eldon Place. During these minutes of idleness he would read
some magazine or newspaper. John Butt took note of this; I
heard him tell the boy that the proper use of such moments was
the test of a good student. This rigorous attitude to work was
shared by his successor. He was tired, as we all were, by the
exceptional demands of that first year, but later he often
regretted that the intellectual demands of students diminished
so drastically when the veteran wave was passed.

Among that set was Ian Gregor, who became a close friend;
Ure was very gratified when, shortly before his death, he heard
the news of Gregor's professorship at Kent. Some account of
how a younger student might see him is provided by Mr Frank
McCombie, who arrived at King's, aged 20, in October 1950.
McCombie remembers both the sustained care Ure gave him
and also a youthful gaiety that could break through the usually
somewhat sombre manner. McCombie notes that not all students
were aware of this natural reserve of humanity, though he was

richly aware that as the years passed this warmth 'found its way securely to the surface of his life, and had come to irradiate his whole personality'. Nevertheless, he knew Ure well enough to see that there was also a reserve of irascibility, and that this could be directed at his colleagues. 'He was very much an old lion in his last days.'

It is very doubtful that undergraduates ever saw much of his unpredictable temper, or experienced the shock which he could administer by a gratuitous violence of language. This was not a consequence of his illness; inexplicable flares of temper were not uncommon in the Ure of 19, perhaps even, as the journal suggests, in the schoolboy. But the illness certainly did not help, and it also limited his movements. He did not care to go abroad, or even to remove himself far from the range of Newcastle doctors. Neville Newhouse remarks that he had little respect for doctors, 'not because they could not cure him but because he found them evasive when he asked them point-blank questions'. He certainly did not fuss about his illness, though many of his friends speak of the pain he suffered during sudden bad moments of it; nor did he spare himself by delegating his responsibilities to others. But there was an inevitable measure of caution. I remember that he wired to Sligo during the Yeats summer school of 1960 that he could not come and speak because of a threatened strike on the railway steamers which might have cut him off from his doctors.

His reluctance to accept the Joseph Cowen Chair in the following year certainly had much to do with his concern for his health. There was no coyness in his *nolo episcopari*; I discussed it with him and he was quite clear that he did not really want the job. There were other reasons: the sense, which he often expressed in his wartime journals, that his work suffered from the distractions entailed by leading, organizing, management of men; the knowledge that if he took it on he would have to compel himself to do it exhaustingly well; and lastly, a genuine but of course erroneous notion that he was unworthy of his predecessors. On the other hand, he told Ernst Honigmann that when the Chair was offered 'the idea of following John Butt . . . was so flattering it was hard to resist'—a confession not inconsistent, as Honigmann remarks, with his saying to Barbara Strang, 'It will kill me before my time.'

Of his eight-year tenure of the Chair I say little. It was impossible, given that selflessness, that austere benignity, that mastery of the subject, for him to fail. In his department he was, though without authoritarianism, master. In Faculty he was effective, though less so in Senate. He accepted responsibility for his subject within but also beyond the University—on the Northern Arts Association, and in the Newcastle English Society. He had enemies, as all heads of department perhaps must have if they are doing their jobs; but many friends remain in the University who will testify to the quality and ease of his intimacy. There are others scattered about the country, many of them old friends, since he was one of those who always take care not to lose possessions so valuable.

Throughout the writing of these pages I have been possessed by so strong an idea of the personality of Ure that I have chosen from the mass of material what seemed most fully to express it, at the expense of the more detailed record of his life that could have been constructed. I have not discussed his scholarship, of which the remainder of this volume anyway contains ample evidence; I have said little of the poetry to which he so passionately devoted his youth, and not much about his achievements at Newcastle. Instead I have given most of my space to the years between 1937 and 1946, believing that they best reveal his mind and his mood. He did not change as much as many of us. The strong runner's physique, the natural grace, were never lost; even the sober but somehow elegant clothes and ties, were always a part of the same image. The voice, and the extraordinarily careful formation and articulation of sentences, expressed a humanist's duty to language and were the outward signs of the intense inner life we glimpse in the journals. For Ure's real motive was to find a life in literature; to discover in poetry reason, vision, justice. The conditions finally imposed by the world were harsh; that he should not achieve what he wanted by the means he proposed, that contemplation must constantly give way to appropriate action. When in his early Newcastle days he turned to the study of Stoicism he must have recognized that he had already felt that philosophy on his pulses. In the world of men, usually lesser men, in whom, when charity failed, he found small interest, another old passion would seize him: the desire to succeed, to do well what others with clear conscience might do less completely. Here one sees the schoolboy, under the intense care of his literary mother, the ironic eye of his successful and civilized father. Old patterns of anxiety lie beneath the strenuousness of both contemplation and action. Holidays from so exacting a consciousness and conscience were rare, perhaps too rare; there are in one's mind memories of a Peter who left early—a Christmas party, perhaps, or a wedding—unable to sail with the wind of public gaiety, or beckoned back to his desk by the demands of work. And then this withdrawal would be a cause of self-scrutiny. Perhaps such a life lacks the kind of spontaneity that as a Yeatsian he most admired; but one can say of it, as of very few, that it was an examined life.

PART I

THE POEMS

I

W. B. Yeats and the growth
of a poet's mind

William Butler Yeats started his poetical career as an admirer,
and to a degree as an imitator of the English pre-Raphaelite
school led by D. G. Rossetti and Edward Burne-Jones. But his
chief master in the last years of the nineteenth century was the
poet William Morris. Morris had rejected much in Victorianism,
including the buoyant commercialism which had set the slum
beside the mansion in so many English cities. His opposition
took the alternative but related forms of an equally buoyant
socialism matched with an eager cultivation of folk-literature,
of medievalism, and of everything that seemed simple and
genuine in the art and crafts of the common people. If the
landscapes and figures in Morris's poetry seem nowadays to be
over-decorated and falsely 'literary' this is perhaps because
Morris shared with the other pre-Raphaelites a common disadvantage: he had little close or enduring acquaintance with the
life of the peasantry.

The comparison between the work of Morris and that of Yeats,
although it has never been worked out in anything approaching
the necessary detail,[1] is an instructive one. Many of the elements
which appear in Morris's work—the love of popular literature,
the desire for unity of culture, the rage against what seems to be
the commercial man's natural love for the ugly—became
fundamental to Yeats's life and thought. Yet Yeats surpassed
his master Morris. This, I suggest, was due to the fact that he
inherited a different social tradition, and a very powerful one,
to which he could and did turn when pre-Raphaelitism broke

Written in 1947 in response to a request from an Italian journal, but not
published.

1. See, however, for one aspect of this relationship the book by D. M. Hoare,
The Works of Morris and of Yeats in Relation to Early Saga Literature (1937).

to pieces through its failure to come to terms with 'this pragmatical, preposterous pig of a world'. This traditon was that of
the Irish Protestant aristocracy. Although Yeats himself was
born very near to Dublin (13 June 1865), he spent much of his
childhood and youth at Sligo on the western Irish coast.[2] His
forebears were Protestant rectors and landowners, the privileged foreign aristocracy in a land of Catholic peasants, the
'hard-riding country gentlemen' of Yeats's later verse. Yeats,
when he spoke of the aristocrat and the peasant, had a real and
contemporary experience in mind, not merely a literary and
historical one. To this experience he added many years of work
for the Abbey Theatre in Dublin, work carried on in collabora-
tion with the leading figures of the Irish literary Renaissance, a
great period in the history of Ireland, during which the acrid
smoke of political struggle cleared many times to reveal patriot,
poet, scholar, and adventurer in attitudes which reminded
Yeats and others of the Italian Renaissance itself. This tradition
and history Yeats partook of and relied upon as a poet—a fact
which he stated many times, uniting with it his belief in the
necessity of cultural unity. Poetry must draw upon popular
culture, speech, and language, said Yeats, in lines in which he
associated with himself the two other principal figures of the
Irish Renaissance:

> John Synge, I and Augusta Gregory, thought
> All that we did, all that we said or sang
> Must come from contact with the soil, from that
> Contact everything Antaeus-like grew strong.
> We three alone in modern times had brought
> Everything down to that sole test again,
> Dream of the noble and the beggar-man.[3]

'Alone in modern times'—the splendid arrogance of that claim
is typical of Yeats when he is reviewing his own position in the
cultural and social scale. In one of his last poems—written in
1938—we can observe the traditional elements set out and concluding in a final triumphant assertion of the value of an integral,
vivid, and self-conscious national culture:

2. The chief authorities for the life of W. B. Yeats are his own masterly *Autobiographies*.
3. 'The Municipal Gallery Revisited.'

Irish poets, learn your trade,
Sing whatever is well made,
Scorn the sort now growing up
All out of shape from toe to top,
Their unremembering hearts and heads
Base-born products of base beds.
Sing the peasantry, and then
Hard-riding country gentlemen,
The holiness of monks, and after
Porter-drinkers' randy laughter;
Sing the lords and ladies gay
That were beaten into the clay
Through seven heroic centuries;
Cast your mind on other days
That we in coming days may be
Still the indomitable Irishry.[4]

The interest of these lines lies partly in the fact that, while sketching a programme for others, Yeats described his own career and achievement. The self-confident tone ought not to deceive us into thinking that the struggle along this way had been an easy one. The injunction to 'cast your mind on other days' had had very different implications in 1889 when Yeats's first collection of lyrics was published, although even then it was being faithfully obeyed. For, backed though he was by the Irish tradition and essential as is the understanding of the value of this tradition to Yeats as a poet, it was not to Yeats a literary tradition primarily, but a social one, whose existence influenced strongly his thinking about society and history but did not provide him in itself with a solution to the problems of poetic form and theme. In order to solve these problems, Yeats looked not purely to Irish but to European letters (and further still indeed to the Japanese drama and the writings of oriental sage and saint). Unlike Synge or Lady Gregory, whom we think of primarily as Irish writers, Yeats was forced to move outside the purely Irish tradition, because his thinking about life and art was profounder than theirs. Consequently, the experiences developed and the needs expressed in his poetry made use of the larger European landscape. The result is that Yeats stands forth not as an Irish poet well known in England but as a European poet who wrote in English. Yet the rootedness, the constant pressure of the

4. 'Under Ben Bulben: V.'

Irish tradition in his work must never be forgotten. For all these reasons, it is convenient and illuminating to regard Yeats's work as a 'search': he starts from Ireland, he returns to it many times, bringing spoils from his journey to enrich that beloved and familiar tradition. In the course of his search Yeats makes himself a poet of European significance. It can be shown, I think, that this search was forced upon Yeats by his sensitivity to the problem of what it is to be a poet in the context of modern European life and letters; that the search was in fact a search for a solution to that problem, and that in the end it became a search for a specific type of theme and poetic process.

In the late poem called 'The Circus Animals' Desertion' (1939) Yeats commented upon his endless search for a theme and upon what he considered his failure to find one. He will abandon what he calls his 'circus animals', his allegorized mythology from Irish classical literature, and turn instead from these 'dreams' to reality:

> I must lie down where all the ladders start,
> In the foul rag-and-bone shop of the heart.

Yeats had from time to time in the course of his poetic career made a similar distinction between old mythologies and 'walking naked'[5] and enjoined upon himself the need for withering into truth:

> Through all the lying days of my youth
> I swayed my leaves and flowers in the sun;
> Now I may wither into the truth.[6]

In fact he never did abandon the search, but he was aware of the conflict and used it as poetic material:

> *The Soul.* Seek out reality, leave things that seem.
> *The Heart.* What, be a singer born and lack a theme?[7]

It is with reference to this pattern of a search for theme, itself conducted against the background of the Irish tradition, that any account of the development of Yeats's poetry may be most coherently set. In the early poems Yeats's main task is the use of Irish themes to express a dreamy sensibility of mixed Celtic and pre-Raphaelite origin. With more than a touch of irony he later

---

5. 'A Coat' (1914).   6. 'The Coming of Wisdom with Time' (1910).
7. 'Vacillation: VII.'

described, in the course of a critical estimate of Morris, what he himself was doing in his early work: he was creating 'new forms of melancholy, and faint persons . . . who are never, no not once in forty volumes, put out of temper'.[8] In his plays, on the other hand, he was trying, both at this time and later, to serve the needs of a real theatre; but his conception of the theatre changed from that of an Irish National Theatre to that of a 'little theatre' of the most exclusive type.[9] While the plays continued to be addressed to a theatrical reality it was one which had changed with the change in Yeats's art. This change, which has been much discussed,[1] was certainly a fundamental alteration of style; but, although Yeats had escaped from the aestheticism of the nineties into the stormy life of 'theatre business, management of men', and even, unlike the pre-Raphaelite heroes, lost his temper continuously throughout a whole volume which contains little but satirical attacks on the stupidity of his countrymen,[2] the poetic need was exactly the same. Pre-Raphaelitism had been one way, and an unsatisfactory way, of solving the dilemma of the poet in the modern world, the dilemma of which Yeats was continually conscious—the lack of a sense of order, the fragmentation of culture, the increasing mechanization and specialization in men and society which Yeats specifically describes and protests against in countless passages in the essays and autobiographical writings.

The search for a theme is one aspect of this poet's intellectual adventure; the search for a solution to the historical and religious problem, the problem presented by a dying and disintegrating social order, is another, and vitally important also. For it is not till Yeats was able to solve this problem, or to see the solution within sight, that he was enabled to become not only a skilful and moving dramatist and lyrist, but a great poet— 'one of those few', in Mr Eliot's words, 'whose history is the history of their own time, who are a part of the consciousness of an age which cannot be understood without them'.[3] The story

8. *Autobiographies* (1955), pp. 142–3.
9. See the essay 'A People's Theatre' in *Plays and Controversies* (1923).
1. For example by V. K. Narayana Menon in *The Development of William Butler Yeats* (1942) and by C. M. Bowra in *The Heritage of Symbolism* (1943).
2. The volume is *Responsibilities* (1914).
3. From Eliot's lecture on Yeats at Dublin in 1940, *On Poetry and Poets* (1957), p. 262.

of that search, the formation of a philosophy of history and of
human personality and fate, and the development of that
philosophy into a 'system', is to be found in Yeats's prose writings, of which the most important, from our point of view, are
Reveries over Childhood and Youth (1915), *Per Amica Silentia
Lunae* (1918), *The Trembling of the Veil* (1922), and *A Vision* (1925).[4]
This body of prose writings, worthy to rank with Keats's *Letters*
as one of the most remarkable and explicit accounts of the
'growth of a poet's mind' which we possess, has been strangely
neglected by students of twentieth-century poetry. Yeats's art
is that of 'a nature, that never ceases to judge itself',[5] and in the
prose writings we have, as one would expect, many anticipations
and echoes of the verse, which help to illuminate and explain
much that is obscure. But the importance of the autobiographical writings goes far beyond this: at the end of his life in his play
Purgatory (1939) Yeats expressed in dramatic form some of the
philosophical ideas which are explained in *A Vision*. There is no
reason to disbelieve Yeats when he declares: 'I have put [into
the play] my own conviction about this world and the next.'[6] It is
not till we have understood what Yeats means by this remark
in this context that we can understand his later poetry.

Speaking of his childhood Yeats wrote in 1914: 'I had as many
ideas as I have now, only I did not know how to choose from
among them those that belonged to my life.'[7] Consciously or
not, Yeats tended to choose ideas not for themselves but for their
function, to satisfy a need, ultimately to satisfy a poetic need. In
1928 he was to make quite clear that he regarded much of the
system of ideas explained in *A Vision* as 'stylistic arrangements
of experience . . . They have helped me to hold in a single
thought reality and justice.'[8] That is to say, they had fulfilled his
need, they had given order, comprehensibility, and unity to the
cruel unintelligibilities of history. In another passage, in *The
Trembling of the Veil*, he writes: 'As life goes on we discover that
certain thoughts sustain us in defeat, or give us victory . . . and
it is these thoughts, tested by passion, that we call convictions.'[9]

4. Dates of first publication only are given. The *Reveries* and *The Trembling of the
Veil* were reissued together as *Autobiographies* in 1926; *Per Amica Silentia Lunae* was
included in *Essays* (1924). The 1925 edition of *A Vision* was for private circulation
only and was reissued with alterations and enlargements to the general public
only in 1937.
  5. *Autobiographies*, p. 332.   6. *Letters of W. B. Yeats* (ed. A. Wade, 1954), p. 913.
  7. *Autobiographies*, p. 83.   8. *A Vision*, p. 25.   9. *Autobiographies*, p. 189.

What then are these 'convictions', which are also 'stylistic arrangements of experience'? From the earliest period of his adult life Yeats had been interested in a phase of human speculation and experience which can only be crudely expressed by the term *spiritualism* and which certainly was not popular spiritualism, a form which Yeats himself condemned in rejecting. In the last decade of the nineteenth century he made use in *The Celtic Twilight* of the legends of ghosts and fairies which still remained to haunt the consciousness and daily life of the Irish peasant; but even before this he had become associated with a body variously described as 'The Hermetic Students' or 'The Hermetic Society', and, under the guidance of MacGregor Mathers, a magician, telepathist, and seer, had dabbled in various kinds of occult and esoteric study. Madame Blavatsky, the theosophist leader, had encouraged these propensities: 'For a period he called on her every six weeks, and felt for her the same kind of admiration which he gave to William Morris.'[1] His interest in esoteric knowledge never faded, although he wrote later of much of his youthful enthusiasm in tones which expressed a certain reflective self-mockery. And he examined Madame Blavatsky's clock in order to discover the hidden mechanism that caused it to hoot like a cuckoo.[2] To this Yeats added the study of Swedenborg, Boehme, and the Cabbala, and of Blake's *Prophetic Books*, which in fact he helped to edit. We can imagine this kind of speculation and experience lying unsystematized—and deliberately unsystematized—in Yeats's mind. But eventually the resistance to forming these ideas into a system of belief broke down. A passage from *The Trembling of the Veil* describes what happened:

I thought it was my business in life [Yeats is describing the 1887–91 period] to be an artist and a poet, and that there could be no business comparable to that. I refused to read books and even to meet people who excited me to generalization . . . I began to pray that my imagination might somehow be rescued from abstraction and become as preoccupied with life as had been the imagination of Chaucer. For ten or twelve years more I suffered continual remorse . . . My very remorse helped to spoil my early poetry, giving it an element of sentimentality through my refusal to permit it any share of an intellect which I considered impure.[3]

1. Joseph Hone, *W. B. Yeats 1865–1939* (2nd ed., 1962), p. 69.
2. The story is told in *Autobiographies*, p. 174.   3. Ibid., p. 188.

The resistance broke down; the systematizing intellect won; and the direct result was the foreshadowing of the complete system of esoteric belief in the Michael Robartes stories and in *Per Amica Silentia Lunae* and the system itself fully expressed in *A Vision*.

Perhaps, from this particular aspect, the most important fact about *A Vision* is that it succeeds in systematizing and explaining the very conflict itself, the conflict which lies at the heart of Yeats's later poetry, which is indeed the subject of much of it— the conflict between the 'fragmentary passionate man' and the abstract intellect. *A Vision* sprang from and was conditioned by a spiritualistic experience.[4] On 24 October 1917, four days after Yeats's marriage, the poet's wife manifested the psychical phenomenon known as 'automatic writing'. She had become, according to Yeats's account, the means whereby certain spirits, whom Yeats called the 'unknown instructors', were able to explain to the poet the nature of the world and of man. The system of *A Vision* claims to be 'a classification ... of every possible movement of thought and of life'.[5] The communication from the instructors continued, first by means of automatic writing, later through verbal messages, and continued irregularly for some six years (1917–24). Such communication was for Yeats 'tongued with fire beyond the language of the living'. We may 'explain' it by supposing that Yeats, passionately concerned as he now was with discovering some kind of formulable truth, 'transferred' his thoughts to his wife, who retailed them back again by means of her mediumistic powers—a process that Yeats, in another connection, called his 'own Daimon, [his] own buried self speaking through [his] friend's mind'.[6] In this way the resistance to intellectual formulation, to the abstraction and generalization which Yeats conceived as the enemy of all the passionate and creative values, was overcome. Perhaps it was the only way in which it could be overcome. It is significant that the instructors forbade Yeats to study philosophy as long as the series of communications was in progress. Equally significant, too, is the fact that when the 1925 edition of *A Vision* had been published and the task imposed on Yeats by the instructors was at an end, he turned eagerly to the study of formal philosophy and even-

4. Although Yeats specifically repudiates popular spiritualism (*A Vision*, p. 24).
5. Ibid., p. 78.   6. *Autobiographies*, p. 371.

tually rewrote much of *A Vision* for the 1937 edition with the excuse that owing to his ignorance of philosophy at the time he had misunderstood much of the instructors' original message.[7]

The instructors, however, encouraged the poet to read and study 'history in relation to their historical logic, and biography in relation to their twenty-eight typical incarnations, that I might give concrete expression to their abstract thought'.[8] The system is essentially an attempt to comprehend within a formula the chaos of the human personality and the unintelligibility of history. The principal symbol is the geometrical double cone: we must think of two fool's caps placed in relation to each other in such a way that the apex of each is in the middle of the other's base, so that one diminishes while the other increases. This symbolizes the way the human personality is divided between its subjective and objective tendencies. (Yeats calls them *antithetical* or natural, *primary* or reasonable.) These tendencies are related in a complicated way, which Yeats explains with the free use of geometrical diagrams, to the 'four faculties' possessed by each personality, which are the will and that which the will seeks, thought and that which thought comprehends.[9] The increasing and diminishing cones of subjective and objective are in their turn symbolized by the waxing and waning of the moon, because, like the cones, the dark part of the moon expands as the illuminated part contracts, and vice versa. Yeats says he has been told to make the movement of the four faculties in relation to the symbolic double cones correspond to the twenty-eight phases of the moon. These represent the twenty-eight types of human being (twenty-six, as it transpires, because human life is not found when the moon is entirely dark or full): the nature of the four faculties that constitute the human personality are rigidly determined by the lunar phase at which he was born, because the lunar phase, or rather the relation between the darkened and the illuminated parts of the moon at any given phase, determines the position of the four faculties in relation to one another and so determines the nature and conduct of the personality. Yeats devotes the central portion of *A Vision* to a discussion of these twenty-eight phases and of the various examples of human types in each phase. He next extends the conception

7. See the 1928 Introduction in the 1937 edition of *A Vision*.
8. *A Vision*, p. 12.   9. I avoid the use of Yeats's technical terms.

to cover the whole of history by reviving the idea of the Magnus
Annus. To this Yeats added the idea of reincarnation and occupies the penultimate section of the book by describing the existence of the dead before their rebirth into a new life—an existence
which is carefully systematized into six stages of purification and
preparation.

   Measured by their analogues in the poetry, two of the most
important ideas within the system are the idea of the anti-self
and the idea of unity of being, the one a psychological, the other
a psycho-historical concept. The idea of the anti-self is set forth
rather more simply and clearly in *Per Amica Silentia Lunae* than
in *A Vision*. The artist, Yeats claims in this work, is continually
seeking his opposite, or anti-self. Out of this struggle, out of this
attempt to escape from the determinism of the phasal pattern,
the 'blind network of the stars', which is however a necessary
part of the whole systemic construction, arises the conflict on
which he is forced to impose the discipline of artistic creation:
'If we cannot imagine ourselves as different from what we are,
and try to assume that second self, we cannot impose a discipline upon ourselves though we may accept one from others.'[1]
In 'Ego Dominus Tuus', a poem printed in *Per Amica Silentia
Lunae*, Yeats makes the same statement:

> I call to the mysterious one who yet
> Shall walk the wet sands by the edge of the stream
> And look most like me, being indeed my double,
> And prove of all imaginable things
> The most unlike, being my anti-self.[2]

Thus Dante, the 'chief imagination of Christendom', but lecher-
ous in life, seeks his anti-self in the purity of Beatrice:

> He set his chisel to the hardest stone.
> Being mocked by Guido for his lecherous life,
> Derided and deriding, driven out
> To climb that stair and eat that bitter bread,
> He found the unpersuadable justice, he found
> The most exalted lady loved by a man.

1. *Per Amica Silentia Lunae*, pp. 27–28.
2. Compare also the Introduction to *The Resurrection* in *Wheels and Butterflies*,
pp. 101 ff.

The history of personality and, by extension of the analogy, the history of nations, is a struggle between the primary or objective, and the antithetical or subjective: it is a struggle between the passionate and fragmentary man and the cold and abstracting intellect. Over this conflict and imposing itself upon it lies unity of being—and, by another extension, unity of culture. The poet achieves unity of being when he finds his anti-self in an act of artistic creation: 'We make out of the quarrel . . . with ourselves, poetry.' Not only this, but all states and civilizations develop according to the phasal system. By Yeats's calculations Byzantium, for example, when at the height of its development, rested in the fifteenth phase, full moon, when

> All thought becomes an image and the soul
> Becomes a body.[3]

I think that in early Byzantium, maybe never before or since in recorded history, religious, aesthetic and practical life were one, that architect and artificers—though not, it may be, poets, for language had been the instrument of controversy and must have grown abstract—spoke to the multitude and the few alike. The painter, the mosaic worker, the worker in gold and silver, the illuminator of sacred books, were almost impersonal, almost perhaps without the consciousness of individual design, absorbed in their subject-matter and that the vision of a whole people.[4]

This is the 'dream of the noble and the beggar-man'.

Enough has been said of the 'system' to indicate its peculiar quality. It is the work of a synthesizing intellect, attempting to reduce what Mr Eliot has called the 'immense panorama of futility and anarchy which is contemporary history' into a significant pattern. It is the task of a scholar to work out in full the exact details and the detailed sources of the system.[5] This must some day be done if we are to find out exactly in what sense Yeats was a great poet. Mr Frank O'Connor wrote recently:

I don't think he was naturally a great poet, though he made himself one. I feel sure he made himself one because he had an unusually fine

3. 'The Phases of the Moon.'   4. *A Vision*, pp. 279–80.
   5. Amongst the works mentioned in the course of *A Vision* as providing ideas are those of Plato and Plotinus, amongst modern philosophers those by Spengler, Vico, Croce, Henry Adams, and Pierre Duhem's *Le Système du Monde*, which Yeats perhaps used more than any other—all mainly philosophers of history, a fact which reflects Yeats's primary interests.

intellect. Not an analytical intellect at all; a synthesising one. He was
the only man I have ever met who from two fallacies and one bit of
nonsense could evolve a theory which worked, and worked in relation
to a system of other theories, so that it illuminated other things besides.
He was the first man who showed me that any theory of life, provided
you do not let it madden you, is liable to contain more truth than any
amount of unrelated facts.[6]

While Yeats was working upon *A Vision*, and after he had
finished it, he was writing poetry which was derived from the
ideas to be found in it. Not more than perhaps half-a-dozen
poems are direct transpositions of the doctrine, or, as Yeats
preferred to call them, 'texts for exposition'. 'The Double
Vision of Michael Robartes' is one of these: the poet is caught
between 'the pull / Of the dark moon and the full', between

> The commonness of thought and images
> That have the frenzy of our western seas.

'Texts for exposition' were not, however, what *A Vision* had
been intended to produce. 'We have come', the unknown
instructors had said, 'to give you metaphors for poetry'.[7] It is
in this sense that *A Vision* plays its part in the later work. The
historical synthesis which is contained in the book and the examples by which that synthesis is illustrated find expression in
poems throughout Yeats's later volumes from *Michael Robartes
and the Dancer* (1921) to *Last Poems and Plays* (1940), and in the
plays of the last period, those plays which carry the ritualistic,
formalizing tendencies of the Japanese drama to the furthest
extreme. Such are *The Resurrection* (1927, 1931), a play about the
breakdown of the historical order involved in the coming of
Christ, or *The Words upon the Window-Pane* (1934), a play about
Jonathan Swift which makes use of the belief about the six states
of the soul between the death of the body and rebirth, as does
Purgatory (1939). One of Yeats's greatest poems, the long elegy
'In Memory of Major Robert Gregory' (1918), depends much
on the idea of unity of being. *A Vision*, or the system which is
described in it, is the mythology for which Yeats had been

6. Frank O'Connor, 'What made Yeats a great poet?' (*Listener*, 15 May 1947,
p. 762).
7. *A Vision*, p. 8.

searching and out of which he was enabled to create poetry. It is essentially a synthesis of the abstract and the passionate, a complex of emotion and judgement. By it Yeats was helped to make use for the purposes of poetry of the very conflict which might otherwise have frustrated him.

Yeats's best work is a continual oscillation, or rather a continual process of poetic choice, between those elements of his thought that we have discussed in this paper. After the early pre-Raphaelite phase of 'faint persons' he rediscovered, perhaps mainly through his work for the Irish theatre, as Dr Bowra has suggested,[8] the beauty and dramatic interest of the human personality, which he expresses in the autobiographical writings and in poems like 'In Memory of Major Robert Gregory', 'Upon a Dying Lady', and 'The Municipal Gallery Revisited':

> You that would judge me, do not judge alone
> This book or that, come to this hallowed place
> Where my friends' portraits hang and look thereon;
> Ireland's history in their lineaments trace;
> Think where man's glory most begins and ends,
> And say my glory was I had such friends.

But at times the abstract intellect conquered, that is to say, it was in the ascendant, it could be allowed its due place in the work without destroying it. Yeats dismisses his friends, being captured and excited by the task of intellectual synthesis. The persons sink into insignificance, even the Irish tradition and background, so closely associated with the gallery of friends and the portraits of heroic ancestors, are laid aside. As he says in 'All Souls' Night', 'names are nothing', 'meditations upon unknown thought / Make human intercourse grow less and less':

> Such thought—such thought have I that hold it tight
> Till meditation master all its parts,
> Nothing can stay my glance
> Until that glance run in the world's despite
> To where the damned have howled away their hearts,
> And where the blessed dance;

8. In his essay on Yeats in *The Heritage of Symbolism*.

> Such thought, that in it bound
> I need no other thing,
> Wound in mind's wandering
> As mummies in the mummy-cloth are wound.

Or the poet turns to analyse civilization and society in terms of the destructive intellect, the 'yellow-eyed hawk of the mind', saying in 'Meru':

> . . . man's life is thought,
> And he, despite his terror, cannot cease
> Ravening through century after century,
> Ravening, raging, and uprooting that he may come
> Into the desolation of reality:
> Egypt and Greece, good-bye, and good-bye, Rome!

Sometimes the conflict becomes formalized and explicit as in the 'little, mechanical songs' which were the last phase of development through which Yeats's lyric style passed. These poems describe a search for truth, the task of old age, yet one which is continually frustrated by the demands of the sensuous and passionate body. 'I long for truth', says the woman in 'A First Confession',

> . . . and yet
> I cannot stay from that
> My better self disowns,
> For a man's attention
> Brings such satisfaction
> To the craving in my bones.

Beyond the power of time, these songs suggest, beyond the power of old age to destroy love, lies a point of reconciliation between old age and youthful desire. The hard work of the systematizing and synthesizing intellect had at times resulted in an affirmation like that in 'The Results of Thought', though in this poem doubt is cast on the achievement in the end:

> Acquaintance; companion;
> One dear brilliant woman;
> The best-endowed, the elect,
> All by their youth undone,
> All, all, by that inhuman
> Bitter glory wrecked.

But I have straightened out
Ruin, wreck and wrack;
I toiled long years and at length
Came to so deep a thought
I can summon back
All their wholesome strength.

What images are these
That turn dull-eyed away,
Or shift Time's filthy load,
Straighten aged knees,
Hesitate or stay?
What heads shake or nod?

But there are poems in which Yeats moves beyond the range of doubt, in which he attains a glimpse of that reality 'whereon the gazing heart doubles its might'. These glimpses are a measure of the skill with which he handled not only the poetic medium but the complex of life and thought and the historical situation in which he found himself. He organized intellect and emotion in such a way that he made that kind of affirmation which is reserved for very few, which proceeds indeed from what Wordsworth called the 'hiding-places of man's power'. This power is related to the value which other poets besides Yeats have named Joy, *Freude*. Wordsworth spoke of the 'never-failing principle of joy', the sense of blessing which occurs when the weight of the 'unintelligible world' is lifted. Yeats writes:

At certain moments, always unforeseen, I become happy . . . Perhaps I am sitting in some crowded restaurant . . . I look at the strangers near as if I had known them all my life, and it seems strange that I cannot speak to them: everything fills me with affection, I have no longer any fears or any needs . . . latterly I seem to understand that I enter upon [this mood] the moment I cease to hate.[9]

A section of 'Vacillation' ('My fiftieth year had come and gone . . .') describes the same experience.

To Yeats the Irish hero Cuchulain, a central figure in much of the old mythology, represented 'creative joy separated from fear' and throughout his life Yeats wrote poems and plays about Cuchulain. But Yeats's principle of joy was the product of something more sensuous and passionate than Wordsworth's. In

9. *Per Amica Silentia Lunae*, pp. 85–87.

Yeats's earlier work Truth was perhaps embodied in high and
invisible gods; later, life was the 'uncontrollable mystery on the
bestial floor', a corporeality whose revelations of truth were
made to the flesh; 'a shudder in the loins' [was the start of a
historical order. Just as 'the annunciation . . . as made to Leda'
'founded Greece',[1] so the tidings brought to Mary, and the
Passion of Christ, founded Christianity.] In discussing the historical significance of Christianity Yeats emphasizes what he
calls that 'shock which will induce a sense of spiritual reality,
whereby the spiritual principle enters into the very bloodstream
of history'. It is Christ the dying God, Christ in his Dionysiac
aspect, the 'odour of blood', which overthrows the Doric
discipline and Platonic tolerance, the old forms of abstract
thought. In the play *The Resurrection* one of the watchers touches
the beating heart in the phantom body of the resurrected
Christ and cries, 'O Athens, Alexandria, Rome, something has
come to destroy you. The heart of a phantom is beating.'[2]

   Thus the life and the history which Yeats accepted and
affirmed did not reveal itself in moments of contemplation
like the night-calm felt, as did Wordsworth's, but it appears in
moments of a sharpened physical sensitivity ('My body of a
sudden blazed'), and his acceptance was stated in terms that
united thought and physical life in 'a single Image' of magnificent power:

> I am content to live it all again
> And yet again, if it be life to pitch
> Into the frog-spawn of a blind man's ditch,
> A blind man battering blind men;
> Or into that most fecund ditch of all,
> The folly that man does
> Or must suffer, if he woos
> A proud woman not kindred of his soul.
>
> I am content to follow to its source
> Every event in action or in thought;
> Measure the lot; forgive myself the lot!
> When such as I cast out remorse

   1. 'Leda and the Swan', and *A Vision*, pp. 267, 268. [The words in square brackets
are a tentative reconstruction from two superimposed lines in the typescript—
C. J. R.]
   2. *Collected Plays* (1960), pp. 593–4.

So great a sweetness flows into the breast
We must laugh and we must sing,
We are blest by everything,
Everything we look upon is blest.[3]

When we review Yeats's achievement, looking along the double
line of his intellectual and poetical career, we observe a continual growth in poetic maturity, accompanied by an increasing
systematization of thought. His poetry had the benefit of at
least two major developments of style and he was continually
experimenting; but the thought of *A Vision* is the logical outcome of his early dabblings in magic and philosophy. From the
beginning he was consciously seeking a means of interaction and
intercommunication between life and thought, which would
allow him to bring his whole personality into play in his poetic
work. (He speaks in a passage in *The Trembling of the Veil* of the
necessity which the poet and philosopher has of 'speaking
[his] whole mind or remaining silent and ineffective'.)[4] The
means which he adopted early in his life to correct what he
considered the deficiencies in his style were peculiar: 'When in
my twenty-second year I had finished *The Wanderings of Oisin*,
my style seemed too elaborate, too ornamental, and I thought
for some weeks of sleeping upon a board.'[5] Later he consulted a
cabbalistic medium in the hope of solving the stylistic problem,
and indeed it was the medium through whom the 'unknown
instructors' finally spoke who may be said to have solved the
problem of poetry and of style. The opening words of the 1937
edition of *A Vision* show Yeats's consciousness of the effect that
the intellectual process had had on his poetry:

The other day Lady Gregory said to me: 'You are a much better
educated man than you were ten years ago and much more powerful
in argument.' And I put *The Tower* and *The Winding Stair* into evidence
to show that my poetry has gained in self-possession and power.[6]

'I think profound philosophy must come from terror', Yeats
wrote in another context.[7] In one respect Yeats's whole poetic
work can be regarded as an elaborate search after profundity,
an attempt to pull the 'golden stopper'[8] out of the neck of the

---

3. 'A Dialogue of Self and Soul.'   4. *Autobiographies*, pp. 357–8.
5. Ibid., p. 371.   6. *A Vision*, p. 8.
7. 'Modern Poetry' (1936) in *Essays and Introductions* (1961), p. 522.
8. Ibid., p. 503.

bottle of reality. As such it is no doubt fallacious, a particularly striking example from the lunatic fringe of human speculation. But it gave Yeats metaphors for his poetry, and in so doing performed a more useful service than many more sober and edifying versions of thought.

2

W. B. Yeats and the Irish theme

I

Several good accounts have already been given of Yeats's formative years between 1887 and 1896: the best written is to be found in *The Trembling of the Veil* itself, although we must look upon that systematized and owlishly wise account of the growth of a poet's mind with the same sort of suspicion that should be active in the study of *The Prelude*—the gap of more than twenty years between the events and the story of the events is greater than in the case of *The Prelude*, and Yeats appears to have been influenced by Moore's method and style in *Hail and Farewell*.[1] There are two dates among the formative years that seem important: Parnell died in 1891, and Yeats first met Lady Gregory in 1896. The end of Parnellism seems to have made clear to Yeats and others the need for the final supersession of the old nationalism in Anglo-Irish literature; the meeting with Lady Gregory meant that the idea of nationality in that literature— for Yeats already an accepted principle—became a formula that worked in practice.

My object is not to give an account of Yeats's work for Ireland or the Irish dramatic movement or of his position and problems as an Anglo-Irish writer—the books by Mr Boyd, Professor Ellis-Fermor, Mr MacNeice, and Mr Hone are there to enlighten

Printed from a completed typescript intended for publication, which bears the note: 'This was originally commissioned for a focus vol. on Yeats in 1947 or 1948 by B. Rajan. The volume reached galley-proof stage, then was abandoned. Publishers went bust, I think.'

---

1. For accounts of the formative years see E. A. Boyd, *Ireland's Literary Renaissance* (1916); Horace Reynolds, introduction to *Letters to the New Island* (1934); Louis MacNeice, *The Poetry of W. B. Yeats* (1941), pp. 39 ff. (on the Irish background); V. K. Narayana Menon, *Development of William Butler Yeats* (1942), pp. 5 ff.; F. R. Higgins, 'Yeats and poetic drama in Ireland' in *The Irish Theatre* (ed. L. Robinson, 1939).

us on all those points. I want only to try to discover what continuity exists between Yeats's early and later use of themes from
Irish history and legend and what poetic need of his own Yeats
desired and expected his use of these themes to satisfy. Even this
limited objective requires, however, a survey of some of the
problems that confronted Yeats as a young writer in the last
years of the nineteenth century—for it was then, I believe, that
he made his choice. Our admiration for the work of his later
years, for his growth in 'self-possession and power'[2] should not
obscure from us the real continuity that exists between *The
Wanderings of Oisin* and *The Death of Cuchulain*: the same powerful but limited intellect was at work throughout, and a copy of
the Cabbala was lying on Yeats's desk in 1887, forty years before
he wrote *A Vision*.

Long before Parnell died Yeats had become preoccupied with
the Irish theme: Standish O'Grady's *History of Ireland* (1878–80)
had announced in rather muffled tones the beginning of the
literary renascence. It is true that Yeats's earliest published
poetry, including *Mosada*, which includes an 'Irish' song about
St Peter, and *The Island of Statues*, which first treats of that
favourite Irish—and European—theme of the earthly paradise,
had not shown much consciousness of the new styles and subjects which that renascence was likely to require. The first
version of *The Wanderings of Oisin* (1889) used Irish mythology
but was inspired by Spenser, Shelley, and Morris. But Yeats was,
none the less, already aware of literary problems which had
perhaps scarcely occurred to the Anglo-Irish poets who preceded
him. Amongst these problems there were two more important
than any of the others: how was the young poet to search for and
find a theme, and how was he to serve the cause of Ireland
through poetry? There is little overt discussion of the first
problem in the earliest writings of Yeats available, although, in
a sense, it is contained in the second problem, and it later
became a constant preoccupation—'The Circus Animals'
Desertion' in *Last Poems* is evidence for that. The second problem
—the Irish cause—had been the justification for the work of
Thomas Davis and was to be the inspiration of Sir Charles
Gavan Duffy, who returned from proconsular duties to activate
the literary revival by the diffusion of bad patriotic poetry. Yeats

2. *A Vision* (1937), p. 8.

was early convinced of the paradoxical truth that Anglo-Irish literature could best serve the Irish cause by deriving its sanctions from a wider principle than patriotic impulse alone could supply. He insisted that the Anglo-Irish poet, faced with the need for reconciling his English tongue with his Irish heritage, must not be content with the inadequacies of the Moore–Davis–Duffy school; and he early felt that the exploitation of Irish mythology and history was the best instrument for the shaping of a distinctive style. In the collection of reviews and gossip entitled *Letters to the New Island*, written between 1888 and 1892 and disinterred by Mr Reynolds from the files of the *Boston Pilot* and the *Providence Sunday Journal*, we find Yeats dealing, in a youthful way, with some of these problems. For example, although he was pleased that poetic drama should win popular acceptance, he could not receive Todhunter's classical pastorals without reserve because Todhunter, as an Anglo-Irish poet, was not cultivating his own potato patch, but was peering over the wall at his neighbour's garden. Yeats adds:

The first thing needful if an Irish literature more elaborate and intense than our fine but primitive ballads and novels is to come into being is that readers and writers alike should really know the imaginative periods of Irish history. It is not needful that they should understand them with scholars' accuracy, but they should know them with the heart, so as not to be repelled by what is strange and *outré* in poems or plays or stories taken therefrom. The most imaginative of our periods was the heroic age and the few centuries that followed it and preceded the Norman Invasion—a time of vast and mysterious shadows, like the clouds heaped round a sun rising from the sea.[3]

In the same collection he praises the work of Standish O'Grady and Samuel Ferguson, who are both almost unreadable nowadays, because they wrote on the heroic themes and so made use of material which had never been exploited before: 'Here in Ireland the marble block is waiting for us almost untouched.'[4] The work of Ellen O'Leary is also commended: her brother the Fenian leader John O'Leary had impressed Yeats by the beauty of his character and principles. It was O'Leary who said, famously, that 'there are things a man must not do to save a nation', and Yeats added to himself that writing bad poetry was one of those things.

3. *Letters to the New Island* (ed. Reynolds, 1934), p. 107.   4. Ibid., p. 159.

One of the difficulties encountered by the Anglo-Irish poet who had no Gaelic (as Yeats himself had none) was the inaccessibility of the texts. Even nowadays accurate but stylish translations are hard to find. This problem, too, was in process of being solved by Kuno Meyer, Nutt, O'Grady, and eventually by Lady Gregory herself. Meanwhile Yeats welcomed the work of Dr Hyde (whose *Beside the Fire* appeared in 1890) and others as 'another link [in] the long chain of Irish song that unites decade to decade'.[5] Hyde's Gaelic League was itself a direct reflection of the nationality that was replacing nationalism after the death of Parnell. Davis, Yeats writes, fails because of his nationalism; Allingham, like Todhunter, because he rejected nationality:

Whenever an Irish writer has strayed away from Irish themes and Irish feeling, in almost all cases he has done no more than make alms for oblivion. There is no great literature without nationality, no great nationality without literature.

How the cultivation of the heroic age could shape a distinctive Anglo-Irish style was another problem discussed by Yeats at this time. He could not praise the Irishism of McAnally, which was, indeed, judging from the quotations which Yeats gives in his review of *Irish Wonders* (1888), a particularly curious perversion of peasant speech, although one doubts also the entire accuracy of the dialect speech of Lady Gregory and of that 'sedulous linguist' Synge, which eventually satisfied the poet.[6] Theirs is the speech, as Mr MacNeice points out, of an idealized peasantry, as McAnally's was that of the comic stage. Yeats reserved his enthusiasm for the matter rather than for the manner of McAnally's book, which was a collection of Irish folk-beliefs. He welcomed this kind of activity as a useful cultivation of the Irish potato patch likely to provide food for poets. It is perhaps incidental to my theme that Yeats's welcome was all the warmer because he had already taken a lively interest in the supernatural: his association with MacGregor Mathers and, a little later, with Madame Blavatsky had begun about 1887, and in 1889 the *Scots Observer* printed some of the stories that were later to appear in his own *Celtic Twilight*. This intertwining of interests is characteristic of Yeats and even in discuss-

5. Ibid., p. 122.
6. Ibid., pp. 103–4 for Allingham, pp. 192 ff. for McAnally.

ing Yeats and the Irish theme one ought not to neglect those other themes which are cognate to it.[7]

After the meeting with Lady Gregory Yeats began to found and establish a school of literature and drama on narrower, more clearly defined, and more personal lines than had been possible in the case of the Irish literary societies in London and Dublin, although these had fulfilled many of the hopes expressed in *Letters to the New Island*.[8] When we read Yeats's later essays on the prospects and duties of Irish poets, whether those from *Samhain* or those collected together in *Ideas of Good and Evil*, we are reading the work of an older man to whom the problems seemed, if not simpler, at least sharper in outline. Yeats has become the Master. '[Mr Yeats]', wrote the defeated Edward Martyn, unkindly, '. . . has above all a weird appearance which is triumphant with middle-aged masculine women, and a dictatorial manner which is irresistible with the considerable bevy of female and male mediocrities interested in intellectual things.'[9] Definition is clearer and confidence greater still in *The Trembling of the Veil*, a retrospective work.

It is, then, as the leader of a school and one of the founders of the Irish Literary Theatre that Yeats wrote between 1901 and 1907 the articles in *Samhain* which were later reprinted, in part, as 'The Irish Dramatic Movement' in *Plays and Controversies*. Ireland must escape from the phantoms of propaganda and rhetoric, because Ireland alone, which has preserved the Gaelic tradition, has thereby the means to revive and re-create 'a portion of the old imaginative life'.[1] The Gaelic tradition lies in spoken and sung stories, the 'most beautiful literature of a whole people that has been anywhere since Greece and Rome',

7. From *The Celtic Twilight* itself it is difficult to discover whether Yeats's primary interest is in the Irish quality of his supernatural titbits or generally in the supernatural as a manifestation of what he elsewhere describes as the 'precise, inexplicable teeming life [which] starts up all around us'. Much later, when he annotated *Visions and Beliefs in the West of Ireland* for Lady Gregory, he shows wide acquaintance with the general literature of the supernatural.

8. For an account of the formation and development of these societies see Boyd, pp. 84 ff.

9. Denis Gwynn, *Edward Martyn and the Irish Revival* (1930), pp. 154–5.

1. *Plays and Controversies* (1923), p. 100. The Chadwicks provide an impartial testimony that this belief was not unfounded: 'Until recently the heroic stories were widely known among uneducated people both in Ireland and in the Gaelic-speaking parts of Scotland . . . Indeed, there are persons still living, at least in Ireland, who can recite some of the stories' (*The Growth of Literature*, vol. i, 1932, p. 15).

in sharp contrast to the literature of England that has 'shaped itself in the printing press'.[2] Hyde is again praised for his work because it is not propaganda, but the discovery of the 'idiom of the English-speaking country-people'.[3] A national literature is 'the work of writers, who are moulded by influences that are moulding their country'[4] but it must not take a narrow view of its functions nor reject foreign influences.[5] The new literature and the new theatre must be 'a natural centre for a tradition of feeling and thought' by means of the stirring up of 'the old imaginative life', but this does not imply imitation of the external forms of the old literature.[6] Of his own part Yeats writes in 1901, now that the theatre is organized: 'I want to go down again to primary ideas ... I hope to get our heroic age into verse.'[7]

I refer to these scattered passages not because of their part in moulding the principles upon which the Abbey Theatre was conducted, for that story has been told elsewhere, but because they help to explain why Yeats chose Irish themes. When, for example, he declares that the new literature must not reject foreign influences, the remark is more applicable to his own work, whether the influence be that of Shelley or Blake or the Noh plays, than to the Abbey Theatre as such. When Edward Martyn tried to introduce the intellectual drama of Europe in the form of his own Ibsenite plays into the Abbey, he had little success and after the second year dropped out, because Yeats and Lady Gregory both thought that 'romantic and historical plays, and plays about the life of artisans and country-people' were the most suitable.[8] Thus the work of the Abbey Theatre was far more parochial than Yeats's own work was to be, and his status as a European writer, a status neither Lady Gregory nor even Synge possesses, depends upon that fact. The discovery of Synge, indeed, seemed to prove for the time that the narrower policy was the right one so far as concerned the Theatre. But in *Ideas of Good and Evil*, generously though Yeats speaks of Synge, he is really engaged in evolving a scale of values in relation to the Irish theme which is more nearly relevant to his own work. In the first essay in the collection his rejection of the propaganda poetry of Davis and of the 'popular' poetry of Longfellow and

2. *Plays and Controversies* (1923), pp. 169–70.   3. Ibid., pp. 28–29.
4. Ibid., p. 106.   5. Ibid., p. 109.   6. Ibid., pp. 172–4.   7. Ibid., p. 9.
8. See Gwynn, pp. 113–70, and *Plays and Controversies*, pp. 32–33.

Macaulay is related to his own programme of work; true popular poetry is poetry of the folk, not of the middle classes; it depends upon an unwritten tradition and an ancient religion; it is a craft and a mystery. The modern Bard can satisfy the same impulses and needs if he avoids rhetoric and abstraction:

There is only one kind of good poetry, for the poetry of the coteries, which presupposes the written tradition, does not differ in kind from the true poetry of the people, which presupposes the unwritten tradition. Both are alike strange and obscure . . . and both, instead of that manifest logic, that clear rhetoric of the 'popular poetry', glimmer with thoughts and images whose 'ancestors were stout and wise', 'anigh to Paradise,' 'ere yet men knew the gift of corn.'[9]

But poetry must draw its strength from a national tradition: 'I could not endure . . . an international art, picking stories and symbols where it pleased', Yeats writes in The Trembling of the Veil;[1] and in the essay on 'Poetry and Tradition' (1907): 'While seeing all in the light of European literature [I] found my symbols of expression in Ireland.'[2] A literature based on Irish landscapes, legend and history—even modern political history—we are told in the essay on 'Ireland and the Arts' (1901), is the need of the future,[3] and Yeats's own style has been re-formed and shaped by the Irish theme:

I could not now write of any other country but Ireland, for my style has been shaped by the subjects I have worked on, but there was a time when my imagination seemed unwilling, when I found myself writing of some Irish event in words that would have better fitted some Italian or Eastern event, for my style had been shaped in that general stream of European literature . . . It was years before I could rid myself of Shelley's Italian light, but now I think my style is myself. I might have found more of Ireland if I had written in Irish, but I have found a little, and I have found all myself.[4]

We may observe here that the kind of relationship—a mysterious one—between 'style' and 'subject', the matrix of style, as here perceived by Yeats, is not invalidated by his later development. In the later work the relationship remained thus organic: what altered was Yeats's conception of Ireland and that in turn changed the style into something quite different.

9. 'What is "Popular Poetry"?' in Ideas of Good and Evil (Essays, 1924, pp. 9–10).
1. Autobiographies (1955), p. 193.   2. Essays, p. 307.
3. Ibid., p. 253.   4. Ibid., pp. 256–7.

Yeats adds that Ireland is the creator and guardian of certain heroic values[5] and that there is a continuity in her tradition that draws its strength from the popular imagination:

It is not a difference in the substance of things that the lamentations that were sung after battles are now sung for men who have died upon the gallows.[6]

Synge himself had been seeking some of these values: it was to find again the Ireland of the stubborn family tradition, of the 'duellists and scholars of the eighteenth century' and of 'generations older still' that Synge returned again and again to the Atlantic coasts.[7] Irish mythology, too, has a special meaning and value, because the great mythological cycles, of which the Irish is one (a claim which Yeats for one would never have doubted and which is indeed hardly doubtful), 'take mankind between their naked arms, and without putting off their divinity'.[8] When Lady Gregory's two collections of Irish heroic legends, *Cuchulain of Muirthemne* and *Gods and Fighting Men*, appeared in 1902 and 1904, Yeats praised them too highly because he thought that she had solved the problem of 'getting a style'—Synge had not yet shown all he was capable of—and that she had finally made the legends available for the use of poets, fulfilling the need which he had expressed in *Letters to the New Island*.[9] Finally, Yeats wrote in *The Trembling of the Veil* with the clarity of retrospect:

Might I not, with health and good luck to aid me, create some new *Prometheus Unbound*; Patrick or Columcille, Oisin or Fion, in Prometheus' stead; and, instead of Caucasus, Cro-Patrick or Ben Bulben? Have not all races had their first unity from a mythology that marries them to rock and hill?[1]

II

I put the first section of this essay into evidence to show that Yeats evolved all those literary principles having relation to the Irish theme that were important to him as a poet prior to 1910—

5. As manifested, for example, in lives like that of O'Leary (ibid., pp. 317 ff.).
6. Ibid., p. 262.   7. Ibid., p. 401.
8. Yeats's preface to *Cuchulain of Muirthemne* (1902) in *Explorations* (1962), p. 10.
9. Ibid., pp. 4 ff.   1. *Autobiographies*, p. 194.

that is to say, before the period in which his most valuable poetry was written. He used the example of Ireland to support his conviction that poetry must go deep to the levels of the racial heritage; he found in it nationality and the native mythology which the English poets had been deprived of by an accident of history,[2] and for which Blake was 'crying out'.[3] He found in it a scale of heroic values and a spontaneous and imaginative life which seemed the antithesis of the pragmatism and abstractions of the leader-writer, which he early hated. Such were the values residing in the Irish theme. They contributed much to Yeats's early poetry, inducing him to choose the heroic legend and to cultivate the *elaborate*, the *intense*, the *obscure*—the adjectives are battle-cries rather than critical judgements, statements of value rather than canons of style. In addition, Yeats went on to formulate principles necessary for the creation of an Irish national literature. That activity was only an aspect of the effort he was making to 'get a style' for himself—to rid his work of 'Shelley's Italian light', for example. (Another writer would merely have said 'to escape from Shelley's influence', a desirable thing to do in any case, but Ireland had made Yeats conscious of the foreign.) He tried therefore to write in a style appropriate to the leader of a new national literature, a style which would give expression to the values associated with 'Ireland', for he believed that style was shaped in the matrix of subject, and subject here meant not merely the bare story of Oisin and Finn but the values read into their tale and implied in the manner of its ancient versions. None the less, his early poetry, built on these principles, and perhaps so far as it is built on these principles, is inferior; and its style, the way it is written, the mannerisms that torment it, is the principal reason for its inferiority. In short, the ambitious and complex effort failed, for a number of reasons: one reason was that Yeats never completely thought out the meaning and implications of his style-subject relationship; again, he was not so single-minded about Ireland as Synge, for example, was— the *elaborate*, the *intense*, the *obscure*, these are also the battle-cries of the 'international' art of the 1890s. These points can be made clearer by looking at the mutations of the Irish theme in some of Yeats's later work. For the values early perceived in it remained valid, were revivified, and yet left Yeats free to write

2. *Essays*, p. 133.   3. Ibid., p. 140.

great poetry without too conscious a pursuit of a national
style.

It is true that, in spite of the difficulties, the stylistic problem
was solved by Synge and Lady Gregory, and this fact accounts
for the high praise which Yeats bestowed upon their work. But
Yeats moved out of their range, and in only one or two of his
earlier plays attempted to occupy the limited kingdom that
belonged by right to them. He liked to think of his plays, in his
general conspectus of the Abbey Theatre movement, as complementary to theirs—the 'romantic and historical' by the side
of their 'plays about the life of artisans and country-people', and
that is one way, though not, I think, a very satisfactory way of
evaluating them. His later poetry, however, and his later plays
too, are quite outside so limited an estimate; the theatre and the
readers they were written for was not the Abbey but the ideal
'unpopular' one with an 'audience like a secret society' which
he described in the 'Letter to Lady Gregory' written in 1919.[4]

There is one exception to my generalization that Yeats discovered the peculiar virtues of the Irish theme early and added
little to it after 1910. Yeats did become increasingly aware of the
continuity of the Irish tradition, of the fact that a statue of Cuchulain stands in Dublin Central Post Office. This is shown by his
acceptance, first critically, and then for poetic purposes, of the
eighteenth-century Protestant tradition in Ireland. In 1889 he
writes as follows in the *Boston Pilot*, criticizing the portrait of the
'blackguard adventurer' Chevalier Burke in Stevenson's *Master
of Ballantrae*:

He is really a broken-down Norman gentleman, a type found only
among the gentry who make up what is called 'the English garrison'.
He is from the same source as the Hell Fire Club and all the reckless
braggadocio of the eighteenth century in Ireland; one of that class who,
feeling the uncertainty of their tenures, as Froude explains it, lived the
most devil-may-care existence. One sometimes meets even at this day
vulgar, plausible, swaggering 'Irishmen', who are its much decayed
survivals . . . No one who knows the serious, reserved and suspicious
Irish peasant ever held them in any way representative of the national
type.[5]

---

4. 'A People's Theatre: A Letter to Lady Gregory' (*Plays and Controversies*,
p. 212).
5. *Letters to the New Island*, pp. 90–91.

As we have seen, Yeats had already grown to accept the mode of life of the 'duellists . . . of the eighteenth century', which he here attacks, when he praised Synge, but he accepted it much more completely after 1910. The fullest critical discussion of it comes in the introduction (1934) to *The Words upon the Window-Pane* (1930), where he describes the eighteenth century as 'that one Irish century that escaped from darkness and confusion'.[6] In poems like 'In Memory of Major Robert Gregory' and 'The Tower', the Protestant tradition plays its part with other elements, but is itself a manifestation of a sharpened awareness of the continuity of Irish history, viewed not as a means of 'getting a style', but as a standard of historical, political, and social values. This is not, of course, to say that it was separated from conflict, from the doubt and disorder that Yeats expressed in 'The Man and the Echo', and from the task of justifying 'all those renowned generations'.

This task was, indeed, one which seems to have inspired much of the poetry written on Irish themes after the Easter Rebellion. That event, because it provided poetic material and in some sense revivified the Irishism in Yeats, which had weakened over the years of 'theatre business, management of men' and 'the obscure spite of blind Paudeen', made Yeats freer to exploit the actualities of modern Irish history in his poetry. But his poetic welcome was not given to something new but to a rediscovery of the heroic values which Cuchulain and John O'Leary had typified in his youth: a terrible beauty was reborn:

> O but we talked at large before
> The sixteen men were shot,
> But who can talk of give and take,
> What should be and what not
> While those dead men are loitering there
> To stir the boiling pot?[7]

As befits martyrs, Pearse and Connolly shed personality and become symbols within the greater theme, but to the theme are attached in a sharpened and revivified form the meanings and values which Yeats had already set out in the essays I have discussed. The old and valued sense of nationality bears fruit in

6. *Wheels and Butterflies* (1934), p. 7.
7. 'Sixteen Dead Men' (*Collected Poems*, 1950, p. 205).

later poems like 'The Ghost of Roger Casement', 'Parnell's
Funeral', and 'The Curse of Cromwell'. For these poems go
beyond nationalism, and owe their exciting quality to that emotion potent everywhere in western Europe. The paradox is that
Yeats had to rediscover his own Irish nationality in order to
supersede mere Irishism in his poetry; but the poetic theme is
firmly 'married to rock and hill' and draws its strength from
that marriage. This, indeed, was the paradox which Yeats
appreciated in the early essays and whose realization he urged
then upon contemporary writers. By comprehending it himself
in poetic terms he owes part of his claim to European and not
merely Anglo-Irish stature.

Out of conflict round this theme he makes poetry:

> Justify all those renowned generations,
> Justify all that have sunk in their blood,
> Justify all that have died on the scaffold,
> Justify all that have fled, that have stood,
> Stood or have marched the night long
> Singing, singing a song . . .
>
> Fail, and that history turns into rubbish,
> All that great past to a trouble of fools;
> Those that come after shall mock at O'Donnell,
> Mock at the memory of both O'Neills,
> Mock Emmet, mock Parnell:
> All the renown that fell.[8]

Poems like this are not amongst Yeats's best work, but they are
vigorous and exciting without being abstract and rhetorical.
That Yeats in our time was able to write poetry of this kind at all
is a tribute to the accuracy of his early diagnosis of the situation
in Irish letters and a sign of the continuity which he himself
perceived and now makes his readers aware of—'lamentations
that were sung after battles are now sung for men who have died
upon the gallows'.

Some of the perceptions outlined in the early essays on Ireland
contribute also to the making of the Crazy Jane poems in *The
Tower*, *The Winding Stair*, and *Last Poems*. There are, of course,
many other elements in these 'little mechanical songs', for
perhaps more than any other of Yeats's verses they compress

8. *Collected Poems*, p. 322.

into tightly organized forms the poetic experience of a lifetime.[9] Behind them lies the idea of the Fool and of the folk-mind, of which the Fool is a representative, and a singularly Irish representative. It is true that the Fool is rendered more significant by the new idea of the Fool's position in the phasal system outlined in *A Vision*, but he originates in the Fool of such early plays as *The Pot of Broth*, a stock character in the plays about country people.[1] Crazy Jane herself is Mary Battle and 'daft Mary' who walked in Sligo, of whom we read in *Reveries over Childhood and Youth*, and Yeats's interest in the folk-mind which here culminates in this greater, this more Shakespearian figure, had begun before he reviewed McAnally and set the value for Irish literature on the 'people' (and the 'little people') which found a fuller, though not a final, manifestation in *The Celtic Twilight*.

> Many times man lives and dies
> Between his two eternities,
> That of race and that of soul,
> And Ancient Ireland knew it all.

Ancient Ireland, as preserved in the imaginative life of the people, which, according to 'The Irish Dramatic Movement', it is the task of Irish writers to awaken and to use, still provides for Yeats, as these poems show, the best examples of the folk-mind functioning in its proper sphere, equipped with its mysterious knowledge and understanding of grief and change and the loss of love.

It seems, then, that a continuity can be established between the poetic values which Yeats early perceived in the Irish theme and certain of the later poems, in which the same values reappear in the context of an immensely improved poetic. The tradition of heroism, the continuity of Irish history, the imaginative life ascribed to the people—these things started into poetic life again after 1916, but the poems that resulted contained not new discoveries of value but ampler justifications of the old. No such continuity exists between the way that the early poems

9. Which is not the same as saying that the Crazy Jane poems are Yeats's best poems. For some discussion of their other elements see my *Towards a Mythology* (1946), pp. 99–114.

1. For the importance of the Fool as poet, prophet, and jester in early Irish literature, see Enid Welsford, *The Fool: His Social and Literary History* (1935), pp. 88–112.

and these later poems are written. We nowhere find in *The Wanderings of Oisin*, or *The Rose* or *The Wind among the Reeds* (in their earliest versions), the vigour and muscularity of *A Full Moon in March* or the 'little mechanical songs'. This suggests that in the later work the Irish tradition became for Yeats primarily a repository of social, historical, and political values, whereas in the earlier phase it had seemed also a guide to literary style. The debility of the early work may partly be explained by the fact that Yeats drew illegitimate conclusions about the way poetry should be written from a version—his own and others' version—of the Celtic complex. Miss Hoare has commented acutely upon the retreat from 'actuality' in the direction of dream and fantasy which is operative in Yeats's poetry during the early period so that he becomes 'a poet of a vain searching for the past, and through that, of unreality'.[2] In the poetry the values which were so plainly enunciated in the essays were themselves distorted and resulted in the languid and hypnotic cadence so characteristic of the early style. Yeats was helped to do this by a number of stylistic predilections which made the mysterious melancholy of the Celtic twilight seem more appropriate to the writing of modern European poetry than it was, but which in themselves had nothing much to do with the Celt—the admiration for Morris, for Arthur Symons and his teaching, for the world-weariness cultivated in *Axël*, and by the Rhymers' Club. It is interesting, for example, to find how much 'your Celt in London'—a phrase at which the later Yeats shuddered—accepts of Renan's and Arnold's diagnosis of Celtic melancholy and strangeness, and how he relates it to pre-Raphaelitism, the symbolist movement, Wagner, and Maeterlinck in the 1897 essay on 'The Celtic Element in Literature'.

But this interaction of style and values is only a part of the story of Yeats's acceptance of the Irish theme. For, in that same essay, he reiterates the claim that the discovery of Celtic literature, that 'untouched marble block', had opened 'a new fountain of legends' for Europe. It had done so for his own work, and was to continue to do so, though style and meanings changed. It is perhaps the most important function fulfilled by the Irish theme.

2. Dorothy M. Hoare, *The Works of Morris and of Yeats in Relation to Early Saga Literature* (1937), p. 93.

III

Yeats never achieved his early ambition of 'getting our heroic age into verse', perhaps because after the literary renascence began to flourish, it no longer seemed so necessary, and certainly because it was no longer the method which he chose to fulfil his own poetic needs.[3] Even so, it is impossible here to survey the many plays and poems that deal with Irish mythological subjects. I will discuss only his different treatments of the Cuchulain legend in an attempt to show the changes that took place in Yeats's handling of Irish mythology as well as the continuity preserved in it. For the Cuchulain theme is perhaps the most 'permanent image' of all the images that Yeats took from the Irish sagas.

Between 1904 and 1939 Yeats wrote five plays with Cuchulain as their hero. The early poem in *The Rose* entitled 'The Death of Cuchullin [or Cuhoollin]' (later renamed after many revisions 'Cuchulain's Fight with the Sea') is based not on the more accepted account of Cuchulain's end given in one of the tales subsidiary to the *Tain bo Cuailgne*, the major saga of the Red Branch heroes of the heroic cycle, but on a version preserved in Curtin's *Myths and Folklore of Ireland*.[4] The first play of the Cuchulain series, *On Baile's Strand* (1903), makes more elaborate use of the same material. In the early versions the poem reflects only a series of moods, the familiar cadences of Celtic melancholy. The play, written for the Abbey Theatre, is a dramatically effective version of the legends in Elizabethan blank verse. Yeats makes clever use of the Fool and the Blind Man who use the speech of peasant drama and behave in its tradition. But the play is a simple transposition of the legend, a clear and conventional dramatic structure: Yeats makes no attempt to explore what he later called the 'heart-mysteries' of the Cuchulain theme:

> And when the Fool and Blind Man stole the bread
> Cuchulain fought the ungovernable sea;
> Heart-mysteries there, and yet when all is said

3. Thus, in speaking of the group of Cuchulain plays in the introduction to *Fighting the Waves* (*Wheels and Butterflies*, p. 71) Yeats writes: 'I would have attempted the Battle of the Ford and the Death of Cuchulain, had not the mood of Ireland changed' and given place to satire and realism. But he lived to write of Cuchulain's death after all.   4. *Poems* (Fisher Unwin, 1899), p. 293.

It was the dream itself enchanted me:
Character isolated by a deed
To engross the present and dominate memory.
Players and painted stage took all my love,
And not those things that they were emblems of.[5]

Many years were to pass before Yeats was to make Cuchulain an 'emblem', and to repudiate the 'character isolated by a deed'. 'The Death of Cuhoollin' and *On Baile's Strand* reflect the Celtic 'retreat from actuality' and the subservience to the practical needs of the literary theatre, but little more.

The Green Helmet (1910) is awkwardly written; but it marks a new stage in that it deals not with legend but with folk-tale and consequently approaches nearer in tone and manner to the later plays.[6] And the folk-tale is an 'international' one, and therefore by implication less tied to the Irish theme.[7] The source of the play is a tale in *The Feast of Bricriu*, and Yeats probably used the translation by Kuno Meyer.[8] He also made use of the portion of *The Feast of Bricriu* known as 'The Women's War of Words'.[9] Indeed, the 'flyting' occupies too much of the play, and Yeats could more appropriately have chosen peasant play dialogue for this kind of material. The play is inferior because it is transitional: on the one hand, Yeats keeps too faithfully to his sources and to the business of 'getting our heroic age into verse'; on the other hand, he looks forward to the simplified but emblematically significant treatment of original folk-tale material that is found in plays like *A Full Moon in March* and *The Herne's Egg*.

In *At the Hawk's Well* (1917) Yeats began to explore the heart-mysteries of the Cuchulain theme, and to use Irish mythology in a different way by making free variations upon his sources or inventing new material. Cuchulain becomes an embodiment of heroic values, of 'creative joy separated from fear', and *At the Hawk's Well* is a play about the heroic nature. Yeats is, in fact,

5. 'The Circus Animals' Desertion' (*Collected Poems*, p. 392).
6. I use the distinction made and explained by Janet Bacon in her *Voyage of the Argonauts* (1931), chap. i, and by W. R. Halliday in his *Indo-European Folk-Tales and Greek Legend* (1933), pp. 5–7.
7. See G. L. Kittredge, *A Study of Gawain and the Green Knight* (1916), especially pp. 147–223.
8. A version of the story built up from the work of Henderson and Meyer is given by Kittredge, pp. 10–14.
9. On which see Eleanor Hull, *Text Book of Irish Literature*, vol. i, 1906, pp. 73, 81. For Lady Gregory's effective version see *Cuchulain of Muirthemne* (1903), pp. 48 ff.

weaving his personal *mythos* into the national mythology, enlarging it, setting it significantly into the context of Europe. He had not, however, forgotten the scale of heroic values which could be read into the Irish theme: although formally he here adopts for the first time the Noh technique, he has made it clear in his essay on 'Certain Noble Plays of Japan' (1916) that he values the Japanese plays partly because their attitude to life seems to him to resemble that of the 'Gaelic-speaking country people':

. . . it pleases me to think that I am working for my own country. Perhaps some day a play in the form I am adapting for European purposes may excite once more, whether in Gaelic or in English, under the slope of Slieve-na-mon or Croagh Patrick, ancient memories.[1]

The story of *At the Hawk's Well* is largely an invention of Yeats's own, though it is plainly indebted to Morris's *The Well at the World's End* (Book III, chaps. xx ff.). The old man, as I interpret the play, who desires and yet fears to gain the water of life lacks the heroic valour which alone can win it. The dancing hawk-guardian represents abstract thought and political hatreds; she leads Cuchulain (heroic and creative joy) away from the Unity of Being that can be found in the draught of sacred water and so dooms him to a prophesied frustration and the curse of a fragmentary life. Cuchulain, be he historical, or solar, hero, Irish Hercules, or even, as Mr Graves fantastically suggests, the sacred Brown Bull, is here made into a master figure in Yeats's mythology.[2] He is one also which bears a close relation to that imagined, solitary and ideal figure, the 'wise and simple man', 'who does not exist' in the poem called 'The Fisherman'. He becomes like the thought of *A Vision* 'metaphor for poetry', and is absorbed into the vortex of the personal task. He is a 'heroic or grotesque type' that keeps 'always an appropriate

---

1. *Essays*, pp. 287, 292.
2. Robert Graves, *The White Goddess* (1959), p. 219. Professor T. O'Rahilly in his *Early Irish History and Mythology* (1946) concludes that the figures of what Yeats unscientifically called the 'Irish heroic age' are entirely fabulous. I do not know how far O'Rahilly's conclusions are accepted by other Irish scholars, but it is interesting to note that his attack on euhemerizing methods does not seem to be paralleled in the development of classical mythological study, for example, L. R. Farnell's insistence on the historicity of the heroes of classical legend (*Greek Hero Cults*, 1921, *passim*) or Bacon's laborious euhemerization of the Argonauts.

distance from life' and so becomes an image 'of those profound emotions that exist only in solitude and in silence'.[3] The Noh masks helped.

In *The Only Jealousy of Emer* (1919), similarly, 'character isolated by a deed' is no longer Yeats's primary interest. In his essay on 'The Tragic Theatre' (1910) he had already urged the exclusion and lessening of 'character': into the places which it leaves empty 'rhythm, balance, pattern, images that remind us of vast passions' will be summoned.[4] *The Only Jealousy* is ultimately derived from one of the tales preserved in the *Book of Leinster* (*Cuchulain's Sickness*), but in that version the struggle for Cuchulain's love is between the supernatural Fand and Emer alone: Yeats introduces from elsewhere or invents the part played by Cuchulain's mistress Eithne Inguba. A prose version of the play, called *Fighting the Waves*, was acted in 1929 and published in 1934. It is even more marmoreal and ritualistic than *The Only Jealousy*, and Yeats could scarcely conceal his delight when a critic, intending to be severe, wrote: 'Mr Yeats's play is not really original, for something of the kind doubtless existed in Ancient Babylon.'[5] The conflict in both versions is between human love and the abstraction of death, Emer and the Woman of the Sidhe, and is followed by a further struggle between Emer whose beauty is that of 'a plummet-measured face' and Eithne Inguba, the truly loved. This second conflict repeats and utilizes ideas found in poems like 'A Prayer for my Daughter' and 'The Statues'. The play is not an allegory (a word which we must be cautious of using in connection with Yeats's poetry in view of the dislike which he expressed for what he regarded as an abstract and barren device), but a manipulation of the Irish legend to make it include Yeats's fresh discoveries, personal discoveries as well as the philosophical integrations that found their final form in *A Vision*. It is written not for Ireland (as *On Baile's Strand* had been) but for:

some country where all classes share in a half-mythological, half-philosophical folk-belief which the writer and his small audience lift

---

3. Note to *At the Hawk's Well* in *Four Plays for Dancers* (1921), p. 87. Yeats's later plays should be read in this edition, and in *Plays and Controversies* and *Wheels and Butterflies* rather than in the 1934 *Collected Plays* [and later editions, C.J.R.], which omits much interesting material.

4. *Essays*, p. 300.

5. Introduction to *Fighting the Waves* (*Wheels and Butterflies*, pp. 78–79).

into a new subtlety. All my life I have longed for such a country, and always found it quite impossible to write without having as much belief in its real existence as a child has in that of the wooden birds, beasts, and persons of his toy Noah's Ark. I have now [1921] found all the mythology and philosophy I need (in the papers of my old friend and rival Robartes).[6]

It is written in fact for Byzantium.

The Death of Cuchulain (1939) is the completion of this series of Cuchulain plays which Yeats persistently thought of as a coherent group. Unlike *On Baile's Strand* it uses the more traditional account of Cuchulain's death after the great battle at Muirthemne.[7] In this play the last stage of satire has been reached, of grim and tragic irony, with a tone which reminds us of 'The Circus Animals' Desertion'—the masterful, heroic image is reduced to a mound of refuse, old iron, old bones, old rags. The vanquished Cuchulain is beheaded by the Blind Man (reintroduced from *On Baile's Strand*) for he has been promised some pennies in exchange for the hero's head, and Cuchulain is content to die thus—'What better reason for killing a man?' (This incident, of course, was invented by Yeats.) In the play itself, as the prologue shows, little distinction is made between the heroism of Cuchulain and that of Padraic Pearse. Can the renowned generations be justified? This play, like *The Herne's Egg*, whose conclusion is very similar, answers No, and history turns to rubbish—'All that great past to a trouble of fools.' This was not Yeats's final answer but it is a measure of how faithfully the Cuchulain theme was made to mirror his immediate problem, whether 'defending Ireland's soul', and, by implication, his own life's work, was justified. Yeats gave no final answer, but the doubt and conflict animates many of the last poems and is an emblem of a larger problem—has life any meaning? It is quite as simple as that.

> . . . All that was sung,
> All that was said in Ireland is a lie

6. Note to *The Only Jealousy* in *Four Plays for Dancers*, p. 106. The 'Robartes papers' is of course Yeats's 'fustian' description of *A Vision* on which he had been working since 1917. The sentence in round brackets was omitted when the note was reprinted in *Plays and Controversies*, p. 434.

7. An abridgement of Whitley Stokes's translation is given in Eleanor Hull, *Cuchullin Saga in Irish Literature* (1898), pp. 253–63.

and therefore:

> . . . all seems evil until I
> Sleepless would lie down and die.

But even in the last poems and in the play the affirmative as well as the negative answer is given: Cuchulain still stands in the Post Office, the emblem of heroic endeavour, a heroism from which the despairing casuistry of the defeated cannot escape:

> What stood in the Post Office
> With Pearse and Connolly?
> What comes out of the mountain
> Where men first shed their blood?
> Who thought Cuchulain till it seemed
> He stood where they had stood?

By isolating the Cuchulain theme in this way we can legitimately draw a series of conclusions about Yeats's use of the national mythology, legend, and folk-tale. That Yeats was conscious from the earliest period of the 'need for a mythology' we have seen from the early essays; that the mythology he chose was largely adequate as poetic material there can be no doubt—the mythology and the folk-beliefs associated with what endures of the civilization from which it sprang make a quarry well stocked enough for most poets, although its blocks are not so well polished by time and long usage as those of Greece. But its adequacy for Yeats is to be measured by the degree of ease with which it lent itself to adaptation to Yeats's developing needs. The Cuchulain theme, perhaps because Cuchulain can so easily be made into an emblem of the heroic nature, did so adapt itself, which is the reason that that 'masterful image' is also a 'permanent image'. Cuchulain, too, is made to exemplify the continuity of the Irish theme as well as the larger meanings which Yeats attached to that theme.

It is far more difficult to admit that the Irish legends, other than that of Cuchulain, would have proved adequate to the strain that they might have been made to bear after the 'growth in self-possession and power': Yeats's poetic *savoir faire* was shown in his comparative neglect of them in his later verse. He developed beyond them, because his poetry outstripped the needs of Ireland: the imagined country for which he writes

At the Hawk's Well—'a civilization very unlike ours'—is not Ireland, although it is a civilization which in his early work Yeats seems almost to have believed *did* exist in Ireland. 'Blind Paudeen' and the 'day's war with every knave and dolt' showed him that this was not so, but none the less *The Celtic Twilight* and the work for Ireland contributed a good deal towards building up the picture of Byzantium. But Yeats was obliged to look elsewhere—in the 'Robartes papers'—for the mythology and philosophy that he needed. Yeats was no exception to the general rule that poets who search for a mythology will tend to depart from its traditional meanings; and the task of 'getting our heroic age into verse' was never so simple or satisfying as it might have been to Standish O'Grady or Lady Gregory, or as it seemed momentarily to Yeats himself in the enthusiastic dawn of a movement conceived as the rehabilitation of Irish letters. Nor, reading the early essays, can we be convinced that it could have seemed at any time an entirely sufficient programme for a poet who considered so many other literatures important and who was even then cultivating in his work a good deal of sophisticated Europeanism—the symbolists, Morris, the 'Celtic' Maeterlinck. It was likely to prove much less adequate when those early interests (which sprang from poetic needs) began to develop, and when, by dint of long gazing at the trembling of the veil, Yeats had added the cubit of *A Vision* to his stature. The purely Irish folk-tale, too, perhaps the more readily because of the folk-tale's inherent internationalism, turned out to be not enough: the Queen of the Great Clock Tower is not Maeve nor even Fand, though she is of their kin.

This is not to deny the vitality of the contribution made by the Irish theme. Yeats, even in his latest work, spoke often and directly to the 'indomitable Irishry' as well as to Byzantium. He believed that the poet must be national to be European; the struggles of Irish history, the values associated with Yeats's reading of that history and the continuity which he perceived in it, continually nourish his poetry. I have scarcely mentioned the many more subtle and potent ways in which the Irish heritage must have affected his work. The landscape of Sligo, the speech of its inhabitants (who included his friends and his ancestors) contribute a great deal to the best poems in *The Tower* and *The Winding Stair*. The obvious stylistic affinity which unites Yeats with Joyce and both with Swift suggests a common factor of nationality; 'that something hard and harsh' to which Yeats referred in connection with Swift and which is generally present in his own later work seems the product of a non-English strain running in the very blood of language.

3

'The Statues'
A note on the meaning
of Yeats's poem

The main theme of 'The Statues', which is printed in *Last Poems and Plays* (1940, p. 57), is made clear by a passage in *On the Boiler* (1938):

There are moments when I am certain that art must once again accept those Greek proportions which carry into plastic art the Pythagorean numbers, those faces which are divine because all there is empty and measured. Europe was not born when Greek galleys defeated the Persian hordes at Salamis, but when the Doric studios sent out those broad-backed marble statues against the multiform, vague, expressive Asiatic sea, they gave to the sexual instinct of Europe its goal, its fixed type.[1]

The last stanza of the poem affirms that the Irish, in a movement of history which brings about the return of the Pythagorean philosophy, must and will adopt a like artistic principle.[2]

Yeats habitually draws conclusions about history and intellectual climates from sculpture, and associates with sculpture the idea that the 'arts [are] . . . among those things that return for ever.'[3] The notion that the beauty and power of certain sculptures—those, for example, of the Mausoleum of Halicarnassus—are founded upon calculation and measurement was not a recent one:

[Maud Gonne's] whole body seemed a master-work of long labouring thought, as though a Scopas had measured and calculated, consorted

First published in *Review of English Studies*, xxv, 1949, 254–7.

1. Mr MacNeice, in his *The Poetry of W. B. Yeats* (1941), p. 175, also quotes this passage when referring to the poem.
2. Cf. 'Under Ben Bulben' (*Last Poems*, p. 91).
3. For example, in 'Discoveries' (*Essays*, 1924, p. 359).

with Egyptian sages, and mathematicians out of Babylon, that he might outface even Artemisia's sepulchral image with a living norm.[4]

'World-famous golden-thighed Pythagoras',[5] therefore, 'planned it' in the sense that the whole manifestation of artistic creation which made the 'statues' possible was prepared for by Pythagoras' doctrine of numbers, although Pythagoras was no sculptor himself. What, however, does Yeats mean by the distinction between 'character' and 'passion' in the first stanza of 'The Statues'? Some light is thrown on this by passages in Yeats's essay on 'The Tragic Theatre' written in 1910. There Yeats had stated his belief that tragic art must 'exclude or lessen character' in the sense of the individual characteristic and idiosyncrasy, the 'little irrelevance of line', the cultivation of the feeling '"How well that man is realized, I should know him were I to meet him in the street"'. Into the places left 'empty' of the 'real world', 'rhythm, balance, pattern, images that remind us of vast passions' will thereby be summoned. Yeats adds:

And when we love, if it be in the excitement of youth, do we not also, that the flood may find no stone to convulse, no wall to narrow it, exclude character or the signs of it by choosing that beauty which seems unearthly because the individual woman is lost amid the labyrinth of its lines as though life were trembling into stillness and silence, or at last folding itself away?[6]

In the theatre, therefore, passion brings 'character enough':

. . . for it is always ourselves that we see upon the stage, and should it be a tragedy of love we renew, it may be, some loyalty of our youth, and go from the theatre with our eyes dim for an old love's sake.[7]

Both the first and the second stanzas of 'The Statues' deal, it would appear, with the 'Doric' sculptures of the fifth century: Pythagoras, of the sixth century, was the forerunner of the Phidian work. Yeats has much to say in *A Vision* about the historic significance of the differences between the archaic sculpture of the sixth century, and the Ionic and Doric modes; he read

4. *The Trembling of the Veil* (1922), (*Autobiographies*, 1955, pp. 364–5).
5. 'Among School Children', *The Tower* (1928), (*Collected Poems*, 1950, p. 244).
6. 'The Tragic Theatre' in *The Cutting of an Agate* (*Essays*, 1924, pp. 297–301). Cf. also 'Estrangement' and 'The Death of Synge' (both 1909), in *Autobiographies*, pp. 471, 500–2.
7. *Essays*, pp. 297–8.

Furtwaengler and thought that the Ionic and Doric united in the work of Phidias. He makes none of these distinctions in the poem before us, and omits the idea, which would have wrought confusion on the principal theme of the poem, but is necessary to the 'system', that 'measurement' came *after* 'those riders upon the Parthenon' and that 'the dancing-master outlive[d] the dance', although in his later analysis of Roman portrait sculpture the predominance of 'character' is emphasized with distaste.[8] In the second stanza the Phidian sculptors are, however, considered 'greater than Pythagoras', because Pythagoras, as Yeats might have read in Taylor's translation of Iamblichus' *Life of Pythagoras*, spent many years in Egypt and Babylon, where he learnt the secrets of the Magi and therefore may be said to have become infected with the 'Asiatic vague immensities' which did not trouble Phidias.[9]

The third stanza is the most difficult and also the last of the four which requires analysis of this kind. If Yeats had been attempting a complete exposition of the historical cycle, he would perhaps have written a stanza describing the rise of the 'Asiatic and anarchic Europe' of the Middle Ages,[1] which is the 'many-headed' of the first line of the third stanza, and is consequently analogous to the 'many-headed foam at Salamis' that symbolizes the Asiatic armies of Xerxes. The Hamlet 'thin from eating flies' (or 'eating the air promise-crammed') is the spirit of modern speculation,[2] and the 'fat / Dreamer of the Middle Ages' is the medieval monk, isolated within his 'few courts and monasteries',[3] as well as William Morris and Titian's portrait of Ariosto—all antitheses of Hamlet. A passage from *The Trembling of the Veil* (1922) explains the conjunctions. Yeats has been recalling his memories of Morris and writes of Watts's portrait of Morris:

8. *A Vision*, pp. 268–77. I use the edition of 1937, but there are no important variations in this respect from the 1925 edition.

9. For the looking-glass in this stanza, by whose means women both discipline themselves and live a sensuous life where 'all thought . . . Becomes a body', cf. 'Michael Robartes and the Dancer' (*Collected Poems*, p. 198) and the 'heroic discipline of the looking-glass' ('Discoveries' in *Essays*, p. 334).

1. *A Vision*, p. 283.

2. Cf. Oscar Wilde's epigram given in *The Trembling of the Veil* (*Autobiographies*, p. 135): Hamlet invented modern pessimism: 'The world has become sad because a puppet was once melancholy.'

3. *A Vision*, p. 283.

Its grave wide-open eyes, like the eyes of some dreaming beast, remind me of the open eyes of Titian's *Ariosto*, while the broad vigorous body suggests a mind that has no need of the intellect to remain sane, though it give itself to every fantasy: the dreamer of the Middle Ages. It is 'the fool of Faery . . . wide and wild as a hill', the resolute European image that yet half remembers Buddha's motionless meditation, and has no trait in common with the wavering, lean image of hungry speculation, that cannot but because of certain famous Hamlets of our stage fill the mind's eye.[4]

This passage foreshadows and explains the greater part of the third stanza of the poem. The idea of the 'empty eyeball' of the 'empty man' who 'saw all that could be seen from very emptiness'[5] is one which Yeats had used before in commenting upon the various conventional methods of representing the human eye in sculpture and portrait. He concluded that a difference in method implied a different world-view.[6] Grimalkin, the cat, is seen 'crawling' to Buddha's emptiness, because the cat is the animal whose eyes are the most responsive to the altering of the moon (with all that those phases mean to the author of *A Vision*). Because of this, Yeats writes in the 1934 introduction to *The Cat and the Moon*, the cat becomes a symbol of the 'normal man'. 'When gong and conch declare the hour to bless', the normal man responds at length to the need for contemplative emptiness by worshipping or fleeing for refuge to the Buddha symbol, the 'fat / Dreamer of the Middle Ages'.[7]

The meaning of the last stanza is plain in the light of the quotation from *On the Boiler* and 'Under Ben Bulben'. A statue of Cuchulain now stands in the Central Post Office, Dublin.

'As life goes on', Yeats wrote in *The Trembling of the Veil*, 'we discover that certain thoughts sustain us in defeat, or give us victory . . . and it is these thoughts, tested by passion, that we call

4. *The Trembling of the Veil*, in *Autobiographies*, pp. 141–2. With the references to Titian's *Ariosto*, a picture with a special meaning for Yeats, cf. *A Vision*, p. 294; *Autobiographies*, pp. 116, 293. The effect of the portrait and that of the Phidian marbles are compared by implication in *A Vision*, p. 270. For another example of the connection in Yeats's mind between medieval contemplativeness and Buddhism, see the introduction to *The Cat and the Moon* in *Wheels and Butterflies* (1934), p. 138.

5. See the parable related in 'At Stratford-on-Avon' (*Essays*, p. 131).

6. As in *A Vision*, pp. 276–7, 280.

7. The cat is found subserving this symbolic purpose first of all in the poem called 'The Cat and the Moon' (1918); then in the play of the same title (1926). The symbolism is explained in the introduction to the play in *Wheels and Butterflies*.

convictions.'[8] The poem is seen to be crowded with convictions of this kind, and few of them are, in fact, of recent growth. It demonstrates the remarkable continuity of his ideas and his ability to make metaphors out of them for one of his finest lyrics.

8. *Autobiographies*, p. 189.

4

The integrity of Yeats

I

In *After Strange Gods* Mr Eliot tells us how Yeats created his own tradition. He accepts I. A. Richards's view that Yeats 'made a violent repudiation, not merely of current civilization but of life itself, in favour of a supernatural world'. But—Mr Eliot goes on—

Mr Yeats's 'supernatural world' was the wrong supernatural world. It was not a world of spiritual significance, not a world of real Good and Evil, of holiness or sin, but a highly sophisticated lower mythology summoned, like a physician, to supply the fading pulse of poetry with some transient stimulant so that the dying patient may utter his last words. In its extreme self-consciousness it approaches the mythology of D. H. Lawrence on its more decadent side.

There are two points, at least, to be noted about this criticism: first, the comparison between Yeats the exploiter of Celtic mythology and (presumably) that D. H. Lawrence who wrote the deplorable novel *The Plumed Serpent*; second, the charge that Yeats's mythology is a *lower* mythology. I am not sure according to what scale of value Eliot places some mythologies in a 'lower' and others in a 'higher' category, but one gathers from this passage that what constitutes the lowness of a mythology (and also what makes for a resemblance between Yeats and the author of *The Plumed Serpent*) is sophistication, self-consciousness, and spiritual insignificance. Dr Richards's criticism is not unlike Mr Eliot's, although his charge bears more heavily on what might be called Yeats's invented or constructed mythology— the world of *A Vision*—rather than on the use made by the poet of the old Irish stories:

He turns [writes Dr Richards] to a world of symbolic phantasmagoria about which he is desperately uncertain. He is uncertain because he has

A paper read to the Durham Branch of the English Association, 1 March 1949. First published in *Cambridge Journal*, iii, 1949, 80–93.

adopted as a technique of inspiration the use of trance, of dissociated phases of consciousness, and the revelations given in these dissociated states are insufficiently connected with normal experience.

Lastly, Mr Stephen Spender may speak for what Yeats would have thought of as the younger generation, though they are now middle-aged: 'Yeats's poetry is devoid of any unifying moral subject', writes Mr Spender in *The Destructive Element*; 'although he has much wisdom, he offers no philosophy of life, but, as a substitute, a magical system . . . not socially constructive . . . the thought is hopelessly inadequate to the situation.'

These are heavy accusations. That they were later in part withdrawn does not seriously diminish their force. I want to supplement these accusations by stating the case against Yeats more thoroughly—or rather in a less generalized way—before attempting to show the measure of his integrity.

When we have absorbed a good deal of Yeats we are conscious of a satiety which has nothing to do with the feeling of organic satisfaction. It can be on occasion something more akin to positive disrelish. There is sometimes a lack of delicacy in what Yeats offers, and very often what he offers, perhaps because it seems intended for the gourmet, is distinctly 'high'. There is the cloistered prose of the *Autobiographies*, in which some of the mannerisms of George Moore have got entangled with the rhythms of Pater; many of the early poems are a mingle-mangle of pre-Raphaelitism, Morris, and the weakly beautiful gestures that theosophy makes to what Yeats later called 'this pragmatical, preposterous pig of a world'. The weakness of the early work needs no emphasizing, though the search after faint beauty, after the intense and the elaborate, can be justified as Yeats's reaction against 'Victorian rationalism'. Yeats's work at this early period mirrors too faithfully the disunity of late nineteenth-century letters. But turn to the later work, and we shall also at times writhe our jaws with disrelish. The sensuous coarseness is sometimes overdone: Yeats is on occasion merely the theosophist with his nose in the garbage can—the house-lights are out and the ill-paid actors quarrel in the wings. The reversion to reality can be a reversion to something as highly stylized and fundamentally 'unreal', phantasmagoric, as the Irish Never-Never Land. Yeats bought his properties and manner at a different shop, but they were properties and manner still; he talked a good deal about walking naked, but his nakedness was the dramatized nakedness of poor Tom in *Lear*: the 'foul rag-and-bone shop' of which he spoke in 'The Circus Animals' Desertion' supplied the very best bones, the most dramatically ragged of rags, but there is still the lingering smell of grease-paint, the sense of a pose histrionically—perhaps almost hysterically—adopted.

I have jumped from the earliest to the latest Yeats, but at all times there is the danger that we may be sickened by that eternally professional manner, and may cry, with Yeats himself: 'Seek out reality, leave things that seem.' Indeed, the accusation may go deeper still. Is there not about all this a suspicion of charlatanism? A charlatan is one who offers the very dead sea fruit itself from

> the baneful tree of hell,
> That Zoacum, that fruit of bitterness,
> That in the midst of fire is ingraffed,
> Yet flourisheth as Flora in her pride.

But charlatanism in the arts is the sign of a profound disorganization in the personality of the artist. I am not of course here concerned to rebut the parrot-cry against the arts that Yeats himself reacted against so fiercely and which Ibsen put into the mouth of the complacent Mayor in *Brand*:

> A little poetry pleases me,
> And all our folks, in their degree;
> But—moderation everywhere!
> In *life* it never must have share,—
> Except at night, when folks have leisure,
> Between the hours of seven and ten,
> When baths of elevating pleasure
> May fit the mood of weary men.

It is the constant refusal of the Mayor and his kin, in Ibsen's words, 'at once to *plough* and *fight*' that inspired the whole immense campaign waged against them by William Morris, and Yeats was for a long time Morris's disciple. The hint of charlatanism lies not on this level at all: it lies rather in the suspicion that Yeats had been floated too far out by the cross-currents of action and reaction ever to recover dry land; that he was torn to pieces between Brand and the Mayor, and that he ever afterwards gives us substitute only for a real resolution of the conflict, some constructed patchwork universe.

One can perhaps see traces of a disordered intention in the relation of Yeats's work to the Irish literary movement. There is, first of all, a peculiar nexus of fallacies, revealed in the earlier essays, about the relationship of a literary movement with national and patriotic roots to the acquisition of a style. Just as Yeats reacted against the Victorian rationalism that dominated his childhood, so he rejected the purely pragmatic Irish writers of his young manhood—Sir Charles Gavan Duffy, the Young Irelanders, all those who wished to use verse for political propaganda; he rejected also those Irish writers who, like Allingham, forsook Irish themes. He vigorously urged Irish writers to exploit the Irish mythology—that 'untouched marble block' as he called it, and did so himself in *The Wanderings of Oisin* and many later poems and plays; and urged them also to exploit the Irish peasant traditions—and did it himself in *The Celtic Twilight*, *The Hour-Glass* and other 'peasant plays', and the Crazy Jane poems. In so doing he was serving the needs of an Ireland inhabited exclusively by beggermen and nobles, of an Ireland that did not exist, but was merely the back of England's mirror, the imagined wish-created opposite of the rational, unhierarchical Anglo-Saxon world. It is not my intention to examine the paradoxical structure of Yeats's early politico-literary preoccupations. It so happened that he got his way, at least as far as the Abbey Theatre was concerned, with the powerful support of Lady Gregory. But he had his critics, and their question was: Why, if you wish Irish literature to serve our cause by becoming 'European' and ceasing to be chauvinistic, should you move in such a crab-wise direction, retrogressing to an Ireland that is but a gesture of revolt against the modern world? Edward Martyn, whose pro-Ibsenite policy for the Abbey Yeats defeated, accused Yeats almost directly of charlatanism.[1] But more important than Edward Martyn's fit of pique was the contempt of James Joyce, the one other great Irish writer of our time: 'Michael Robartes', Stephen Dedalus wrote in his diary, 'remembers forgotten beauty and, when his arms wrap her round, he presses in his arms the loveliness which has long faded from the world.'

1. Denis Gwynn, *Edward Martyn and the Irish Revival* (1930), pp. 154 ff.

Joyce is the Brand of this particular drama, just as the Catholic
bourgeois Dublin that cried out against *The Countess Cathleen*
and *The Playboy of the Western World* is Ibsen's Mayor, and Yeats
came to terms with neither. For within ten years came the reaction against the imaginary Ireland—a reaction stimulated by
Yeats's discovery that the 'obscure spite of blind Paudeen' and
Biddy's halfpence were the real factors in the Irish situation.
What followed was another construct, another substitution:
Yeats spent his middle period putting Byzantium in the place
of Ireland, another imaginary eclectic culture that bore the same
stamp of unreality. His play *On Baile's Strand* was written, he
wrote in 1921, not for Ireland but for:

some country where all classes share in a half-mythological, half-
philosophical folk-belief which the writer and his small audience lift
into a new subtlety. All my life I have longed for such a country, and
always found it quite impossible to write without having as much
belief in its real existence as a child has in that of the wooden beasts,
birds and persons of his toy Noah's ark.

Yeats goes on to say that he has now found all the mythology
and all the philosophy he needs in the work for *A Vision* (the
Michael Robartes papers, as he calls them at this stage). In this
passage it is Yeats himself who contributes the suggestion that the
thing is a toy, a plaything invented to still a crying need. We
might remark, with Joyce in *Finnegans Wake*: 'condemned
fool . . . you have reared your disunited kingdom on the vacuum
of your own most intensely doubtful soul'—only Yeats's
Byzantium was not a 'disunited kingdom', but the world of a
somnambulist, mortared with all the hierarchical coherence
of the perfectly realized wish—and perhaps none the better for
that.
    This Noah's ark was a raft, a *Nancy* Brig whose captain, Yeats,
was mate, passenger, and crew as well; and we know of what
materials it was constructed—of 'phantasmagoria' in Dr
Richards's words, of 'folklore, occultism, mythology and symbolism, crystal-gazing and hermetic writings' in Mr Eliot's.
Scholars are at this moment engaged in feeling their way back,
like spiders in a web, to the sources from which Yeats gathered
his heterogeneous materials. We can be confident in the assur-

ance that Yeats will prove the better spider; but—said the bee in Swift's fable—'in that building of yours, there might, for aught I know, have been labour and method enough: but by woful experience for us both, 'tis too plain the materials are naught'.

In reading Yeats, then, we may be irritated by the hieratic pose, by the constant assumption of fresh sets of priestly garments; we may feel, as Joyce appears to have felt, that he misdirected the Irish revival in the direction of the folksy and the esoteric, in the direction of what Eliot calls 'the provincial in time and place', and we may in the end, climbing along the threads to the heart of the matter, find only a spider spinning a uniquely useless web. Lastly, we may think ourselves entitled to state, as Dr Richards draws near to doing, that Yeats's poetry claims too exclusive an absorption, too total a sympathy, that his references to the esoteric or to the merely personal and private unduly strain our willingness to enter into bonds to a poet who demands that we turn our attention to such things as Madame Blavatsky's cuckoo-clock, or Porphyry's *Life of Plotinus*—an important document no doubt but hardly one which is central to our civilization. And Dr Richards, as a psychologist, has a severer admonition: Yeats's 'revelations' are 'insufficiently connected with normal experience'. In short, Yeats's elaborately wrought poems demand 'that ideal reader suffering from the ideal insomnia', but apparently—since all Yeats's constructs are false—do not undertake to reward him with any meaningful experience, any significant vision of life. Where, in the reading of Yeats, can contemporaneity be enriched as it is by the moral vision and lofty order of Turgenev, or Ibsen, or Henry James? This is a serious question, for some time Yeats's position *vis-à-vis* the other great writers of the age must be more fully determined than it is at present. Every modern poet who has succeeded in writing at all well appeals to us as someone saved from a shipwreck—so difficult, so seemingly irrelevant to the storms and rocks of the modern world is this apparently inconsequent art. But, as Henry James made one of his characters remark, 'There are wrecks that are not adventures', so surely as there are very few adventures that are not wrecks. Can it be that Yeats's Noah's ark is merely a wreck, and that the adventure, in spite of his loud asseverations to the contrary, never occurred?

II

There is always the danger when one states the case against a writer in this summary way that one may be fair neither to him nor to his accusers, but that is a risk which I have been prepared to run. There is one way in which I do not think the case should be answered, and that is the way chosen by Mr Eliot. 'We admire Mr Yeats for having outgrown' his earlier manner, he writes, 'for having packed away his bibelots and resigned himself to live in an apartment furnished in the barest simplicity. A few faded beauties remain: Babylon, Nineveh, Helen of Troy, and such souvenirs of youth: but the austerity of Mr Yeats's later verse, on the whole, should compel the admiration of the least sympathetic.' Yeats has perhaps enjoyed for too long the privileges of subdivision of this kind; these changes in manner and method are signal enough, but they should not be allowed to obscure the continuity which is their base. Yeats, indeed, displays an extraordinary consistency of outlook in his poetic work; he is always pursuing the same poetic objective. It can be shown, for example, that Yeats's poetic values were established by him quite early in his career and that they never underwent any serious or fundamental change, although they underwent a number of mutations which have helped to conceal the persistency with which the original scale of values is employed. His attitude to Ireland is an example. On the evidence of the early essays it can be said that Yeats evolved all the literary principles having relation to the Irish theme that were important to him as a poet prior to 1910—that is to say, before the period in which his most valuable poetry was written. Furthermore, the example of Ireland, imaginary or real, was used by him to nourish and support convictions that remained with him always: that poetry must go deep to the levels of the racial heritage, that it must be national rather than nationalistic (a distinction which he explains at some length in the early essays), that it must employ a native mythology, that it must be the index of a spontaneous, heroic, imaginative life, the antithesis of pragmatism and abstraction. Yeats himself fostered in his work that sense of continuity which seemed to him to animate and bestow value upon the Irish theme as that could be utilized in poetry. 'It is not a difference in the substance of things', he wrote in an early essay, 'that the lamentations that were sung after battles are now sung for men who have died upon the gallows.' The mutations that the Irish theme underwent were many and cannot be described here. But our admiration for the work of his later years, for what he called his growth in self-possession and power, should not prevent us from recognizing that the same powerful but limited intellect was at work throughout—that the Cabbala was lying on Yeats's desk in 1887, forty years before he wrote *A Vision*.

It is, then, not accurate to assume an opposition of values in Yeats's early and his later work. Moreover—and on a different level of objection—this 'apartment furnished in the barest simplicity', to which Mr Eliot likens the later poetry, is nearly as wide of the mark. *The Tower*, *The Winding Stair*, and *Last Poems* contain writing more elaborate and obscure and intense—and I am using adjectives which Yeats was using as far back as the 1890s to describe the sort of art that Ireland must cultivate—than anything in the early poetry. And those three volumes make a very conscious use of the 'phantasmagoria' of *A Vision*. Indeed, *Purgatory*, Yeats's last play, which might seem to be a bare apartment, is most elaborately furnished with the mythology of *A Vision*.

The paradox contained in this coincidence of bareness and elaboration brings me to the first point I want to make in defence of Yeats's integrity. What Mr Eliot had neglected to emphasize in this part of his critique, is Yeats's habit of self-dramatization. In the reading of Yeats's poetry we come across a number of statements of poetic intention; they are declarations that in future the poet will 'walk naked', that he will cast off that coat embroidered with old mythologies. The last of the series is that fine poem 'The Circus Animals' Desertion':

> I sought a theme and sought for it in vain,
> I sought it daily for six weeks or so.
> Maybe at last, being but a broken man,
> I must be satisfied with my heart, although
> Winter and summer till old age began
> My circus animals were all on show,
> Those stilted boys, that burnished chariot
> Lion and woman and the Lord knows what.

If nothing else is, the contents of the rest of *Last Poems* are evidence that Yeats never really abandoned the circus animals and the embroidered coat. But he made drama of the self out of their deficiencies and his reluctances. The self which he dramatizes is indeed that disordered self, that disorganized personality, which I earlier put in the scale against Yeats. Yeats himself is the first of his critics to realize that the struggle of Brand is taking place in himself and that, in today's world, the issue remains in doubt always. The disorder is the poetry's 'cause'; in the poetry, Yeats turns the shipwreck into an adventure. By being made the subject of a process of poetic choice, the grand professional manner is itself altered from a possible liability into an asset. So it is that much of Yeats's poetry is 'about' conflict, choice, disorder: the macrocosm of world confusion is mirrored in the microcosm of drama or lyric. *At the Hawk's Well* is Yeats's own version of *Brand*, a struggle between heroic virtue and spiritual death. The theme that runs through the Crazy Jane poems is one conceived and born in disorder: the fight between old age and youthful desire, between the thwarting shadow of Urizen and 'spontaneous joy and natural content', between man and woman—these are the elements of that drama: 'I struggled with the horror of daybreak,' cries Crazy Jane, 'I chose it for my lot!' Yeats's theory of the anti-mask expressed in *Per Amica Silentia Lunae* and *A Vision* is a parable which systematizes a conflict seen even in the poet's search out of subjectivity for an objective art. Yeats can render with new force also the ancient struggle between Stoic and Epicurean, as well as that between Emperor and Galilean. Indeed there is no point in his poetry, whether he is dealing with Christ and Dionysus, or with Parnell and Mr de Valera, where one can say that choice is avoided and conflict glossed over. Always in his verse the fierce horsemen ride from mountain to mountain. One of Yeats's last poems, 'The Man and the Echo', mirrors such a conflict. The Echo suggests to the ageing poet, netted in worry and disillusion, to let the Id have its way, to 'lie down and die'; but strength is found to reply:

> That were to shirk
> The spiritual intellect's great work . . .
> Nor can there be work so great
> As that which cleans man's dirty slate.

In the long run, the conflict is one waged between Death and Life; Yeats is busy keeping alive in a special sense, preoccupied with detecting the insidious advance of spiritual death, much as

are the characters of Henry James and E. M. Forster; Yeats
refused to believe, as he wrote in *The Trembling of the Veil*, that
'great men must live in a portion of themselves'. But the issue
is constantly in doubt because the conflict is archetypal. The
claim can, then, be made that the disorder inherent in the poet
and the poet's relationship to a hostile and confused world, so
far from being a frustration of the poetic work, is rather a means
by which vitality and relevance are added to it.

We have, however, the right to demand something more
from a great poet than the recapitulation of our disorders. Nor
have I gone any way towards justifying the use of that farrago
of mythology and esoteric teaching, the 'phantasmagoria' of
which Dr Richards disapproves. These two questions, which are
really interdependent, must be approached in a roundabout
though not, I hope, in a tendentious manner. Yeats was, of
course, as well as raising the conflict between extremes of experience to poetic level, seeking to impose an order upon that
experience. It is the constant effort of his life and art—which
may much more plausibly be described in terms of a search for
an objective order than as a mere galloping over rough country
in search of the 'right' style, the sort of style which appeals to
the contemporaries of Eliot. Yeats, like the Dante he described,
seeks an 'unpersuadable justice'. 'One goes on year after year',
he wrote to his father, 'getting the disorder of one's mind into
order, and this is the real impulse to create.' This is the task of
the 'spiritual intellect', as Yeats conceived it, to 'arrange all
in one clear view', to 'prepare my peace' as he said in various
poems—and this task is a necessity to him. It is this side of Yeats's
task, one may judge, for which Mr Eliot feels greatest sympathy,
with an understanding also of how this objective grows pro-
gressively more difficult of attainment in a context of ship-
wrecked values. 'We sing in spite of our terror', commented
Yeats. As early as 1887 Yeats seems to have become content with
the heroic order that he believed to be manifest in the Irish
legends. 'I hope', he wrote sixteen years later, 'to get our Irish
heroic age into verse.' Later, he sought the unpersuadable
justice in strange places, on the margins, away from the central
traditions of European Christianity. It was then that he combined
early with later interests to make what Eliot calls 'the wrong
supernatural world'. The immediate discovery is reported upon

in *A Vision*, a few essays, and a handful of poems which Yeats called 'texts for exposition'.

It is important to judge this assortment of 'semi-mythological, semi-philosophical' beliefs in our argument, not for itself, but in regard to the function which it performs in Yeats's work, and to remember the way in which Yeats himself contemplated it. Speaking of his childhood, Yeats wrote in 1914: 'I had as many ideas as I have now, only I did not know how to choose from among them those that belonged to my life.' Consciously or unconsciously, Yeats tended to select ideas not for themselves but for their function, to satisfy a need, ultimately to satisfy a poetic need. In 1928 he wrote in the proem to *A Vision*:

Some will ask whether I believe in the actual existence of my circuits of sun and moon . . . To such a question I can but answer that if sometimes, overwhelmed by miracle as all men must be when in the midst of it, I have taken such periods literally, my reason has soon recovered; and now that the system stands out clearly in my imagination I regard them as stylistic arrangements of experience . . . They have helped me to hold in a single thought reality and justice.

That is to say, they have brought for the space of 'a single thought'—a poet's thought, not a philosopher's or a theologian's —order and understanding into the cruel unintelligibilities of history and human life. Again, he writes in *The Trembling of the Veil*: 'As life goes on we discover that certain thoughts sustain us in defeat or give us victory . . . and it is these thoughts, tested by passion, that we call convictions'—the kind of convictions Yeats was describing when he wrote to Lady Wellesley about his last play *Purgatory*: 'I have put [into this play] my own conviction about this world and the next.'

It is important that we should preserve an awareness of the function of the system in relation to the poetry, since by so doing we shall the more easily understand Yeats's claim that it was that 'incredible experience' that accounts for the growth of 'self-possession and power' in the later poetry. 'We have come to give you metaphors for poetry', declared the 'unknown instructors' in *A Vision*, and in a sense this is the only part of their work that need concern us. 'To hold in a single thought reality and justice' is, for Yeats, the necessary preliminary to poetic composition: it is more than that, perhaps, for the 'single thought' is itself the resultant poem, a construction in which 'passion' and 'truth', the mortal world and the immortal order, are held in an intricate balance. Such seems to be one of the ways of defining the effect, if not the nature, of some of the best of Yeats's poems. It is in this sense that Yeats believed in the 'system', and it is doubtful if we are entitled to question the validity of that kind of belief, without also considering it in terms of its poetic progeny, which excels. The 'system', or the 'unknown instructors', are like the old mythological Muse: a stylization of the experience of writing poetry, of 'hold[ing] in a single thought reality and justice', a good Genius to be invoked, who can raise to the creative level the 'intensely doubtful soul' of the poet and bestow upon it the coherence and power necessary for the practice of his art. But Yeats's poems, with the exception of the few 'texts for exposition', are not *about* the 'system', any more than *Paradise Lost* is about Urania. The Muse is the Muse under whatever disguises, provided she performs her function. Milton saw her as the seraphim, touching and purifying the lips of whom the Eternal Spirit pleases. But it would be a mistake to regard *Paradise Lost* as a poem necessarily superior to the *Aeneid* because Virgil invoked not the Christian Muse but the pagan one whom Milton called 'an empty dream'. Though the 'system' may be amongst the wilder sorts of nonsense, as indeed is the idea of the Heavenly Muse, if interpreted literally or euhemeristically, it functioned well.

I have, in that excursus, moved slightly away from Mr Eliot's charge that Yeats's supernatural world is not a world of real Good or Evil, of holiness or sin. I have done so in order to show that I think the attitude of mind which informs that charge is open to criticism from two angles: first, in that it takes insufficient account of the functional relation of the system to the poetry; and, secondly—a quite different kind of objection—in that it makes the same kind of rather limited presuppositions about the relation of poetry to its intellectual background that Sir William Davenant and other seventeenth-century critics made when they threw overboard the pagan fables because a Christian poet little needs the aid of such false inventions. But Davenant's confidence, or Mr Eliot's, in the possession of a means of measuring the rightness or wrongness of supernatural worlds, is strictly irrelevant to the *datum* of Yeats's situation. *He* did not feel that confidence—he had been 'deprived [of it] by Huxley

and Tyndall'. It is out of the disorder, out of the loss of confidence, that he makes his poetry, and that is the measure of his
achievement.

Yet there is a broad sense in which every poet's work has to be
judged by these two standards—does it deal with a world of real
Good and Evil? Does it—to use the old phrase which is fast
recovering its old validity—'persuade to virtue'? By a broad
sense one means the broadest possible sense within which these
commonplaces can still remain effective. The force of Eliot's
criticism of Yeats lies precisely in its delicate hinting at these two
larger queries, and it must be met.

Yeats sees Good and Evil in terms of the conflict which I have
already described as archetypal in his work. It is quite true that
he doesn't see them in terms of the Christian analyses. Indeed,
although he believes in miracle he rejects the Christian explanation of it:

> Must we part, von Hügel, though much alike, for we
> Accept the miracles of the saints and honour sanctity?

But Yeats's poetry involves a metaphysical analysis of the conditions of human life, conducted by a man profoundly aware of
the dualisms which may frustrate it. It is these dualisms which
express themselves in the conflicts whose general nature I have
already sketched—the opposition between Truth and Passion,
between Christ and Platonic tolerance, between the labour and
the blossoming, the christened and the unchristened heart.
Yeats's world, besides being a personal landscape of symbolic
beauty, an 'island of statues' (which is the title of his first published play), is a battleground of these forces, a constant pattern-
ing of antitheses—just as Henry James's very different-seeming
world, a furnished world where the furniture is continually
thinking and the cities decay slowly by the water's edge, turns
out to be a world where Good and Evil, under many disguises,
are the main preoccupation of the inhabitants. But it is not possible to extract from Yeats's work an ethical system, as it is, for
example, from Spenser's—which is no doubt what Mr Spender
meant when he said that it offers us no philosophy of life and is
not socially constructive. On the other hand, just as we can say
that James seems to be concerned with the creation and preservation of a value which he redefines many times but which we

here can summarize as something of 'quality', of 'fine-
grainedness' in human living, so in Yeats's case we can say that
his work, too, is concerned with the creation and preservation
of a value, though one very different from the novelist's. Yeats's
value is heroic life, passionate, sensuous, aristocratic living,
charged with an awareness of the antitheses that I have mentioned—the 'whirl[ing] upon a compass-point' and the finding of
'certainty' which he celebrated in the poem called 'Coole Park,
1929', all that Yeats meant when he said 'Homer is my example
and his unchristened heart'. This is the virtue to which Yeats
persuades us. Stated in this way, it may sound thin and pagan
enough, certainly not socially constructive and probably 'insufficiently connected with normal experience', and perhaps it is
time that Yeats was recognized as being nearer akin to Nietzsche
and Stendhal than to Spenser and St Thomas Aquinas. But
to state it thus is not quite fair to Yeats or to the effect which his
work has upon us. Yeats is a poet, and a poet of a kind once rare
but now increasingly the norm—a poet engaged in salvaging
the practice of his art from the 'dolphin-torn, [the] gong-
tormented sea' of the modern world, in turning his shipwreck
into an adventure. It follows that the poet himself, by all the
subtle means which he has at his command in poetic practice,
creates the value which he wishes to preserve—as I implied
earlier when I spoke not only of the preservation but also of the
creation of values. The modern poet, for the most part, cannot,
as Spenser did, re-apply the Christian ethic, or write in the
happy confidence that he is expressing more delightfully and
more precisely the valued commonplaces of his age. Yeats must
have regretted this, for his was the mind that conceived Byzantium, where culture is a unity. But it was a condition of his mind,
as formed by his century, which he was forced to obey. We
are left then with the poet's claim that the world which
he has created in his poetry is a more intense and elaborate
version of reality than the dolphin-torn world, the normal
confusion in which the shipwreck occurred. Yeats makes this
claim:

> ... art
> Is but a vision of reality.
> What portion in the world can the artist have
> Who has awakened from the common dream?

The proof of the claim is, of course, to be found in the poetry itself, nowhere else at all. And it does seem that in Yeats's poetry, and strictly within the context of that poetry, there are poems which provide us with the special kind of intense illumination, the achievement of a positive equilibrium, that is found only in the greatest poets. This equilibrium is achieved by a reconciliation, by a momentary transcendence of the many antitheses, so that the poem and the reading of it become, if another Jamesian phrase may be used, something which is completely and intensely *there*. Yeats has described the process and its effects in the oblique language of poetic symbolism:

> A tree there is that from its topmost bough
> Is half all glittering flame and half all green
> Abounding foliage moistened with the dew;
> And half is half and yet is all the scene;
> And half and half consume what they renew,
> And he that Attis' image hangs between
> That staring fury and the blind lush leaf
> May know not what he knows, but knows not grief.

This kind of experience and effect may be described as a reconciliation, as a 'vision of reality', as a realization, to reverse Seneca's phrase, that 'There are Gods'. It is of course an experience within the poetic context, and one fostered by the discipline of poetic study. It is, if you like, self-created and self-sustained, but the watchful eye of the eternal Wisdom is upon it:

> And yonder in the gymnasts' garden thrives
> The self-sown, self-begotten shape that gives
> Athenian intellect its mastery,
> Even the grey-leaved olive-tree
> Miracle-bred out of the living stone;
> Nor accident of peace nor war
> Can wither that old marvel, for
> The great grey-eyed Athena stares thereon.

Such lines as these have the weight of all Yeats's achievement behind them. They rise up, as Forster has said of great poetry, from that anonymous part of a man which 'cannot be labelled with his name. It has something in common with all other deeper personalities, and the mystic will assert that the common quality is God.' One can carry that remark further; for such an achievement may seem to have as little—or as much—relevance to Good and Evil, to holiness and sin in the real as well as in the supernatural worlds, as the experience of the religious mystic. I am prepared to admit as much or as little relevance to these things on the part of the mystical experience as seems proper, provided that the comparison that I am implying between this kind of poetic experience and the mystical experience is allowed to stand. The areas where the comparison is relevant may be few and not central or important to the theological assumptions within which the mystical experience, historically, takes place: Yeats is no St John of the Cross, but he is perhaps the most Dantean poet of our time.

Lest it be thought that I am claiming for Yeats some unique kind of poetic achievement, it is perhaps safer to point out that I merely think Yeats not only the best English poet since Wordsworth, but the English poet, since Wordsworth, who has written most like Wordsworth: the similarity between them lies chiefly in their common ability to charge an object with symbolic power to such a degree that the poetic imagination seems to take an upward leap to that reality of which Yeats spoke, 'wherein the gazing heart doubles her might'. Compare, for example, the seagull in 'On a Political Prisoner' or the stone in the stream in 'Easter 1916', with the leech-gatherer in 'Resolution and Independence'. These are high claims indeed, but, if truth and justice support them, then poets who can write in that way are not, however far they stray from current formulas—theological or political—or from 'normal experience' —living in a world of spiritual insignificance, self-consciousness and sophistication; they are not being nourished on 'phantas-magoria'. They give us, rather, a world where all the ship-wrecked men are saved and their adventures permanently recorded, and that is the measure of their integrity:

> I am content to follow to its source
> Every event in action or in thought;
> Measure the lot; forgive myself the lot!
> When such as I cast out remorse
> So great a sweetness flows into the breast
> We must laugh and we must sing,
> We are blest by everything,
> Everything we look upon is blest.

5

Yeats's 'Demon and Beast'

'The spring-time! The spring-time! Wake up and see it, Yeats,
I cried, poking him up with this objection—that before he met
the Indian who had taught him metaphysics his wont was to take
pleasure in the otter in the stream, the magpie in the hawthorn
and the heron in the marsh, the brown mice in and out of the
corn-bin, and the ousel that had her nest in the willow under the
bank. Your best poems came to you through your eyes.' The
speaker is George Moore, by the lakeside on Stephen's Green,
in the second week of May 1899. Yeats and Moore, if Moore is to
be believed, lingered there watching the children throwing
bread to the waterfowl, while a tumult of gulls passed to and
fro overhead; for Moore the scene was refreshingly different
from the melancholy entertainment in the Antient Concert
Rooms the previous night when the expert keening of the
Galway singers in *The Countess Cathleen* had mingled with the
howls from the gallery. The argument which Moore tried to
start—tried and failed, for 'Yeats's thoughts were far above
nature that morning'—broke out some eighteen years later when
Yeats wrote 'Demon and Beast,' a poem about nature and the
poet, about Stephen's Green, Moore's green-headed sheldrake
and the herring-gull dipping for bread over the ornamental
lake.

There cannot be much doubt that in 1918 Yeats's thoughts
were still 'far above nature' in Moore's sense. But for some
approach to the most pregnant line in 'Demon and Beast'—
'Right mastery of natural things'—we may well go back to the
beginning of the century and to the book of that period, *Ideas
of Good and Evil*. Yeats says in one of his essays on Blake that the
'sleep of nature where all is soft and melting' tempts the artist
away from the 'labours of inspiration'. Nature is a 'net woven by
Satan', and the artist who is contented in its toils may, like

First published in *Irish Writing*, xxxi, 1955, 42–50.

William Morris, be happy as he contemplates nature's delight in mere profusion; but Yeats's genius was, like Rossetti's, stirred to reject the profusion. Nature for its own sake, as his readers and critics know, does not appear in his poetry; the art that celebrated nature in Morris's or Wordsworth's way was for him an art founded not upon experience and imagination, but upon observation, generalization, and the quiescent eye; it was a kind of indolence, not a creative energy, and led too easily to what Yeats wrote of in *A Vision* as Wordsworth's reduction of mankind to 'a few slight figures outlined for a moment amid mountain and lake'. Yeats owed a good deal, as Miss Marion Witt has shown, to the aesthetic of Blake's disciples Samuel Palmer and Edward Calvert; when he turned to their writings he found grounds for his rejection of false mimetic art, the fruit of observation and of 'seeing like a naturalist', with its laws dictated by reasoning from sensation, in favour of true severe art, which is 'expressive and symbolic, and makes every form, every sound, every colour, every gesture, a signature of some unanalysable imaginative essence'. 'Terrestrial spring showers blossoms and odours in profusion,' wrote Palmer, but

the perfection of nature is not the perfection of severest art: they are two things. The former we may liken to an easy, charming colloquy of intellectual friends; the latter is 'Imperial Tragedy'. *That* is graceful humanity; *this* is Plato's Vision; who, somewhere in untracked regions, primigenous Unity, above all things holds his head and bears his forehead among the stars, tremendous to the gods! . . . *General* nature is wisely and beneficently adapted to refresh the senses and soothe the spirits of general *observers* . . . General nature is simple and lovely; but, compared with the loftier vision, it is the shrill music of the 'Little herd grooms'. . . . Everywhere curious, articulate, perfect and inimitable of structure, like her own entomology, Nature does yet leave a space for the soul to climb above her steepest summits.[1]

Yeats held, with Palmer, that there must 'after all . . . be the study of this creation [the dominion of nature] as well as art and vision; tho' I cannot think it other than the veil of Heaven . . .' As he wrote in *The Cutting of an Agate*, 'Art bids us touch and taste and hear and see the world and shrinks from what Blake calls mathematic form, from every abstract thing, from all

1. A. H. Palmer, *The Life and Letters of Samuel Palmer* (1892), pp. 175–6.

that is of the brain only, from all that is not a fountain jetting from the entire hopes and memories and sensations of the body.' The 'loftier vision', the world of the divine, was prevented in Yeats's poetry from falling into fantasy or abstraction away from nature and the processes of observation and experience by his lifelong search for the symbolic correspondences between the natural and the supernatural. The symbols in his poetry are the places where the 'world of essences, of unmixed powers, of impossible purities', for which Rossetti craved, is incarnated in human moods and, often, in birds and beasts. The relating of emotion to emotion through a system of ordered images was a means of correcting the fantasy and lack of substance which might arise when the images of poetry were broken, fleeting, and uncertain owing to some vague or over-contemplative strain in the artist. Thus, Yeats tells us, he transformed the void and luminous poetry of Shelley into a symbolic art by massing Shelley's recurring images in his own mind and relating them to each other so as to produce a world which grew 'solid underfoot and consistent enough for the soul's habitation'. Such a method, Yeats wrote in the essay on 'The Symbolism of Poetry', entailed a 'casting out of descriptions of nature for the sake of nature'.

To achieve, then, 'Right mastery of natural things' the poet must relate images drawn from nature to the intelligible world of 'Plato's Vision' by a system of symbolic correspondences— 'the more his mind is on fire or the more creative it is, the less will he look at the outer world or value it for its own sake'; if he is content merely to rejoice in nature's lovely profusion, to observe it and record his sensations, he sinks passively into the sleep of nature and its 'multiplicity', and rests from the spiritual labour that can alone produce great imaginative art:

I knew an old man who had spent his whole life cutting hazel and privet from the paths, and in some seventy years he had observed little but had many imaginations. He had never seen like a naturalist, never seen things as they are, for his habitual mood had been that of a man stirred in his affairs; and Shakespeare, Tintoretto, though the times were running out when Tintoretto painted, nearly all the great men of the Renaissance, looked at the world with eyes like his. Their minds were never quiescent, never as it were in a mood for scientific observations, always an exaltation, never—to use known words—founded upon an elimination of the personal factor; and their attention and the attention of those they worked for dwelt constantly with what is present to the mind in exaltation.[2]

The distinction between the observer and the visionary and their contrasting attitudes to nature seems to have been as thoroughly established by the time *Ideas of Good and Evil* (1903) appeared as Yeats's inaccurate history and transcendental language (when he wrote of such matters) permitted. I think that this same distinction underlies 'Demon and Beast', but it has been magnified in power and suggestiveness by Yeats's new researches into man and nature. Of these the chief published expression at the time when the poem was written was *Per Amica Silentia Lunae* (1917), the prolegomenon to *A Vision*. I doubt if 'Demon and Beast' can be fully appreciated unless we are aware of the new form the distinction had assumed. The objective man has replaced the 'general observer' (to use Palmer's phrase), and the subjective man the visionary. 'Demon and Beast' is about the subjective man's struggle against the sleep of nature and about his happiness in the 'mere profusion' of nature that attends upon a momentary rest from the labours of inspiration. These labours, too, have changed their quality; the source of creative energy is more precisely specified and more esoteric: the mind 'stirred in its affairs', that is never quiescent, 'always an exaltation', is now described as one that had 'long perned in the gyre / Between my hatred and desire'.[3]

As a description of sudden happiness and of a joyful understanding of creatures in the external world, the poem is related to the fourth section of 'Vacillation' (1931) and to the prose version of this later poem which is found in the much earlier *Per Amica Silentia Lunae*:

At certain moments, always unforeseen, I become happy, most commonly when at hazard I have opened some book of verse . . . Perhaps I

2. *Essays* (1924), pp. 345–6.
3. *Perne* means to 'travel in a spiral'; the *gyre* is a circular or spiral turn, and was used by Yeats to describe the spiral line traced round the imaginary cones by means of which he diagrammatized the antitheses in history and human life. All the recent books on Yeats have something about his gyres, but see especially D. Stauffer, *The Golden Nightingale* (1949), pp. 38 ff.; A. N. Jeffares, '"Gyres" in the poetry of W. B. Yeats', *English Studies*, xxvii, 1946, 65–94 and 'Yeats's "The Gyres"': sources and symbolism', *Huntington Library Quarterly*, xv, 1951, 88–89; R. Ellmann, *The Identity of Yeats* (1954), pp. 151–7.

am sitting in some crowded restaurant, the open book beside me, or closed, my excitement having overbrimmed the page. I look at the strangers near as if I had known them all my life, and it seems strange that I cannot speak to them: everything fills me with affection, I have no longer any fears or any needs . . . It may be an hour before the mood passes, but latterly I seem to understand that I enter upon it the moment I cease to hate.

These experiences have in common the cessation of hatred and the invasion of the personality by things from outside it that mollify its harsh self-absorption; in the restaurant it is the book of verse, in 'Demon and Beast' the portraits in the gallery, that seem to be the agents that effect the change. Similar experiences happened earlier still: in *The Trembling of the Veil* Yeats writes of 'certain half-dreams, if I can call them so, between sleep and waking':

It was during 1897 and 1898, when I was always just arriving from or just setting out to some political meeting that the first dreams came. I was crossing a little stream near Inchy Wood and actually in the middle of a stride from bank to bank, when an emotion never experienced before swept down upon me. I said, 'That is what the devout Christian feels, that is how he surrenders his will to the will of God'.

This surrender of the will is characterized elsewhere in *The Trembling of the Veil*:

[There] are those who must seek no image of desire, but await that which lies beyond their mind—unities not of the mind, but unities of Nature, unities of God—the man of science, the moralist, the humanitarian, the politician, Saint Simeon Stylites upon his pillar, Saint Anthony in his cavern, all whose preoccupation is to seem nothing; to hollow their hearts till they are void and without form, to summon a creator by revealing chaos, to become the lamp for another's wick and oil.

In *A Vision* Yeats classified such men as objective; they abandon the self to dedicate everything to God or a cause; they include poets whose imaginations grow 'more vivid in the expression of something which they have not themselves created'. The extreme examples of such objectivity are found in the Saints, and 'Demon and Beast' is not to end before the life of St Anthony in the desert is adduced as an analogue to the condition of self-surrender and absorption in nature which the poet experiences in the gallery and beside the lake.

As he contemplates the portraits and the birds the poet ceases from the labours of inspiration and sinks into the sleep of nature; so, at least, he would have put it before the experience recorded in *A Vision* came to override the Blakean terminology with one still more esoteric, and to help in the shaping of this poem. Labouring inspiration, the creative energy of the poetic imagination, is now called the gyre of hatred and desire, the work of demon and beast in the self, and to resign from that struggle is to resign from the hope of right mastery of what lies beyond the mind. Cleanth Brooks, in the only comment of any length on this poem which I have seen,[4] takes the words to refer, perhaps more precisely than they appear to do in the poem itself, to what Yeats called in *Per Amica Silentia Lunae* and *A Vision* the warfare with the Daimon, or 'ultimate self of [a] man'. The elements of this warfare also are hatred and desire, for there is 'a deep enmity between a man and his [Daimon]', and yet a man loves nothing but it. I think, though, that the language of the poem does not oblige us to interpret it in terms of so obscure and transcendental a part of the System. In the poem the struggle is more broadly and more poetically described as a war between extreme passions, the demon of hatred and the beast of desire. These images adequately depict a state of intense self-absorption and subjectivity; they do not need to be made more specific because they already indicate vividly enough that they are the antithesis of that objective state which entails a neutralization of the energy of the self. This antithesis is the groundwork of the poem.

Because it has ceased to struggle, the poet's mind becomes a thoroughfare for others' thoughts. In the second stanza the painted dead live in a world of vast tolerance where antitheses have ended; Luke Wadding, the rebel patriot, and Lord Deputy Strafford are 'folded in a single party'. Like and unlike mingle, too, amongst the birds on the lake. The seagull may be a complex symbol here. It seems to resemble those lonely birds of which Yeats wrote in his note to *Calvary*, which are the 'natural symbols of subjectivity, especially when floating upon the wind alone or alighting upon a pool or river'. (It may be objected that the gregarious gull is not a very good symbol for subjectivity, but it is so used in the contemporary poem 'On a Political

4. In *The Permanence of Yeats* (ed. J. Hall and M. Steinmann, 1950), pp. 80–81.

Prisoner'.) In 'Demon and Beast' the point made about the gull is that, like the poet, it has given up its natural station in the air for the sweetness of a 'bit of bread'; the verbs that describe its action, with the sudden cessation of the winding movement in 'splashed'—'Now gyring down and perning there / He splashed . . .'—are an indication that it has become soft, ridiculous, 'absurd' like the portly duck whose prize it is trying to share: the seagull loses its dignity in this narrow place. The gull represents, therefore, not, as Richard Ellmann thinks, 'the poet's sense of joyful freedom', so much as the poet's surrender of his self to nature's sweetness and his latent uneasiness about this. This uneasiness is openly expressed in the fourth stanza:

> Yet I am certain as can be
> That every natural victory
> Belongs to beast or demon,
> That never yet had freeman
> Right mastery of natural things.

With all their brevity, the lines make the distinctions about which, as we have seen, Yeats had written so constantly. Every 'victory over nature' (*every natural victory*) is an idea that derives from and is given meaning by his view of the poet's relation to nature which he worked out from his study of Blake and Palmer; the victory pertains to the condition of subjectivity, of warfare in the self (*Belongs to beast or demon*), because Yeats knows more surely than he did before *Per Amica Silentia Lunae* how the tormented visionary is distinguished from the free and happy naturalist.

Yeats seems at times to have thought that the 'quarrel with ourselves' out of which poetry is made was the only way poetry could be made:

> *Hic.* Yet surely there are men who have made their art
>   Out of no tragic war, lovers of life,
>   Impulsive men that look for happiness
>   And sing when they have found it.
> *Ille.*   No, not sing,
>   For those that love the world serve it in action,
>   Grow rich, popular and full of influence,
>   And should they paint or write, still it is action:
>   The struggle of the fly in marmalade.

The last line is Yeats's expressive phrase for the endeavour to make art out of the love of this world of nature; the diction has changed, but the sentiment is perfectly Blakean. The bitter-sweet of the marmalade is relevant to 'Demon and Beast', because the absorption in nature has in retrospect the same mixed flavour in that poem. The enjoyment of it may be aimless, like the joy of the Fool in *A Vision*, but it is sweet enough to fill the whole being with desire for more. In the poem Yeats attributes to advancing age the breakdown of subjectivity and the pleasurable inflowing of the sleep of nature into the unwarring self. He speaks of this temptation also in the last section of 'Anima Hominis' in *Per Amica Silentia Lunae*, and says there that if the ageing poet rests from 'loving and hating' he will lose the favour of the muses and perhaps, like Wordsworth, his wits as well.

What is the connection of the fifth and final stanza with the rest of the poem? Of course, both the poet 'for certain minutes' and the anchorite, for a much longer time, are freed from the gyre of hatred and desire; yet superficially at least the last stanza would appear to discriminate between, rather than compare, their conditions. 'Starved' and 'withered' suggest the anchorite's deliberate discipline of restraint, that curbing of all images of desire and the awaiting of something 'which lies beyond their mind' of which Yeats wrote in *The Trembling of the Veil*; the poet enjoys, by contrast, a momentary liberation from demon and beast which comes about through sudden chance and is unforeseen; *he* has not renounced his 'blood-sodden heart' by a deliberate choice. The real ground of the analogy between the two, however, is the fact that the poet, suddenly free, and the anchorite, devoted to the new God described in *A Vision* as 'something outside man and man's handiwork', share the condition of objectivity and have renounced the warring self:

If [the Saint] possesses intellect he will use it but to serve perception and renunciation. His joy is to be nothing, to do nothing, to think nothing; but to permit the total life, expressed in its humanity, to flow in upon him and to express itself through his acts and thoughts. (*A Vision*)

Into some degree of this objectivity the poet has himself advanced, albeit momentarily, so that the portraits and the birds, things outside himself, pour their life into him. This experience is so sweet that he seeks to prolong it, and reflects: 'If I in this momentary phase of objectivity, of selflessness, experience such sweetness, how great must have been the sweetness enjoyed by such wholly objective men as were the selfless saints!' (Yeats frequently discriminated between the types of the Artist and the Saint; because the Artist has here become partly assimilated to the Saint, it is implied of course that the subjectivity which is the ground of his power to create is weakened—hence the reluctance which mingles with his pleasure.) The last line—'What had the Caesars but their thrones?'—makes a rhetorical point. The Caesars, too, were objective men, complementary to the Saints, but, like them, antithetical to the Artist:

The typical men of the classical age (I think of Commodus, with his half-animal beauty, his cruelty, and his caprice) lived public lives, pursuing curiosities of appetite, and so found in Christianity, with its Thebaid and its Mareotic Sea, the needed curb. But what can the Christian confessor say to those who more and more must make all out of the privacy of their thought, calling up perpetual images of desire, for he cannot say, 'Cease to be artist, cease to be poet', where the whole life is art and poetry. (*The Trembling of the Veil*)

But even the Caesars, objective in their concern with the public life outside the self, cannot enjoy such sweetness as follows from a total renunciation of the self.

The poem, then, describes how the artist is momentarily seduced by the beauty and profusion of nature into relinquishing his proper task. He is suddenly abandoned by the passions that ensured his subjectivity and his power to create; he grows objective—his mind becomes a vessel, instead of a vortex of energy, the fountain's basin instead of its abundant jet. Behind the pleasure that this brings there lurks the threat of impotence, but the dominant mood of the description is sweet, not fearful. The intellect alone, long-trained in the anti-naturalistic aesthetic, asserts a half-hearted disapproval; it expresses its uneasiness in the symbolic birds, in the touch of contempt ('bag of bones') when the anchorites are described, and in the explicit worry of the fourth stanza.

The thoughts that shaped 'Demon and Beast' arose directly out of Yeats's study of the poet's relation to nature. This is an interest characteristic of the romantic poets, and it is not mere chance that the name of Wordsworth recurred so often to his mind. He felt some compulsion to settle his attitude to that master; 'Demon and Beast' is as good a starting-point as will be found anywhere in his writings for the attempt to reckon the scale of his achievement in relation to that of his great romantic predecessors. Did Yeats impoverish his verse by some failure to understand what Wordsworth meant by 'a heart / That watches and receives'? That is the question moved, in his own way, by George Moore; despite all Moore's calculated frivolity, it is not an idle one.

6

Yeats's supernatural songs

'Aimer, c'est la vie de l'ange!'
BALZAC, *Louis Lambert*

Eight of these poems were first published in *The King of the Great Clock Tower, Commentaries and Poems*, a Cuala Press volume of 1934;* the entire group of twelve appeared the following year in *A Full Moon in March*. When he read one of them to Frank O'Connor, Yeats told F. R. Higgins, 'O'Connor was rude and said he didn't understand a word of it.'[1] Some perplexities may perhaps be resolved if the first four poems, to which I am going to confine the discussion in this paper, are read as the expression of a single movement of poetical thought. Since the poems are by Yeats, this thought is of the kind which, in Richard Ellmann's phrases, focuses contradictory attitudes and 'presents reality as if by antithesis'.[2]

Thus the four poems contrast with one another in verse-movement and pattern; they are poems of different shapes, longish and meditative, and little and mechanical. In tone, they vary between vehemence and calm assurance. The first and the third recount experiences of a magical or mystical character—perhaps we may call them *supernatural*, as Yeats did, and so describe both kinds. The second and the fourth present frag-

---

First published in *Review of English Studies*, NS, vii, 1956, 38–51.

* Actually, they first appeared in *London Mercury* and *Poetry* (Chicago) in December 1934. See *Bibliography* (ed. A. Wade and R. K. Alspach, 3rd ed., 1968), pp. 183, 389—C. J. R.

---

1. F. O'Connor, 'What made Yeats a great poet?', *Listener*, 15 May 1947, p. 762. O'Connor reports Yeats as saying that the poem read was 'Meru', the last in the published series but the first composed. Yeats used, however, to refer to the whole series by this title. It is not clear why Ellmann (*The Identity of Yeats*, 1954, p. 282) states that the poem read on this occasion was 'Ribh denounces Patrick', unless he has been misled by O'Connor's claim that the first lines of the next poem ('Ribh in Ecstasy') refer to this incident. This claim seems to me very doubtful. The point is of some importance, since it affects the interpretation of 'Ribh in Ecstasy'. [The mistake is corrected in Ellmann's second edition, 1964, p. 282—C. J. R.]
2. Ellmann, p. 244.

ments of theology. But the second pair does not seem to illustrate or support the first pair; or, if it does so, the comment is
oblique and even contradictory. Then again, the experience
recounted in the first poem, 'Ribh at the Tomb of Baile and
Aillinn', is very different from that of the third, 'Ribh in Ecstasy':
the vision in the first poem is a reward bestowed upon an initiate,
the fruit of his purity and fabulous old age, and leaves Ribh in
solemn, supernatural light; the ecstasy in the third poem comes
and vanishes suddenly—unasked and unexpected, it seems—and
leaves Ribh desolate in the common light of day. The second
poem, 'Ribh denounces Patrick' (originally entitled 'Ribh
prefers an Older Theology'), is concerned with the birth and
generation of the gods, while the fourth poem, 'There', is
about the heavenly condition, the end of time. This effect, as of
elements straining in different ways, yet all obviously having
something in common, is a system of stresses contrived by an
architect who was expert at building structures such as this.

I

What the poems most obviously have in common is their speaker or singer, Ribh. He can express and suffer these different
things because he is himself a creature who embodies in his own
person a Yeatsian distinction between kinds of men. Yeats tells
us that he is an 'old hermit',[3] 'an imaginary critic of St Patrick'.[4]
As such, it is fairly obvious that he revives the long-abandoned
role of Oisin, who argues with the apostle of Ireland in the
Agallamh na Senorach and in Yeats's earliest narrative *The
Wanderings of Oisin*. The name Ribh, Yeats says also, has been
conferred upon his own thoughts. This is plain enough, too:
Ribh is a stylized poetic self, the Blakean and Byzantine 'aged
man' who recurs in *Purgatory* and elsewhere. Yeats has made
him venerable and holy by adding twenty years to his own age.
The hermit's Christianity 'comes perhaps from Egypt'.[5] Yeats
is no doubt thinking of the anchorites who joined St Anthony by
the Mareotic Lake and there

> Starved upon the shore
> And withered to a bag of bones![6]

3. *The King of the Great Clock Tower*, p. 45.
4. *A Full Moon in March*, p. vi.
5. Ibid.   6. 'Demon and Beast' (*Collected Poems*, 1950, p. 210).

The figure, then, if we generalize about it from what Yeats tells
us in his comments in *The King of the Great Clock Tower* and *A Full
Moon in March*, is an imaginary hermit and theologian conflated
with an aged Yeats, who is not austere but irritable and 'coarse',
like the 'wild old wicked man' in the poem of that title. So the
monk's devotion and the old man's sexuality may coexist in
Ribh as in him:

> '*Because* I am mad about women
> I am mad about the hills,'
> Said that wild old wicked man.[7]

But in the two poems 'Ribh at the Tomb . . .' and 'Ribh in
Ecstasy' the experiences recorded are very different from each
other. They help to separate the two elements in the personality;
they suggest perhaps that this personality is not meant to be seen
as a harmonious concord, or, at the least, that we cannot see it
fully unless we trace its inward articulations.

In the first poem, as Yeats wrote to Olivia Shakespear,

> a monk reads his breviary at midnight upon the tomb of long-dead
> lovers on the anniversary of their death, for on that night they are
> united above the tomb, their embrace being not partial but a conflagra-
> tion of the entire body and so shedding the light he reads by.[8]

Ribh is able to behold this vision of the unearthly intercourse of
the dead lovers because his eyes are

> By water, herb and solitary prayer
> Made aquiline[9]

—like an eagle's, like the old man's of the later poem 'An Acre
of Grass', who prays to attain this eagle mind so that he may
perceive the truth. But unlike the old man of that poem, Ribh
has no need to pray for enlightenment through frenzy; the air
is calm and the vision achieved. After his austerity has brought
this reward, Ribh is able not only to look upon it but to expound
it to us in a decisively catechistical manner, as T. R. Henn has
remarked.[1] He is the teacher addressing his disciples: 'Mark
and digest my tale, carry it afar . . . speak what none have heard.'
In 'Ribh in Ecstasy' all this is quite gone:

---

7. Ibid., p. 356. My italics.   8. *Letters* (ed. Wade, 1954), p. 824.
9. The text of all quotations from '*Supernatural Songs*' is that of *A Full Moon
in March*.
1. *The Lonely Tower* (1950), p. 294.

> What matter that you understand no word!
> Doubtless I spoke or sang what I had heard
> In broken sentences.

The ecstasy itself—leaving undiscussed for the moment what kind of ecstasy it is—is spasmodic and incoherent, something given rather than achieved; it does not, apparently, crown a lifetime's disciplined effort, but with sudden violence takes Ribh 'out of himself' and then returns him to the common day. In both poems, therefore, things are seen or heard which lie beyond nature, but they are experienced in very different ways. These ways correspond to a distinction that Yeats had drawn many years before in *Per Amica Silentia Lunae* (1917):

I think that we who are poets and artists, not being permitted to shoot beyond the tangible, must go from desire to weariness and so to desire again, and live but for the moment when vision comes to our weariness like terrible lightning, in the humility of the brutes ... We seek reality with the slow toil of our weakness and are smitten from the boundless and the unforeseen. Only when we are saint or sage, and renounce Experience itself, can we, in the imagery of the Christian Caballa, leave the sudden lightning and the path of the serpent and become the bowman who aims his arrow at the centre of the sun.[2]

The Sage who renounces Experience and travels straight towards Vision, and the Artist who is smitten from the boundless and unforeseen, as by the lightning flash, are the two modes of Ribh's existence as it is expressed in the first and the third poems respectively. That they are present together, and strive against one another in the same *dramatis persona*, reminds us of Yeats's psychological system, which he had worked out very elaborately in *A Vision*: by this, each man has a self and an anti-self, a hidden opposite which he pursues. Another way of saying this was to describe the selves as primary, or objective, and antithetical, or subjective. Yeats wrote in a diary:

The antithetical man works by flashes of lightning. He was the burden of himself and must lose himself to rest—Primary man does not lose himself, he may be perfect, a saint or a sage ... The antithetical man is always impure and lonely—though pure in the lightning flash.[3]

So the primary Ribh, the Sage of the first poem, is pure and has a vision of heaven which is external to himself, achieved through

2. *Essays* (1924), pp. 503-4.
3. Quoted by A. N. Jeffares, *W. B. Yeats: Man and Poet* (1949), p. 335.

training and discipline; during it he maintains his self-possession. In the third poem, Ribh is caught up into something in which the coherent speech of the self is lost. If we look at them in this way, in the context of Yeats's earlier thoughts, the first and the third poems appear to complement and complete each other in a meaningful way.

II

So far I have been discussing the poems in order to show how the study of Ribh's personality may help us to understand their system of antitheses. The poet, however, was concerned not only with character—'the emotions of a soul'—but with ideas as well —'the emotions of a soul dwelling in the presence of certain ideas'.[4] There are thoughts, he wrote in *The Trembling of the Veil*, which 'sustain us in defeat, or give us victory'; tested by passion, they become our convictions.[5] To these he referred when he told Dorothy Wellesley: 'I have put [into *Purgatory*] my own conviction about this world and the next.'[6] We are bound to ask who Ribh is, and equally bound to inquire about the convictions which Yeats put into him. What is the character of his supernatural experiences? What does his theology teach or imply? We turn, therefore, to look at the poems in sequence in order to discover their materials and their relationship to each other. Here again reality is presented by means of diverse and antithetical elements.

Why did Yeats choose for Ribh's first visionary experience this fable and this manner of description as they are found in the central portion of 'Ribh at the Tomb . . .'?

> Of Baile and Aillinn you need not speak,
> All know their tale, all know what leaf and twig,
> What juncture of the apple and the yew,
> Surmount their bones; but speak what none have heard.
>
> The miracle that gave them such a death
> Transfigured to pure substance what had once
> Been bone and sinew; when such bodies join
> There is no touching here, nor touching there,

4. Quoted by Ellmann, p. 43, from an uncollected article in *Bookman*, August 1894.
5. *Autobiographies* (1955), p. 189.
6. *Letters*, p. 913.

Nor straining joy, but whole is joined to whole;
For the intercourse of angels is a light
Where for its moment both seem lost, consumed.

Here in the pitch-dark atmosphere above
The trembling of the apple and the yew,
Here on the anniversary of their death,
The anniversary of their first embrace,
These lovers, purified by tragedy,
Hurry into each other's arms. . . .

One reason is that they had long been present in his mind. The germ of the poem, mentioned in letters to Mrs Shakespear in 1933, is 'that saying of Swedenborg's that the sexual intercourse of the angels is a conflagration of the whole being'.[7] Yeats first read Swedenborg when he was a very young man and reread him in 1913; about this time he wrote the essay on 'Swedenborg, Mediums and the Desolate Places', which was published in Lady Gregory's *Visions and Beliefs in the West of Ireland* (1920). Swedenborgian ideas have some influence on *A Vision*. What A. N. Jeffares[8] calls his obsession with Swedenborg's description of the intercourse of angels is present in the essay on 'The Irish Dramatic Movement' (1919)[9] and in *Per Amica Silentia Lunae*, the prolegomenon to *A Vision*:

I do not doubt that [the dead at a certain stage of their discarnate existence] make love in that union which Swedenborg has said is of the whole body and seems from far off an incandescence.[1]

The lovers in the poem are in the 'condition of fire', the 'God's holy fire' of 'Sailing to Byzantium',[2] which Yeats described as a heavenly state where is 'all music and all rest':

When all sequence comes to an end, time comes to an end, and the soul puts on the rhythmic or spiritual body or luminous body and contem-

---

7. Ibid., p. 805. See also pp. 807, 824.

8. Jeffares, op. cit., p. 283.

9. *Plays and Controversies* (1923), p. 201. Another passage in the same essay throws light on Yeats's use of the word *straining* in the poem: 'great dramatic persons . . . those men and women of Plutarch, who made their death a ritual of passion; for what is passion but the straining of man's being against some obstacle that obstructs its unity' (p. 209). Baile and Aillinn, being without earthly passion, love unobstructedly. I do not think that Henn's reference of the word to the Leda poem (p. 296) will work out.

1. *Essays*, p. 523.

2. On the condition of fire, see C. Brooks in *The Permanence of Yeats* (ed. Hall and Steinmann, 1950), p. 85.

plates all the events of its memory . . . in an eternal possession of itself in one single moment.[3]

There can be little doubt that the notion of the luminous, purified and incandescent condition of the souls of the dead, which is also found in Henry More and other neo-Platonic writings that Yeats knew, acquired fresh life in the 1930s through Yeats's reading of Berkeley's *Siris*,[4] and his rereading of Balzac's Swedenborgian stories *Séraphita* and *Louis Lambert*. On the latter Yeats wrote an essay in 1934, which guides us back to the poet's young manhood and to a visionary experience of his own which proved of lasting imaginative importance to him:

Passages in *Séraphita* suggest [Balzac's] familiarity with a state known to me in youth, a state transcending sleep when forms, often of great beauty, appear minutely articulated in brilliant light, forms that express by word or action some spiritual idea and are so moulded or tinted that they make all human flesh seem unhealthy.[5]

When Yeats was 22, a guest of Edward Martyn at Tulira Castle, he had a vision, later recorded in *The Trembling of the Veil* (1922), of 'a naked woman of incredible beauty, standing upon a pedestal and shooting an arrow at a star. I still remember the tint of that marvellous flesh which makes all human flesh seem unhealthy.'[6] In *Per Amica Silentia Lunae*, as we have seen, this

3. *Essays*, p. 524.
4. Section 171, *Works of George Berkeley* (ed. Luce and Jessop, 1953), vol. v, p. 89: 'Galen likewise taught that, admitting the soul to be incorporeal, it hath for its immediate tegument or vehicle a body of aether or fire, by the intervention whereof it moveth other bodies, and is mutually affected by them. This interior clothing was supposed to remain upon the soul not only after death, but after the most perfect purgation.' Imagery of light is of course endemic in Swedenborg: his angels are regularly seen 'in their own light' and can be observed only by the purified spiritual sight (eg *Heaven and Hell*, 1899, p. 41); the heavens and hells in the *Arcana Celestia* are managed in terms of light and dark symbolism. A passage in Yeats's essay on *Prometheus Unbound* gathers together one or two other links: 'There is much curious evidence to show that the Divine Purpose . . . descends into the mind at moments of inspiration, not as spiritual life alone but as what seems a physical brightness. Perhaps everybody that pursues that life for however short a time, even, as it were, but to chase it, experiences now and again during sleep bright coherent dreams where something is shown or spoken that grows in meaning with the passage of time. Blake spoke of this "stronger and better light", called its source "the human form divine", Shelley's "harmonious soul of many a soul", or, as we might say, the Divine Purpose. The stationary, joyous energy of certain among his figures . . . suggests radiating light. We understand why the first Christian painters encircled certain heads with light' (*Essays 1931 to 1936*, 1937, pp. 59–60).
5. Ibid., p. 65.   6. *Autobiographies*, pp. 372–3.

shooting at the star becomes a symbol for the straight path which the Saint or Sage takes towards the supernatural reality. Thus the chosen figure in 'Ribh at the Tomb . . .' of angelic, luciferent intercourse has correspondences over the whole period of Yeats's creative life.

To this image Yeats attached the legend of Baile and Aillinn. This again draws commentary back towards past work. The short narrative poem *Baile and Aillinn* (1902) is one of several poems on the theme of dead lovers who achieve the consummation of their love after death. Baile of the Honey Mouth and Aillinn, daughter of the King of Leinster's son, died of grief when each heard that the other was dead; it was Yeats's imagination, rather than the Irish original,[7] which interpreted this act of Aengus, the Master of Love, as a means whereby the lovers might achieve an everlasting bliss of communion in his own land of the dead:

> Their love was never drowned in care
> Of this or that thing, nor grew cold
> Because their bodies had grown old.
> Being forbid to marry on earth,
> They blossomed to immortal mirth.

The fullest treatment of the theme that it is better to renounce earthly love, whose perfection is certain to be flawed by trouble and disillusion, and dedicate all to a consummation beyond time, is found in *The Shadowy Waters*, a play on which Yeats worked for over twenty years.* Forgael, the hero, voyaging through waste seas, seeks a love

> of a beautiful, unheard-of kind
> That is not of this world.

> *Aibric.*   And yet the world
> Has beautiful women to please every man.
> *Forgael.*   But he that gets their love after the fashion

---

* For a detailed account of Yeats's work on this play, see *Druid Craft: The Writing of The Shadowy Waters* (ed. Michael J. Sidnell, George P. Mayhew, and David R. Clarke, 1971)—C. J. R.

7. A version of the story is given in Lady Gregory's *Cuchulain of Muirthemne* (1903), pp. 305–6; see also Dorothy M. Hoare, *The Works of Morris and of Yeats in Relation to Early Saga Literature* (1937), p. 117.

> Loves in brief longing and deceiving hope
> And bodily tenderness, and finds that even
> The bed of love, that in the imagination
> Had seemed to be the giver of all peace,
> Is no more than a wine-cup in the tasting,
> And as soon finished.
> *Aibric.*   All that ever loved
> Have loved that way—there is no other way.
> *Forgael.* Yet never have two lovers kissed but they
> Believed there was some other near at hand,
> And almost wept because they could not find it.[8]

The aspiring hero at last encounters, in Dectora, a woman who is ready to sail away with him from the ordinary world to 'grow immortal' in his company. The source of this theme is to be found in no more recondite a place than the earliest and most notorious of Yeats's many sacred books, Villiers de l'Isle-Adam's *Axël*, which the youthful poet painfully spelled out with the aid of a dictionary and remembered all his life. In the fastnesses of his castle at Auërspurg Axël persuaded Sara to die with arguments very like those used by Forgael to justify his disdain of ordinary loves.[9] Nor must we forget the contribution made towards the permanent establishment of this theme in Yeats's art by his admiration for the Japanese Noh play *Nishikigi*. Ezra Pound published his translation of this in 1916, but Yeats had read the work in progress. It tells the moving story of how two lovers, parted in life owing to the girl's unconscious cruelty, are united in death through the piety of an old priest. The cave which they inhabit blazes with light as a sign of their union:

> Strange, what seemed so very old a cave
> Is all glittering-bright within,
> Like the flicker of fire.[1]

If we bear these analogues in mind, the nature of the thought or 'conviction' in 'Ribh at the Tomb . . .' becomes clearer. We learn something of the mystery—what it is that Ribh wishes his disciples to 'mark and digest and carry . . . afar', the secret part

8. *Collected Works* (1908), vol. ii, pp. 195–6.

9. See, for example, Axël's speech, Villiers de l'Isle-Adam, *Axël* (*Œuvres complètes*, 1923, vol. iv, pp. 262–3).

1. *The Translations of Ezra Pound* (1953), p. 293.

of the story that no one else has heard. All the tales which corre-
late with the Baile and Aillinn legend are tales of lovers who were
disunited and distressed on earth, or who longed for something
greater and less perishable than mortal love. To achieve this,
they pass beyond the natural world. Their bodies are consumed
away, gathered into the 'artifice of eternity', into the condition
of fire. I quote the phrase from 'Sailing to Byzantium' as a
reminder that this is not just a ninetyish notion which Yeats
outgrew when he outgrew *Axël*, and to avoid the danger of
underestimating the continuity in Yeats's convictions, which
used to mislead his commentators. The Swedenborgian and
neo-Platonic imagery of light comes in to reinforce the theme
of the difference between the mortal and the immortal lovers:
their bodies are composed of a supernatural substance, of purer
fire, and their delights are such as men cannot know. This is
insisted upon in the poem:

> when such bodies join
> There is no touching here, nor touching there,
> Nor straining joy, but whole is joined to whole.

Like Axël and Sara, they enjoy a 'miraculeuse nuit nuptiale'.[2]
The whole image, and all its antecedents, emphasize a division
between the natural and the supernatural world. The scheme
of the poem, Ribh's relation to his vision, supports this emphasis.
The sage looks upon, but is not caught up into, the transcendence. The modes of existence of the two worlds are quite different: on the one hand, the unearthly lovers blazing in their joy;
on the other, the austere, dispassionate, and fantastically aged
solitary, whose relation to the mystery is no closer than that of
an expositor, teaching it to others as a secret thing.

   This needs emphasizing, because it is precisely this conception
of a barrier between natural and supernatural and of a difference
in kind between the two sorts of life that is to meet its antithesis
in the next poems. It was Yeats's skill in creating such antitheses
that helped to turn him from a poet absorbed chiefly in *Axël*-
like fantasy into a poet of the kind that he became in his later
and greater work. 'Ribh at the Tomb . . .', despite its charm and
power, will leave us back where *Axël* found Yeats in the eighties
unless we read it in conjunction with what follows.

2. *Axël*, p. 263.

III

For what follows is a restless and almost violent refusal to admit
that the burden of the body must be thrown off before the soul
can be satisfied. The tone alters, and a simple, rocking, exultant
rhythm takes the place of the meditative paragraphs of the first
poem; in 'Ribh denounces Patrick' theology displaces contemplation and the discursive intellect the purified heart. Nature
and supernature are not separated and need not communicate
only by means of the contemplative vision of the sage. Ribh
rejects the 'masculine Trinity' of Christianity because it implies,
like the contrast of austerity and conflagration in the first poem,
an absolute difference between the two kinds of life:

An abstract Greek absurdity has crazed the man—
Recall that masculine Trinity. Man, woman, child (a daughter or a son),
That's how all natural or supernatural stories run.

Natural and supernatural with the self-same ring are wed.
As man, as beast, as an ephemeral fly begets, Godhead begets Godhead,
For things below are copies, the Great Smaragdine Tablet said.

The rejection of a masculine Trinity may well derive from Yeats's
early theosophical studies. 'The Trinity of the Egyptians and
that of the mythological Greeks', wrote Mme Blavatsky, once
his mentor in these matters, in *Isis Unveiled*, 'were alike represen-
tations of the first triple emanation containing two male
principles and one female.' We remember that Ribh's 'Christianity . . . comes perhaps from Egypt'. 'When I close my eyes',
Yeats had written in 1919, 'and pronounce the word "Christianity" and await its unconscious suggestion, I do not see Christ
crucified, or the Good Shepherd from the catacombs, but a father
and mother and their children, a picture by Leonardo da Vinci
most often.'[3]

But this correspondence between natural and supernatural in
the family, holy and profane, and in the sexual act, is no sooner
established than the theologian discovers the difference between
the two which distinguishes, and limits, the human progenitor.

3. *If I were Four and Twenty* (1940), p. 12. This essay first appeared in 1919. The
version of 'Ribh denounces Patrick' in *The King of the Great Clock Tower* has slightly
different opening lines. In both versions *recall* means 'revoke'. The Great Smaragdine Tablet of line 6 is the *Tabula Smaragdina* attributed to 'Hermes Trismegistus':
cf. with the reference to it here the one in 'Symbolism in Painting', *Collected Works*,
vi.176.

'The point of the poem', Yeats wrote, 'is that we beget and bear because of the incompleteness of our love',[4] and this is developed in the two next and concluding stanzas:

Yet all must copy copies, all increase their kind;
When the conflagration of their passion sinks, damped by the body or
the mind,
That juggling nature mounts, her coil in their embraces twined.

The mirror-scalèd serpent is multiplicity,
But all that run in couples, on earth, in flood or air, share God that is
but three,
And could beget or bear themselves could they but love as He.

Here God becomes like the Presences in 'Among School Children', the undying images which are hailed as 'self-born mockers of man's enterprise'. This enterprise is man's struggle to make exact the correspondence between his way of loving and God's. The theology of the first two stanzas of the poem suggests that success in this enterprise ought to be possible. But it is frustrated by man's possession of body and mind; thereby 'that juggling nature' intrudes with its coils. This symbol for nature as the Serpent and its winding Path is used elsewhere by Yeats: it is the same path which the Artist must tread, caught in 'the winding movement of nature'. This serpent of nature, which has scales like mirrors because it endlessly repeats images, is what makes men endlessly beget and bear, or symbolizes that process. Natural generation, we have been told in the first two stanzas, is a copy of supernatural; we might therefore expect man in the sexual act to be like God, complete and changeless, an eternal Trinity whose number never alters; instead, he falls into 'multiplicity'. This was often a bad word to Yeats: by a misreading in a famous letter of 1827 he makes Blake say that 'amongst the delusions of the goddess Nature' were the 'laws of the numbers' and glosses this phrase as 'the multiplicity of nature';[5] elsewhere Yeats speaks of his fear lest the 'multiplicity of interest and opinion' destroy his absorption in the passionate moment.[6]

4. *Letters*, p. 824.
5. *Collected Works*, vi.167, essay on 'William Blake and his illustrations'; the misreading is preserved in the later reprint in *Essays*, p. 170. What Blake actually wrote was 'Law of the Members' (*Poetry and Prose of William Blake*, ed. G. Keynes, 1927, p. 1139).
6. *Autobiographies*, p. 269.

'Ribh denounces Patrick', therefore, begins as a trenchant expression of Ribh's antithetical self, the self that will not yield, even in placid vision, to being separated from the supernatural life, but proclaims its likeness to that life. In the first poem, Ribh had seemed complete, the perfected Sage; but it was only one of the selves that was complete. As with civilizations, so with men—the more finished and elaborate the primary self, the greater the 'counter-longing' of the antithetical self.[7] This second self resists the perfection of the first, and its theology countervails the fable of Baile and Aillinn. But it, too, is forced to recognize that man and God cannot 'live each other's life', and the Ribh of the second poem falls back also before the barrier —not, like the Ribh of the first poem, in calm acceptance, but in restless dismay.

The two poems have in this way brought us to a crisis in this drama of the self and anti-self. The first, the 'primary' self, the Sage, has achieved its perfection in solemn vision; the second, the antithetical, the Artist, struggling against the other, awaits its own moment of completion. This is what Yeats called 'the two halves of the soul separate and face to face'. But the counter-longing of the second half of the soul, which its theology has given expression to, can only become 'a conscious energy', and so complete itself, 'suddenly, in those moments of revelation which are as a flash of lightning'. We are already familiar with this metaphor as a way of describing the Artist's perception of reality, which smites him 'from the boundless and the unforeseen', 'vision . . . like terrible lightning'.[8]

'Ribh in Ecstasy' records such a vision, resolves the dramatic crisis in the sequence, and completes the second self.

> What matter that you understood no word!
> Doubtless I spoke or sang what I had heard
> In broken sentences. My soul had found
> All happiness in its own cause or ground.
> Godhead on Godhead in sexual spasm begot
> Godhead. Some shadow fell. My soul forgot
> Those amorous cries that out of quiet come
> And must the common round of day resume.

7. See *Plays and Controversies*, pp. 217–18.
8. The phrases quoted in this paragraph will be found in *Essays*, pp. 503–4, and *Plays and Controversies*, pp. 217–18.

It is obvious how completely this is antithetical to the separation of natural and supernatural accepted by Ribh in the first poem. The lines are a way of saying, 'In my ecstasy I, Ribh, became like God', that is to say like the triune God of the theology of the second poem, who begot and bore himself. The experience is so intense that it is compared to the sexual ecstasy of this God:

> My soul had found
> All happiness in its own cause or ground.
> [It was as though] Godhead on Godhead in sexual spasm begot
> Godhead.

This does not mean that Ribh's ecstasy is itself of a sexual character. It is, rather, a realization of the self in the sense found in the *Upanishads* and the *Aphorisms* of Patanjali, which Yeats was studying at this time; they too make use of sexual metaphor to signalize the intensity.[9] Ribh's ecstasy must be distinguished also from the Christian mystical use of sexual imagery, which is used to describe the mystic's union with God; in the poem, the mystic has momentarily become a God—a terrible heresy from the Christian point of view. The experience happens, as we have seen, to Ribh as Artist, or poetic self, not to Ribh as Sage, or austere anchorite. It is tempting, therefore, to identify the ecstasy as artistic ecstasy, the sense of self-completion achieved, for example, in the writing of a poem. There is plenty of material in Yeats's writing that would support such an interpretation. I give two examples both recently made available from unpublished writings:

The end of art is ecstasy . . . It is a sudden sense of power and of peace that comes when we have before our mind's eye a group of images which obeys us, which leaves us free, and which satisfies the needs of our soul. (1915)
. . . We may escape from the constraint of our nature and from that of external things, entering upon a state where all fuel has become flame . . . We attain it always in the creation or enjoyment of a work of art, but that moment . . . passes from us. (1928)[1]

9. For example: 'As a man in the embrace of his beloved wife forgets everything that is without, everything that is within; so man, in the embrace of the knowing Self, forgets everything that is without, everything that is within; for there all desires are satisfied, Self his sole desire, that is no desire; man goes beyond sorrow' (*The Ten Principal Upanishads*, trans. Shree Purohit Swami and W. B. Yeats, 1937, p. 151).
1. Ellmann, pp. 105, 221.

I am not sure how far we need accept this identification of the
God-like ecstasy with the moment of aesthetic joy. If we do
accept it, it shows how enduringly Yeats maintained, like that
very different figure Thomas Hardy, a kind of religion of aesthetics, or substitution of art for religion, which is no longer at all
fashionable. Yet we must remember that the ecstasy, even if it
is of that character, pertains only to one of the selves: the complete reality is the total picture of the struggle of the selves—
their system of antitheses—which is revealed by all three poems
read together.

This system of antitheses is completed by the fourth poem,
'There'. The first three poems have each contained descriptions
of the heavenly state: the dead lovers, the life of God, and
momentary participation in that life. These have been presented
as expressions of the double personality of Ribh. The last antithesis is a ferocious Yeatsian irony, in which the sexual imagery,
which has linked the poems, and the personality of Ribh, even
his voice perhaps, suddenly cease. In *this* description of heaven,
we are presented instead with four highly traditional symbols:

> There all the barrel-hoops are knit,
> There all the serpent-tails are bit,
> There all the gyres converge in one,
> There all the planets drop in the Sun.

There is the ἐκεῖ of Plotinus, the Divine Sphere, the Intelligible
World, 'not to be spoken of, not to be written'.[2] Yeats called it
the Thirteenth Cone or Sphere; it is the one that transcends the
gyres.[3] The poem brashly proclaims itself as a symbolical way
of speaking. Like the private terminology used by the mystics,
it tells us what heaven transcends, but not what it is. It refuses
direct description, and no longer attempts to describe the supernatural by means of sexual imagery and the struggle of the selves.
All that power and force, which has been Ribh's method, is
ironically diminished, and for its bread we are given the stone
of these little mechanical figures. The three other poems all say
that man cannot wholly share the life of heaven: even for the
ecstatic his human condition reasserts itself; he 'must the
common round of day resume'. This last poem says that he

2. *Enneads* (trans. S. MacKenna, 1926), vol. i, p. 125. Yeats bought and read this
translation on publication.
3. *A Vision* (1937), p. 210.

cannot describe it either. It sets Ribh's struggle in a rather grim perspective. Instead of its richness of conflict and its metaphors of sex and light we have this poverty and infertility, as though a diagram had been substituted for a painting and the free imagination bundled into the schoolroom cupboard. We are assigned, as it were, a little handful of cardboard simulacra for the reality which lies beyond the reach of description: since all are mere diagrams, mere attempts by the human intellect to translate into its language what it cannot understand, it scarcely matters which we choose.

It is not wrong, I think, to find the series disappointing when we see it as a whole. The poems are admirable for the intellectual nimbleness displayed in their arrangement; admirable, too, for the way Yeats steers past the danger of too confident affirmation about mystery by instantly directing our minds to the counter-affirmation. But the doctrine of the self and the anti-self, when put into poetry, is too like the spectacle of a ventriloquist playing with a pair of dolls. To give each a voice, Yeats has divided his human voice between them, and to give each passion he has robbed himself of his own. There is left to him only the terrible intellectual energy with which the game is contrived and the movements of the puppets controlled. When we might hope for Yeats to speak with his own voice and to explore the mystery with his own passion, in the last poem, nothing emerges except a handful of cardboard objects: after the dummies, the toys. A good deal of Yeats's later poetry seems to suffer from this kind of limitation, which may become increasingly apparent as the years pass.

> We the great gazebo built,
> They convicted us of guilt.

For a house to live in, readers may turn from his ornamental structures, elaborately pretty but slightly sinister in their obsolescence, and go back to other poets, to Wordsworth, for example, to the undivided voice and the 'essential passions of the human heart'.

7

A source of Yeats's
'Parnell's Funeral'

Sordello di Goito, the thirteenth-century troubadour poet, and
W. B. Yeats are not writers whom one would ordinarily think
of in conjunction with one another. Yet Sordello's famous *planh*
for the Lord Blacatz did, I believe, supply the basic structure
and dominant image of the second part of Yeats's poem 'Parnell's
Funeral', first printed under the title 'Forty Years Later' in the
Spectator on 19 October 1934, then in the Cuala Press volume
The King of the Great Clock Tower and finally in *A Full Moon in
March* (London, 1935). A *planh*, says A. Jeanroy in his *Poésie
lyrique des troubadours* (Paris, 1934 ed., ii.238), is a funeral poem
which normally combines a lament for a dead hero or prince
with a satirical outburst against a corrupt world which has been
left a great deal worse off by his death—a world full of wretches
who would do well to profit by the example of the hero's worthy
life. The *planh* for Blacatz and 'Parnell's Funeral' both follow
this mode, and in both poems the dominant image is that of
eating the heart of the dead man. Stanza by stanza in Sordello's
lament the poet numbers off those who ought to take out the
heart of the dead Count and eat of it because of their great need
of his strength and virtue: first, let the Emperor of Rome eat
of it, then the French king (if his mother will let him), then the
English king, the kings of Aragon and Navarre, the Count of
Toulouse:

> Let the Castilian king eat for two, for he holds two kingdoms, and
>   isn't good enough for one,
> But if he eats, I wager he does it in secret,
> For if his mother knew of it, she would beat him with a stick.

Stanza by stanza in Yeats's poem the same image is carried
forward:

First published in *English Studies*, xxxix, 1958, 257–8.

Had de Valéra eaten Parnell's heart
No loose-lipped demagogue had won the day,
No civil rancour torn the land apart.

Had Cosgrave eaten Parnell's heart, the land's
Imagination had been satisfied, . . .

The link between Yeats and Sordello was, not surprisingly, Ezra Pound. In chapter iii of *The Spirit of Romance* (London, nd, 1910), Pound supplies an English translation in free verse of the *planh*. I do not think it is entirely wrong to perceive, besides the basic resemblances in structure and figure between the two poems, certain rhythmical correspondences as well, although it would be necessary to quote them both *in extenso* in order to demonstrate this.

'The death of Parnell', says Richard Ellmann in a reference to Yeats's poem in *The Identity of Yeats* (p. 208), 'is described as if it were the death of some pagan god, and the ancient rite of eating the hero's heart to obtain his qualities is introduced metaphorically to explain the course of Irish history after Parnell's death.' News of this 'ancient rite' (if such there ever was) was, I suggest, transmitted to Yeats through an older poet's handling of the theme in a quite specifically literary context. This is further suggested by the fact that a quite different secondary meaning appears to be attached to the cutting out and eating of a heart in the *first* part, or poem, of 'Parnell's Funeral'. The image helps to link the two parts, though each one can be read separately from the other. The cutting out of the boy's heart, which is depicted on the Sicilian coin described in the second stanza of the first part (on a possible numismatic source for this, see T. R. Henn, *The Lonely Tower*, 1950, p. 156), seems at first to have suggested to Yeats simply the notion of the brutal destruction of the hero by the mob. This is what is described in the third stanza of the first part, where Parnell is 'murdered' by the frenzied crowd:

An age is the reversal of an age:
When strangers murdered Emmet, Fitzgerald, Tone,
We lived like men that watched a painted stage.
What matter for the scene, the scene once gone:
It had not touched our lives. But popular rage,
Hysterica passio dragged this quarry down.
None shared our guilt; nor did we play a part
Upon a painted stage when we devoured his heart.

This, surely, is primarily a lynching party, a dismemberment substantially and flatly murderous, implying 'This time it is Parnell's own countrymen who bear the blame for their own greedy anger, their hatred of the noble thing.' It contains, it is true, faint overtones of such secondary meanings as 'sacrifice' and 'eating the hero's heart to obtain his qualities', but these are kept entirely subordinate. That, in the second poem, these secondary meanings should become so precise and explicit almost suggests that at some stage in the composition of the two poems which bear the collective title of 'Parnell's Funeral' Yeats refreshed his memory of the more arcane meanings of his dominant image by looking up the Pound version of Sordello in *The Spirit of Romance*, and so was ready to render them more positively, and even, to some degree, to reverse the image's primary significance as it is found in the first poem. The sources of this image certainly appear to exemplify, in a curious and characteristic way, Yeats's habit of combining literary and iconographical material, or poems and coins.

8

W. B. Yeats and the musical instruments

I have been counting the musical instruments in Yeats. It has surprised me not at all that you'd hardly find the constituents of a modern symphony orchestra in his works; there are three flutes and a trombone, it is true, some fiddles, one clarinet, and a number of trumpets and horns; but there are also a lot of bells, a conch, too many drums, four gongs, and a very large number of harps. There are more harps than anything else.

> And once a lady by my side
> Gave me a harp, and bade me sing,
> And touch the laughing silver string;
> But when I sang of human joy
> A sorrow wrapped each merry face,
> And, Patrick! by your beard, they wept,
> Until one came, a tearful boy;
> 'A sadder creature never stept
> Than this strange human bard', he cried;
> And caught the silver harp away,
> And, weeping over the white strings, hurled
> It down in a leaf-hid, hollow place
> That kept dim waters from the sky;
> And each one said, with a long, long sigh,
> 'O saddest harp in all the world,
> Sleep there till the moon and the stars die!'
>
> (*Collected Poems*, pp. 416–17)

At first thought, it does seem surprising that there are so many harps, because we no longer think of Yeats as a harp-and-shamrock bard. Druid harps of applewood may be all right, but late Victorian poets who write of harps may be hideously suspected just of being early Victorian. The harp was a Victorian instrument, too: 'In the early Victorian days', we read in the

A paper read at Liverpool, 1 November 1968.

Oxford Companion to Music, ' when in every refined English family one of the gentlemen played the flute, . . . one of his sisters or daughters was usually capable of accompanying him upon the harp—which of all instruments most incites the performer to graceful action and particularly to the display of well-rounded arms.' Perhaps the harp was always associated with dignity and grace. If we may judge by Ben Jonson's *Irish Masque at Court*, the Elizabethans thought that bagpipes were funny—clownish and rustic, suitable music for the anti-masque dances; but that harps were dignified and splendid: the Gentlemen dance the masque in their Irish mantles to the solemn music of harps and the Bard praises King James to the accompaniment of the harp, too. I wish I knew what the music was for Ford's *Perkin Warbeck* some time later; for there the music of the English morris—bells, pipes, and tabors—is mixed with what one of the characters, ill disposed to Celtic music, calls a 'Hotch-potch of Scotch and Irish twingle-twangles'. This sounds like the harp, here used in an undignified way to accompany a dance of antics in trowses, an Irish garment of the time. The bagpipe of course was originally an English instrument, as it still is in its less noisy form of the Northumbrian pipes: the bagpipe as a symbol of Scottish national behaviour and identity is a relatively recent import, a fact which may give the Scottish nationalists trouble in time to come. The harp as a nationalist symbol, as on the Irish coinage and on the caps of its officials, is on much safer ground, being a genuinely indigenous affair.

But to get back to Yeats: the preponderance of the harp in his work is in fact more apparent than real. Ninety per cent of the harps occur in two early works, *The Wanderings of Oisin*, from which came the passage that I quoted earlier on, and the dramatic narrative or verse play *The Shadowy Waters*, where the harp is a magical harp, representing or symbolizing the hero's poetic facility perhaps: at any rate, it gives him the power to make the people see visions and dream dreams. But, as might be expected, this rather exhausted and conventional symbol disappears from the work of a later Yeats, even less prepared than was the earlier one to attune his work to harp-and-shamrock associations. The harp, though, does not really disappear; it loses its name in his work, or acquires another—it becomes the psaltery, the celebrated stringed instrument wielded by Florence Farr, with

Yeats's enthusiastic support, during the 1900s at a number of poetry recitals. The psaltery is variously described as a kind of dulcimer or a kind of zither—the zither is plucked, the dulcimer hammered. In fact, all three, zither, dulcimer, and psaltery, are stringed instruments with resonator boxes. Florence Farr was a damsel with a dulcimer, of a sort, and it is not so long since women with long necks and vaguely loosened hair, carrying small string instruments of the Irish harp, psaltery, dulcimer, zither sort, were portrayed in tapestries dating from the late Victorian and Edwardian period, on stage-curtains, and other places where 'aesthetic' decoration was supposed to be suitable. It is a little odd to think, by the way, of the damsel in 'Kubla Khan' carrying a small *hammer* as she would have had to do if she had elected to play her dulcimer when singing of Mount Abora. Yeats valued the psaltery, so far as I can judge, because it could be used to enhance the rhythm of the words without in any way interfering with their intelligibility. It was mere accompaniment, of the crudest sort; the notes of the psaltery simply underlined without distorting what I must call the quantities—Yeats being perfectly hostile to the idea of a musical accompaniment being permitted to stretch or distort the words in a way that would be beyond the reach of an expressive, strongly rhythmical speaking voice.

The very last thing that I want to do is to get in any way tangled up with Yeats's theories about music and verse-speaking. But I think that through all of them will be found a sentimental attachment to the harp or some harp-like instrument. One of the most powerfully pictorial of all Yeats's poems is 'Her Vision in the Wood' (from *The Winding Stair*), where the women who move in a throng to music and a song are compared to a procession in Mantegna, but are also singularly like one in Morris or Burne-Jones or their followers:

> But the dark changed to red, and torches shone,
> And deafening music shook the leaves; a troop
> Shouldered a litter with a wounded man,
> Or smote upon the string and to the sound
> Sang of the beast that gave the fatal wound.
>
> All stately women moving to a song
> With loosened hair on foreheads grief-distraught,
> It seemed a Quattrocento painter's throng,

> A thoughtless image of Mantegna's thought—
> Why should they think that are for ever young?
> 				(*Collected Poems*, pp. 312–13)

This is amongst other things a picture of an ideal Yeatsian society, in which music is in a proper relation to song: the music is 'deafening', it has a slightly Maenadic quality, and one feels that this procession could at any moment start rampaging over the mountains and tearing passers-by to pieces; and at the same time there is a kind of pre-Raphaelite decorousness about it— the stately women, the forehead which is grief-distraught beneath the loosened hair—you might meet them in the drawing-rooms of Bedford Park at full grips with the late Victorian servant problem. Nor is the nature of the 'string' on which they smite with such *éclat* beyond all conjecture; obviously it is a zither, dulcimer, psaltery, or *harp*—it hardly matters which, or whether it is an Irish or a Homeric harp. But this harp has lost its name, and become a synecdoche. The same is also true of another stringed instrument, this time from a last poem, 'Lapis Lazuli'. This is the poem where Yeats imagines the particular loop in the cyclical time-process in which he lives with particular vividness: a great war is to overwhelm civilization, but that is no reason why the performers in the tragic play should lose their nerve. There is joy in tragedy, 'All things fall and are built again, / And those that build them again are gay.' As everything prepares to go to rack the poet fixes his attention on the miniature scene carved on the piece of lapis lazuli, and gradually takes us into the scene, much as Keats does with his Grecian urn:

> Two Chinamen, behind them a third,
> Are carved in lapis lazuli,
> Over them flies a long-legged bird,
> A symbol of longevity;
> The third, doubtless a serving-man,
> Carries a musical instrument.
>
> Every discoloration of the stone,
> Every accidental crack or dent,
> Seems a water-course or an avalanche,
> Or lofty slope where it still snows
> Though doubtless plum or cherry-branch
> Sweetens the little half-way house

> Those Chinamen climb towards, and I
> Delight to imagine them seated there;
> There, on the mountain and the sky,
> On all the tragic scene they stare.
> One asks for mournful melodies;
> Accomplished fingers begin to play.
> Their eyes mid many wrinkles, their eyes,
> Their ancient, glittering eyes, are gay.
>
> (*Collected Poems*, p. 339)

The description of the instrument suggests the plucked psaltery again—played, you notice, by the servant. Music is again in its properly Yeatsian subordinate position—the mournful melodies, like the smitten string in 'Her Vision in the Wood', are an *accompaniment*; the gaiety which is the morally paradisal heart of the poem is in the hearts—or eyes—of the two old Chinamen as they survey the 'last scene'.

I have quoted from a later poem and a last poem, both of which have a musical instrument of the psaltery/harp sort in them; and earlier on in my talk I quoted the passage from *The Wanderings of Oisin* about the saddest harp in all the world, where most of the music is of a very different kind—Oisin is a sojourner in the Island of the Living where everybody is happy, where 'God is joy and joy is God, / And things that have grown sad are wicked' (*Collected Poems*, p. 418). The immortal music is that of the unaccompanied voice:

> And once a sudden laughter sprang
> From all their lips, and once they sang
> Together, while the dark woods rang,
> And made in all their distant parts,
> With boom of bees in honey-marts,
> A rumour of delighted hearts.
>
> (*Collected Poems*, p. 416)

It is after that passage that the human Oisin unwittingly half-spoils things with his stringed instrument, which has about it, of course, the clogging air of mortality, lapped in its muddy vesture of decay. But in case you have forgotten the passage about the saddest harp in all the world, here is a passage from another early poem, 'Cuchulain's Fight with the Sea' (1892). This tells how the jealous Emer, Cuchulain's wife, sets a trap for Cuchulain at the hand of his son; she says to the boy, at the point where my quotation begins:

'The Red Branch camp in a great company
Between wood's rim and the horses of the sea.
Go there, and light a camp-fire at wood's-rim;
But tell your name and lineage to him
Whose blade compels, and wait till they have found
Some feasting man that the same oath has bound.'

Among those feasting men Cuchulain dwelt,
And his young sweetheart close beside him knelt,
Stared on the mournful wonder of his eyes,
Even as Spring upon the ancient skies,
And pondered on the glory of his days;
And all around the harp-string told his praise,
And Conchubar, the Red Branch king of kings,
With his own fingers touched the brazen strings.

At last Cuchulain spake, 'Some man has made
His evening fire amid the leafy shade.
I have often heard him singing to and fro,
I have often heard the sweet sound of his bow.
Seek out what man he is.'
                    One went and came.
'He bade me let all know he gives his name
At the sword-point, and waits till we have found
Some feasting man that the same oath has bound.'
                              (*Collected Poems*, pp. 38–39)

In order to prevent any possible confusion, it should be said that
the 'sweet sound of his bow' is not a reference to a fiddle. The
harp with its brazen strings is the only musical instrument
mentioned in this passage; and it is mentioned in a very Burne-
Jones-like context—the composed pictorial fusion of sweetheart, warrior, harper, king.

So we have come full circle in this attempt to retrace the recurrence of the psaltery/harp from the earliest to the latest
Yeats. Perhaps it is with the earlier passages that we may most
connect some of the things that Yeats says in his essay on the
subject, 'Speaking to the Psaltery', written to celebrate the art
of Florence Farr in 1902. But the quotations that I offer from the
beginning of the essay have relevance, I consider, to all the poems
I have referred to—to the Chinamen in 'Lapis Lazuli' as much
as to the Red Branch heroes in 'Cuchulain's Fight with the Sea',
the Ever-Living in *The Wanderings of Oisin*, or the Quattrocento

throng, 'the thoughtless image of Mantegna's thought', in 'Her Vision in a Wood'. Yeats's essay begins thus:

I have always known that there was something I disliked about singing, and I naturally dislike print and paper, but now at last I understand why, for I have found something better. I have just heard a poem spoken with so delicate a sense of its rhythm, with so perfect a respect for its meaning, that if I were a wise man and could persuade a few people to learn the art I would never open a book of verses again. A friend, who was here a few minutes ago, has sat with a beautiful stringed instrument upon her knee, her fingers passing over the strings, and has spoken to me some verses from Shelley's *Skylark* and Sir Ector's lamentations over the dead Launcelot out of the *Morte d'Arthur* and some of my own poems. Wherever the rhythm was most delicate, and wherever the emotion was most ecstatic, her art was most beautiful, and yet, although she sometimes spoke to a little tune, it was never singing, as we sing to-day, never anything but speech. A singing note, a word chanted as they chant in churches, would have spoiled everything; nor was it reciting, for she spoke to a notation as definite as that of song, using the instrument, which murmured sweetly and faintly, under the spoken sounds, to give her the changing notes. Another speaker could have repeated all her effects, except those which came from her own beautiful voice, a voice that would have given her fame if the only art that offers the speaking voice its perfect opportunity were as well known among us as it was known in the ancient world. (*Essays and Introductions*, pp. 13–14)

There is much of interest in this opening: the air of casualness and the touches of intimacy—it is the style of a private letter: 'A friend, who was here a few minutes ago . . .' This essay first appeared in the *Monthly Review*, and this is not the way people wrote generally in the literary journals of the 1900s—they were much stiffer, more facetious or more schoolmasterly. And yet the content in many ways is strangely and characteristically evasive—it is quite hard to find out what Florence Farr actually did on her instrument, at any rate from the opening paragraph of the essay (there is more precision later on). So much is stated as negatives: it was not singing, neither was it reciting. What we are really left with is perhaps a glimpse of an ideal relationship—a portion of an ideal society: the woman with her beautiful stringed instrument (she must, we think, be beautiful too) and the poet. It is a scene out of a Pre-Raphaelite missal. This feeling that what one might call a sociological element or concern underlies the passage and is mediated through its intimacy and pictorial qualities, is much reinforced by the next section of the essay:

Since I was a boy I have always longed to hear poems spoken to a harp, as I imagined Homer to have spoken his, for it is not natural to enjoy an art only when one is by oneself. Whenever one finds a fine verse one wants to read it to somebody, and it would be much less trouble and much pleasanter if we could all listen, friend by friend, lover by beloved. Images used to rise up before me, as I am sure they have risen before nearly everybody else who cares for poetry, of wild-eyed men speaking harmoniously to murmuring wires while audiences in many-coloured robes listened, hushed and excited. Whenever I spoke of my desire to anybody they said I should write for music, but when I heard anything sung I did not hear the words, or if I did their natural pronunciation was altered and their natural music was altered, or it was drowned in another music which I did not understand. (*Essays and Introductions*, p. 14)

The music is again, as in the poems from which I quoted earlier, accompaniment only—reduced to the 'murmuring wires' of Florence Farr's psaltery. But what strikes us most is again the vision of a paradisal society, though one which is curiously affected by reminiscences perhaps of Bedford Park fancy-dress balls and the Greek or pseudo-Greek plays of Dr Todhunter, *Helena in Troas* and *A Sicilian Idyll*, performed there in the 1890s. There is perhaps nothing very surprising in this: even H. G. Wells, writing *The Time Machine* in 1895, borrowed from the *avant-garde* tastes of the decade in which the story was written the 'rich soft robes' and Greek or pseudo-Greek dress of his utopian 'little people' of the future. It was the robes that struck everybody, and Ian Fletcher has reproduced in his book *Romantic Mythologies* a photograph of Florence Farr wearing some in a hammock, 'somewhat voluptuously', as Fletcher says; it was perhaps of her that Chesterton wrote in his lines on Bedford Park:

> There was a velvet long-haired beau
> I could have murdered (which is wrong),
> There was a lady trailing slow
> Enormous draperies along.
> And there was Yeats . . .

As for the Greekism, here is Wells's description of the first of his little utopians, from *The Time Machine*:

He was a slight creature—perhaps four feet high—clad in a purple tunic, girdled at the waist with a leather belt. Sandals or buskins— I could not clearly distinguish which—were on his feet; his legs were bare to the knees, and his head was bare.

Straight out of the *Sicilian Idyll*, in fact, in his flowery, grassy, statued land. The fact, incidentally, that the time-traveller couldn't tell whether the figure was wearing buskins or sandals (both, certainly the latter, appropriate Bedford Park footgear) suggests that Wells himself didn't know the difference, since a sandal is to a buskin as a slipper is to a Wellington boot. Florence Farr herself went on wearing 'purples and ambers and scarlets and great hats and veils' until she was old.

From all the material by Yeats which I have set before you— poems as well as prose, and poems selected from the earliest, later, and last phases of his work—I want to claim this: they are all, as it were, sociological, serious versions of a paradisal state, a social paradise, not a solitary one. Taking them in chrono- logical order of composition, they offer, first, the land of the everliving, and nothing is more striking in that land than the positively Wellsian sense of community, which first presents itself to Oisin the hero as

> a band
> Of men and ladies, hand in hand,
> And singing, singing all together.
> (*Collected Poems*, p. 415)

Everything is done together in a manner reminiscent of holiday camps, but saved for gentility by that extraordinary late Vic- torian phrase, which is several times repeated, 'men and *ladies*'. Then there are the Red Branch heroes settled cosily round their camp-fire amidst the distant glories of Celtic heathendom when the Irish were kings. Then there is a Homeric society, bard and people. Then there is the Quattrocento throng —partly Mantegna, partly a pre-Raphaelite dream. And finally some classical Chinese sages and their musician servant, ima- ginatively animated from a fragment of carved blue silicate. Wordsworth's phrase for the collection as a whole might have been 'a Very pretty piece of Paganism' (the phrase which he applied to Keats's Hymn to Pan in *Endymion*), and parts of it at least might be summed up Byronically:

> And thus they form a group that's quite antique,
> Half-naked, loving, natural, and Greek.

For what strikes us surely about all these societal visions, if we may call them so, is that they are archaic and remote—Greek, Celtic, classical Chinese, Italian Renaissance. They are the work of Yeats the archaizer, of the poet who, as the cliché has it, 'refuses to come to terms with the modern world'. And their archaic quality—that in them which tempts us to use of them the word *antique* in the Byronic-ironic sense—is sufficiently pointed by the presence in them of that ancient musical instrument—more emblem than instrument perhaps—the portative harp, the wild harp that the minstrel boy in Thomas Moore's poem slung behind him when he went to war. But as we all know:

> The harp that once through Tara's halls
> The soul of music shed,
> Now hangs as mute on Tara's walls
> As if that soul were fled.

So we come up against the charge that Yeats is too often an archaizer, that he turns us away from our own time to an unreachable past; that, if we may judge by the societies which he delights to imagine, he has little to say that is relevant to our own problems in society; he is, as Stephen Spender said long ago, 'not socially constructive'. He would therefore be in sharp contrast with a writer such as D. H. Lawrence, who, though he died nearly forty years ago, does seem to have more to say than Yeats to the 'sort now growing up'. And he would contrast too with his own near-contemporary Joyce, whose actualization of the city and whose attempts to celebrate the life of Stephen and Bloom and whose experiments with the language of fiction all seem to class him as a founding father of much that is still going very strong in the contemporary novel. By contrast Yeats was the conclusion of a phase, the final apogee of the romantic movement, the logical consequence of Keats; and poetry after him seemed compelled to turn in other directions.

'Not socially constructive', however, is the portion of the case against Yeats which I want at this point to examine. It is a charge which can, I think, be somewhat modified if we consider what Yeats thought he was doing and the historical circumstances in which he did it. For to Stephen Spender's 'not socially constructive' he might have replied, borrowing his favourite phrase from Bishop Berkeley, 'We Irish do not think so.' Most of his life Yeats was consciously working in order to try to form the new Irish society—not so much perhaps to persuade it to adopt certain recognizable social forms and practices (though there was a certain amount of that too) as to give it a sense of its own identity, a soul. This comparatively restricted historical objective, which fluctuated and varied in detail according as the details of the historical and political situation fluctuated, explains perhaps a certain obliquity and remoteness which we, from a different vantage point, are aware of in Yeats's manner of address.

If we cast our eyes back over the societal visions from poems and prose which I earlier exposed to your view, we shall surely be struck by one thing—the essential gregariousness of Yeats. You will remember how one of the quotations from the 'Speaking to the Psaltery' essay begins:

Since I was a boy I have always longed to hear poems spoken to a harp, as I imagined Homer to have spoken his, for it is not natural to enjoy an art only when one is by oneself. Whenever one finds a fine verse one wants to read it to somebody, and it would be much less trouble and much pleasanter if we could all listen, friend by friend, lover by beloved.

Though Yeats was in many ways a solitary person, especially perhaps in his youth, this essential gregariousness—so contrary to the stereotype idea of the romantic poet—especially in the enjoyment of the arts comes out continuously in his works and in his life. It was perhaps this that induced him to pay so much attention to the place of the arts in society; the community he was interested in was Ireland, and so his concern naturally became the place of the arts in Ireland and the influence that they could exert on Ireland. This combination of interests—gregariousness in the enjoyment of the arts within the Irish context—was the combination that turned him into a playwright and worker in the theatre. He said many years later that

he had always disliked the isolation of the work of art; he thought
of the theatre as a mixture of many different arts and as a means
of, as he put it, plunging art back into social life; he wrote at the
same time:

I wanted a theatre where the greatest passions and all the permanent
interests of men might be displayed that we might find them not alone
over a book but, as I said again and again, lover by lover, friend by
friend.

'It is not natural to enjoy an art only when one is by oneself.'
Yeats realized the socially cohesive power of music. And hence
the harp: the harp is the instrument with which the bard keeps
the tribe awake until dawn listening to the enthralling tale of its
own greatness and past heroes. The harp, therefore, is not
simply a bit of archaistic decoration in keeping with the archaic/
ideal societies displayed. It is an emblem for the gregariousness
in the enjoyment of the arts and for the model-forming virtue
of the arts as a means of bestowing upon a community a sense
of its own power and identity. For Yeats this was reinforced by
his belief that Irish literature was the 'creation of a whole
people', 'made to be spoken or sung', while English literature
was created by individuals for a leisured class, only a portion
of the people. Yeats comes close to saying not only that it is not
natural to 'enjoy an art only when one is by oneself' but that
it is not natural to *create* an art only when one is by oneself—
hence again his work for the theatre, where the playwright has
to learn to create in company with others and in response to
their needs.

I spoke a moment ago of the model-forming virtue of the arts
as a means of bestowing upon a community a sense of its own
power and identity, and perhaps I had better explain a bit more
what I mean by this. As an artist in Ireland Yeats saw the role
of the artist as quite different from that of a propagandist for
a cause; he must not get lost in the 'flood of opinion'. To Yeats
it seemed wholly relevant to Ireland's needs as a political and
social community that the arts should serve them not by lam-
basting the English or flattering the Irish but by releasing some
source of imaginative coherence that would deepen and ennoble
political passion, make the nation more completely alive, create
a kind of social Unity of Being, Yeats's name for the most

precious condition that he knew, for both the individual and society. The theatre was especially the place where such processes could occur, and in his many writings on the subject Yeats works out a fairly elaborate sense of the relationship between the arts and the psychology of a community: in such a theory the arts directly play upon the springs of a community's life. What is worked out in the prose is stated with metaphorical simplicity and force in the play *The King's Threshold*, where the poet Seanchan is catechizing his pupil:

> *Oldest Pupil.* I said the poets hung
> Images of the life that was in Eden
> About the child-bed of the world, that it,
> Looking upon those images, might bear
> Triumphant children. But why must I stand here,
> Repeating an old lesson, while you starve?
> *Seanchan.* Tell on, for I begin to know the voice.
> What evil thing will come upon the world
> If the Arts perish?
> *Oldest Pupil.* If the Arts should perish,
> The world that lacked them would be like a woman
> That, looking on the cloven lips of a hare,
> Brings forth a hare-lipped child.
>
> (*Collected Plays*, pp. 111–12)

One reply to the charge that Yeats's poetry is not 'socially constructive', therefore, might be that on the contrary it is the product of a sustained effort to be just that: an effort to help Ireland realize itself as a society and to hold up before it idealisms which are supposed to spring from a real (if idealized) national past and have consequently a special relevance to its present need for 'unity of being'.

But you might well say that this is too restricted an objective, that the theories by which it is supported are at best non-proven, that the whole operation has become history anyway—interesting if you like history but not otherwise. And you might further add, which would be true, that nothing could be much further from the sort of Ireland that Yeats would have liked to see than the one that actually happened. The bourgeois, puritan, Catholic republic is not exactly a social set-up to start anyone's pulses racing, least of all those of anybody committed (as I, I hasten to say, am not) to Yeats's taste for nobles and beggar-

men. In short, the whole bundle of objections could be summed
up as 'Who cares about Ireland anyway?'

Don't care shall be made to care, as the old nursery proverb
has it. I hesitate about using an old-fashioned and not too well
defined word and idea, but I want to say, as used to be said, that
Ireland is immortalized by the poem. It is this that makes us
care. The *OED* definition of to immortalize is 'To cause to be
remembered or celebrated through all time; to confer enduring
fame upon'. Poetry conducts this operation upon certain conditions and with certain limitations, but before getting entangled
in those, let me remind you what Yeats does for or to that
obscure magician MacGregor Mathers in 'All Souls' Night':

> And I call up MacGregor from the grave,
> For in my first hard springtime we were friends,
> Although of late estranged.
> I thought him half a lunatic, half knave,
> And told him so, but friendship never ends;
> And what if mind seem changed,
> And it seem changed with the mind,
> When thoughts rise up unbid
> On generous things that he did
> And I grow half contented to be blind!
>
> He had much industry at setting out,
> Much boisterous courage, before loneliness
> Had driven him crazed;
> For meditations upon unknown thought
> Make human intercourse grow less and less;
> They are neither paid nor praised.
> But he'd object to the host,
> The glass because my glass;
> A ghost-lover he was
> And may have grown more arrogant being a ghost.
>
> But names are nothing . . .
>   (*Collected Poems*, pp. 258-9)

How beautifully here the plain-speaking of the character
vignette is mixed with and controlled by the rhythms of elegy!
It is the same method that Yeats uses in all his autobiographical
writings: a tenderness which respects the memory and nature
of his fellow workers so that they seem freely to play their parts
in the autobiographical drama that he shapes about them.

This is the kind of immortality that MacGregor Mathers gets (I am not of course concerned with the kind that is conferred upon him by our having to look him up in Professor Jeffares's notes at the back of the book). It is of course a conditional sort of immortality, but it seems to me quite a real one and fitting the dictionary definition. The idea that the poet can immortalize his subject is a very traditional one as everybody knows:

> Not marble, nor the gilded monuments
> Of princes, shall outlive this powerful rhyme;
> But you shall shine more bright in these contents
> Than unswept stone, besmeared with sluttish time.
>
> (Shakespeare, Sonnet 55)

> Goe you my verse, goe tell her what she was;
> For what she was she best shall finde in you.
> Your firie heate lets not her glorie passe,
> But Phenix-like shall make her live anew.
>
> (Daniel, Sonnet 30)

But plainly Shakespeare's 'you' (whether Willie Hughes or the Earl of Southampton) or Daniel's 'she' (Delia) have not the same status as MacGregor Mathers in the Yeats poem. They are as it were excuses for the sentiments, lay figures, neutral. If the Earl of Southampton is in any sense immortalized it is not by Shakespeare, who tells us so little of him that his identity is lost or can only be recovered by the labours of commentators. MacGregor Mathers, on the other hand, is still personally and historically alive, and though he has been fitted for a role in the personal drama of Yeats, he has not been neutralized by it. The poem mimes the form of a seance or a summoning of spirits. The three—Horton, Florence Farr, Mathers—appear, and they have a necessary dramatic life, and share the immortality of the artefact, even though the drama in which they seem freely to be playing their parts is one whose last scene concludes with their dismissal:

> But names are nothing. What matter who it be,
> So that his elements have grown so fine
> The fume of muscatel
> Can give his sharpened palate ecstasy
> No living man can drink from the whole wine . . .
>
> (*Collected Poems*, p. 259)

'All Souls' Night' is one of a number of Yeats's greatest poems which have a common attitude and rank: the Coole Park poems, the elegiac poems, the 'Municipal Gallery Revisited', the many poems which he uses to present himself as *dramatis persona*. What do they resemble each other in? In exhibiting this combination: a conditional freedom allotted to the characters by which they earn their immortality, the poet's own nobility of bearing conveyed through noble speech, through what he called 'passionate syntax'—the whole constituting a drama (perhaps a scene from a continuous extended drama which the body of the poems makes up). And this drama, of course, when it touches on great political or amorous intensities, is very often more theatricalized, more tensioned, strained, and criss-cross than it is in 'All Soul's Night'.

I would say, then, that what engages us with Yeats's world and makes us care about it—about its marginal and eccentric thought system, about its obscure personae, even about its archaic instruments—is this interlocking process of immortalization and dramatization—the one being dependent on the other, neither anything without the other. I would further add that the quality of this process and its contriver seems to me capable of being admired, and even exemplary, if you want your literature to be exemplary. There is not only the care and intelligence exercised about the lives and beings of other people (Yeats, though he creates a personal drama in poem and autobiography, never strikes one as being a self-centred writer in the same sense that Lawrence or Pound or even Eliot does), there is also that combination of ordering and intensity of experience, which seems to have a moral quality. It is perhaps an old bourgeois virtue that Yeats would probably like us to think that he had inherited from his merchant-skipper and Protestant-clergymen ancestors. Parents used to say to their children, 'You ought to make something of your life'. The long procession of Yeats's mature and late poems affords us the spectacle of Yeats making something of his life—and by this I mean perhaps chiefly preserving a fresh sense of experience and what it may contribute to a meaningful pattern; and this is courageous and human enough to anyone who knows how easy it is to lose that sense.

But I don't want to be pushed into making out a case for Yeats as a neo-Victorian moral example, simply because people shout so loud about D. H. Lawrence as one. What I value Yeats chiefly for is that he puts us in possession of works of art which, by dramatizing and immortalizing, combine the intensity and temporality of drama with the finality and changelessness of perfect statement. Amongst the various ideas of the current *avant-garde*, none is more distasteful to me than the notion that the artist is essentially a provider of consumable goodies which are eaten up and thrown away to make room for the next. 'Only an aching heart / Conceives a changeless work of art', said Yeats. The artist, *I* think, gives the human race things to keep: stagnation and connoisseurship are a possible dangerous outcome of this fact, but they are much less dangerous than the idea that confuses the work of the artist with that of the manu-facturer of bric-à-brac.

Another conclusion follows from what I have said about the character of Yeats's work. It is easier to accuse him of being an archaizer if one fastens on a chosen detail of his work as I did in the first half of this talk when I was talking about the musical instruments. In fact, if you return to the Red Branch heroes round their camp-fire or the Chinese sages on their mountain-side you see that they and their stringed instruments form part of an elaborate drama in which the archaism that focuses in the stringed instrument is held in tension and antithesis against the threat of total disturbance from a world outside. In each case the society is about to be split open and crushed. It is this that the poems are 'about' and enact—the coming disaster and madness of Cuchulain and the disruption of the tribe, and the coming cataclysm of world war. In either case the archaic instrument is an accent in a drama which, viewed as a whole, is not really archaic at all. The same is true, *mutatis mutandis*, of 'Her Vision in the Wood' and 'The Wanderings of Oisin'. You can prove almost anything by the distance at which you station yourself from a work of art, and when I was talking about the musical instruments I was standing too near. This is better, if only a little better, than standing too far away—a habit which is res-ponsible for all those dreary books that prove that Dickens was really Kafka or that Shakespeare was just another Elizabethan.

Of course even the most archaic ornaments are subject to mutation by time and may return to fashion. Whoever would have thought that the recorder, of all instruments, would ever be played by massed bands in comprehensive schools? Perhaps we shall all take in time to the dulcimer. Does after Yeats the harp that once through Tara's halls the soul of music shed really hang as mute on Tara's walls as if that soul were dead?

PART II

THE PLAYS

9
Yeats and the
two harmonies

In four of his plays, *On Baile's Strand*, *The Hour-Glass*, *The Shadowy Waters*, and *The King's Threshold*, Yeats mingled verse and prose. In so doing he was contravening current opinion as well as the judgement of a very eminent authority:

I believe that in verse drama prose should be used very sparingly indeed; that we should aim at a form of verse in which everything can be said that has to be said . . . to introduce prose dialogue would only be to distract [the audience's] attention from the play itself to the medium of its expression.[1]

So far as I know, this matter has not been discussed in any detail in relation to Yeats, except by Dr Denis Donoghue in his chapter on Yeats in *The Third Voice* (1959). It may, like other questions concerning Yeats's plays, be worth looking at again, though I am of course indebted to Donoghue's treatment of the subjects. The facts, briefly, would seem to be as follows:

1. The first play in which Yeats used both prose and verse was *On Baile's Strand*, both in the first version (first printed in 1903) and in the second much revised version (first printed in 1906). The only characters who speak in prose are Fintain the Fool and Barach the Blind Man; they appear only at the beginning and end of the play. In the 1906 version the prose at the beginning is very much rewritten, at the end hardly at all.

2. Next, conveniently but perhaps not quite accurately, comes *The Hour-Glass*. This was first printed—a version wholly in prose—in 1903, and it remained a prose play through many printings thereafter including those of 1904 (*Plays for an Irish Theatre*, vol. ii), 1908 (the Stratford-upon-Avon *Collected Works*,

First published in *Modern Drama*, vii, 1964, 237–55.

1. T. S. Eliot, *On Poetry and Poets* (1957), p. 74.

vol. iv) and 1911 (*Plays for an Irish Theatre*, Stratford-upon-Avon, in one volume). But in January 1903 Yeats is writing to Lady Gregory:

Then (I am afraid you will be sorry to hear) I propose to put certain parts of *The Hour-Glass* into verse—only the part with the Angels and the soliloquies. I have got to think this necessary to lift the 'Wise man's' part out of a slight element of platitude.

And again:

I do not agree with you that *The Hour-Glass* when I have put the verse into it would be out of tune with the rest. It repeats practically the Fool and the Blind Man of [*On Baile's Strand*] and would have something the same proportion of verse and prose.[2]

It is some indication of Lady Gregory's influence that it was perhaps her disapproval that at the first prevented the 'putting the verse into it'. But the inhibition lasted nearly ten years, and there were graver reasons for it. The play remained resignedly prose, and there is no further word of a poetical version until Gordon Craig and his screens came on the scene for the Abbey revival of the play in 1912. It was apparently for this performance that Yeats now at length put the verse in, about March 1912.[3] The mixed version was first printed in Craig's periodical *The Mask* in 1913 (followed by a private printing in 1914[4]) and then in *Responsibilities* (Cuala Press, 1914, and London, 1916). As Yeats told Bullen in February 1913, the new version is 'practically a different work of art'[5] from the old. The changes amount to far more than the mere 'putting . . . verse into it' that he had proposed to Lady Gregory in 1903. The Wise Man speaks mostly in verse; what little prose is left (that of the Fool, Bridget, the Children, and the Pupils—these last also have verse as well) is radically rearranged and rewritten. The Wise Man no longer kneels to the Fool at the Faustian end of the play ('Have pity upon me, Fool, and tell me!'[6]) but says to him:

> Be silent. May God's will prevail on the instant,
> Although His will be my eternal pain.
> I have no question.[7]

2. *Letters of W. B. Yeats* (ed. Wade, 1954), pp. 391, 393.
3. Ibid., p. 567.   4. Wade, *Bibliography*, no. 108.   5. *Letters*, p. 576.
6. *Plays for an Irish Theatre* (1911), p. 177.   7. *Responsibilities* (1916), p. 178.

In a 'Note' to the play Yeats makes it plain that it was not Lady Gregory's disapproval that had held him up but his dissatisfaction with the story and the moral of the original version:

I have for years struggled with something which is charming in the naïve legend but a platitude on the stage. I did not discover till a year ago [see the new version's 'Preface' in the *Mask* printing of 1913] that if the wise man humbled himself to the fool and received salvation as his reward, so much more powerful are pictures than words, no explanatory dialogue could set the matter right. I was faintly pleased when I converted a music-hall singer and kept him going to Mass for six weeks, so little responsibility does one feel for those to whom one has never been introduced; but I was always ashamed when I saw any friend of my own in the theatre. Now I have made my philosopher accept God's will, whatever it is, and find his courage again, and helped by the elaboration of the verse, have so changed the fable that it is not false to my own thoughts of the world.[8]

Regrettably, this 'Note', and with it perhaps the most Wildean sentence that Yeats ever composed, disappeared after 1916, to be replaced, when the play was next reprinted in *Plays in Prose and Verse* (1922), by a shorter one explaining that a certain Mr Alan Porter had been persuaded—though with no real dramatic gain, as Professor G. B. Saul remarks[9]—to put certain passages into medieval Latin:

I found that in performance verbal repetitions which did not get on the nerves in the prose version, did so when all the first half of the play was in verse. We listen more intently to verse than to prose, and therefore notice verbal repetition more quickly.[1]

The process of revising, then, certainly did not cease with the version performed at the Abbey in 1912. It is, however, a fair inference from the 'Note' which accompanied the printing of that version that the revision of the play had hung fire until then because Yeats was ashamed of the naïveté of the original ending and could not at once discover a more sophisticated one, not because he had any doubts or inhibitions, despite Lady Gregory, about mingling verse and prose in the same play.

   3. Yet, in the case of *The Shadowy Waters*, although he had his own example in *On Baile's Strand* and his own (as yet unfulfilled)

8. *Responsibilities*, pp. 186–7.
9. *Prolegomena to the Study of Yeats's Plays* (1958), p. 61.
1. *Plays* (1922), p. 428.

plan for *The Hour-Glass* as precedents, Yeats was extraordinarily
slow in taking action. This does not appear from Professor
Parkinson's well-known account of the evolution of the play,
for he ignores the mixed version altogether.[2] The tale of Forgael
and Dectora remained substantially the same in the three major
printed versions (1900, the 'poetic version' of 1906 [later revised],
and the 'acting version' also of 1906 and also later revised); it
was to represent in symbol 'the whole story of the relation of
man and woman'.[3] From the first it was intended for theatrical
performance. Yeats conceived the subject when he was eighteen,[4]
and we find him working on it in 1894, but confessing to his father
that it will prove so overloaded with legendary detail as to be
useless for theatrical purposes.[5] It is laid aside for two years, but
in 1896-7 it is resumed and recast: 'magical and mystical beyond
anything I have done . . . a wild little play . . . probably the best
verse I have written'.[6] Its keynote is to be 'a kind of grave
ecstasy'.[7] In 1899 it is being prepared for publication in the *North
American Review* (May 1900), and is 'wilder and finer'; it is still
meant to be a stage play, for Yeats has thought out the staging
carefully to get a strange dreamlike effect.[8] This text, never
reprinted by Yeats after 1901, is in fact a dramatic poem, overloaded with symbolism impenetrable to an audience; the
characters murmur their speeches in their heads. Yeats himself
provided an exact enough criticism of it when he wrote from
New York in the same month in which this version was being
performed in Dublin (January 1904):

I had a different feeling about [the] stage when I wrote it—I would not
now do anything so remote, so impersonal. It is legitimate art however
though a kind that may I should think by this time prove itself of the
worst sort possible for our theatre. The whole picture as it were moves
together—sky and sea and cloud are as it were actors. It is almost religious, it is more a ritual than a human story. It is deliberately without
human characters.[9]

The accent of apology should not deceive us; it was 'our theatre'
that Yeats was to find inadequate, not the kind of play that is
described in that passage. When he returned from America, the

2. *W. B. Yeats: Self-Critic* (1951), pp. 59–75.   3. *Letters*, p. 324.
4. *Autobiographies* (1955), pp. 73–74.   5. *Letters*, p. 236.
6. Ibid., pp. 280, 320.   7. Ibid., pp. 280, 322.   8. Ibid., p. 331.
9. Ibid., p. 425.

players put on a private performance for his benefit, and in June 1905 he is busy reshaping it for performance at a theosophical convention in London in July, but was already toiling at a second version 'getting rid of needless symbols, making the people answer each other, and making the groundwork simple and intelligible'.[1] The performance in July had shown him how bad the first version was; he spends the summer of 1905 at Coole rewriting and is filled with fresh enthusiasm: now there is jealousy and anger and strong simple scenes: 'I let them play it in London . . . that I might find out what was wrong.'[2] The play is at last, Yeats considers, filled with homely phrases and the idiom of daily speech; the sailors (Forgael's crew) are rough as sailors should be:

It has a simple passionate story for the common sightseer . . . I am now correcting the last few lines and have very joyfully got 'creaking shoes' and 'liquorice-root' into what had been a very abstract passage.[3]

This version was first published in *Poems 1899–1905* (1906) and is, with some later revisions, the version in *Collected Poems*. And it is all still in verse.

It proved too profuse for the Abbey production in December 1906, despite the improvements described by Parkinson—less obscurity, characters who stand out more from the background and who do at least speak to one another. Yeats had spent years revising the play with the theatre in mind, yet when it came to that test it was still no good. Part of the trouble seems to have been that it was simply too long. And so for the Abbey performances a great deal of the earlier dialogue between Aibric, Forgael's lieutenant, and Forgael, was cut, as well as some of the exchanges between Forgael and Dectora at the end. For the first time prose was introduced, the common sailors using it throughout and Forgael and Aibric occasionally: Allan Wade says that the prose 'seems to be largely the work of Lady Gregory'.[4] This would seem to be true of the lengthiest prose passage, the one with which the play now begins; much of the original subject matter is eliminated; the language is kiltartanized and withal refined.

1. Ibid., p. 453.　　2. Ibid., p. 459.
3. Ibid., p. 462. For the passage see the Variorum *Poems*, pp. 227–8.
4. Wade, *Bibliography*, no. 66.

> I am so lecherous with abstinence
> I'd give the profit of nine voyages
> For that red Moll that had but the one eye,[5]

disappears to be replaced with this kind of locution: 'What is worse again, it is the way we are in a ship, the barrels empty and my throat shrivelled with drought, and nothing to quench it but water only.'[6] But, elsewhere, the prose is mostly the verse, transposed and contracted. The text which emerged from all this was the mixed or 'acting version', first printed separately in 1907, and next included as an appendix in both the New York *Poetical Works of William B. Yeats*, volume ii (1907) and in volume ii of the Stratford-upon-Avon *Collected Works* (1908). Yeats prevented the poetic version ever again being printed as a theatrical piece and in 1911 is found insisting that the acting version should be included in *Plays for an Irish Theatre* as well as the poetic one:

I am most anxious that this book, which I hope will go about among people who have a technical interest in the stage, should show that I understand my trade as a practical dramatist. It will injure me if it contains a play which is evidently unfit for the stage . . . actable plays or nothing.[7]

4. Lastly, *The King's Threshold* provides the most surprising case of all. The play remained wholly poetical, despite all the revision it underwent,[8] until *after* its printing in *Plays in Prose and Verse* in 1922. Then, at a date unknown to me, Yeats put the whole of the episode involving the Mayor of Kinvara into prose, and the play was printed for the first and only time during Yeats's life in this mixed form in the 1934 edition of *Collected Plays*.[9] The new prose is mainly, though not entirely, a mere transposition of the verse, but there are some passages[1] where more radical changes have been effected.

5. *Poems, 1899–1905* (1906), p. 10.

6. *Collected Works*, Stratford-upon-Avon (1908), iv.232.

7. *Letters*, pp. 561–2. [For a recent, very full history of the manuscript (and also the printed) versions, see *Druid Craft: The Writing of the Shadowy Waters* (ed. Michael J. Sidnell, George P. Mayhew, and David R. Clark, 1971)—C. J. R.]

8. For an account of this, see my *Yeats the Playwright* (1963), p. 34.

9. Saul's entry on the play (*Prolegomena*, pp. 38 ff.) fails to mention this, and is therefore quite misleading about the texts.

1. Compare, for example, *Plays in Prose and Verse* (1922), pp. 77–78, with *Collected Plays* (1934), p. 115.

5. It is relevant to mention here three other plays which were printed in alternative prose or verse versions. *The Golden Helmet*, the prose version of *The Green Helmet*, was printed twice only, in a separate American edition and in volume iv of the Stratford-upon-Avon *Collected Works* (both in 1908); it was then superseded by the poetical *The Green Helmet* (Cuala Press, 1910, and many later reprintings). Reversing this process, *The Only Jealousy of Emer* (first printed 1919) was turned into prose in 1927 and printed in that form as *Fighting the Waves* for the first and last time in *Wheels and Butterflies* (1934). Once more vice versa, *The King of the Great Clock Tower* with the dialogue in prose (printed by the Cuala Press in 1934) was followed by a wholly poetical version in 1935 (in the volume called *A Full Moon in March*). Of course all these three (or six) plays contain songs, but I have not counted these as 'verse' in this record.

There are two ways—which are interrelated—of looking at some of the functions of the prose in the four plays: prose as something that helps to define the status of certain characters who speak it in their relation to those who generally eschew it; and prose as mingling with verse within a single episode of a play—what I shall call '*local* mixing', in order to distinguish it from the common Jacobean and Yeatsian method of composing an entire episode in prose followed by an entire episode in verse and so on.

From the first point of view, the mixed versions of *The Shadowy Waters* and *The King's Threshold* pair together in a relatively un-complicated way. The sailors in the first play, the Mayor and the cripples in the second, speak in prose because they represent the greedy and fickle common men, the way of the market-carts and not the way of the bird, of Forgael and Seanchan; and they are therefore intended to emphasize the lonely pride of heroic character, trembling into passion and still intensity. Most of the prose in both plays, however, is too close in idiom, rhythm, and vocabulary to the verse it once was to make much difference—it is simply the verse melted into prose by the removal of line-endings and capital letters. The exception to this is the rewritten opening episode of the sailors' expository conversation in *The Shadowy Waters*. Apart from an occasional false—in the circum-stances—note of pastiche Jacobean rumbustiousness the sailors in the poetical versions sound as dreamy and wildered as Forgael

—a fitting crew, one would think, for him to take with him to the Ever-Living. I cannot agree with Parkinson that in the poetical version of 1906 they have become 'ordinary men with a normal endowment of sensuality'[2]—their rhythms betray them. Such rhythms have not been banished even from the prose, but at least the prose sheds the load of mythological references and self-consciously contrived answering half-lines, as in:

> *Second Sailor*. 'Twas Aengus and Edain, the wandering lovers,
>   To whom all lovers pray.
> *First Sailor*. But what of that?
>   A shadow does not carry sword or spear. (*Collected Works*, ii.189)

Parkinson's point that the poetical sailors of 1906 see visions, too, and so make Forgael's dream appear less vague and false—'for if the sailors have seen magical birds and gods, they may truly exist'[3]—is amply satisfied by the mixed version of 1906, where they also report on their visions:

> *First Sailor*. I was sleeping up there by the bulwark, and when I woke in the sound of the harp a change came over my eyes, and I could see very strange things. The dead were floating upon the sea yet, and it seemed as if the life that went out of every one of them had turned to the shape of a man-headed bird—grey they were, and they rose up of a sudden and called out with voices like our own, and flew away singing to the west. Words like this they were singing: 'Happiness beyond measure, happiness where the sun dies.'
> *Second Sailor*. I understand well what they are doing. My mother used to be talking of birds of the sort. They are sent by the lasting watchers to lead men away from this world and its women to some place of shining women that cast no shadow, having lived before the making of the earth. But I have no mind to go following him to that place. (*Collected Works*, ii.232–3)

This prose is probably as good a compromise as Yeats and Lady Gregory between them could achieve—for obviously it would not do to make the sailors go right over the edge into market-cart language and so introduce too abrupt a contrast between the two ways of life. But, although its claims to contribute to the needed antithesis seem more justified than those which are advanced by Parkinson on behalf of the 1906 poetical version, the play is fundamentally of such a kind that the difference between the two 1906 versions is never *very* considerable. The

2. Parkinson, p. 70.   3. Parkinson, p. 70.

conflict had to be always somewhat muffled; otherwise the whole fragile texture would have split into pieces.

On Baile's Strand and *The Hour-Glass* present much more complex cases. In *On Baile's Strand* Fintain and Barach represent the life of unheroic circumstance in contrast to Cuchulain's; but they also do much more. The relationship of this Fool with his Blind Man mirrors Cuchulain's with Conchubar; that implicit parody lingers suggestively in our minds as we watch the nobler scenes. It is doubtful if the prose, simply by being prose, contributes anything to this particular effect that verse could not have done. What counts—and it is not a method very common in early Yeats—is the *sight* of Fool and Blind Man on the stage, the spectacle of maimed crafty age and maimed discontented youth, each unwillingly dependent on the other. The language only underpins this, and it therefore must be prose, because the verse of these early plays, which is always the passionate and ordered expression of personality and energy and intensity (even if it is the intensity of the dreamer), cannot so subordinate itself to what is here being shown primarily by the actors' gesture and stance—but which needs speech as well. Furthermore (although it is impossible to imagine even Yeatsian verse which might have had the same effect), the Blind Man's *silent* expectation of fate, the fearful constraint with which he nourishes his secret, the *suppression* of speech in Cuchulain's presence at the end of the play, contrasted with the Fool's loose chatter, justify a prose exhibiting an inexpressiveness and disorder completely contrary to all the qualities that Yeats cultivated in his dramatic poetry. Understandably, Yeats never needed to reconsider his decision to make *On Baile's Strand* a play of the mixed kind.

But from one point of view at least the mixed version of *The Hour-Glass* is not an improvement over the one written in prose. The introduction of verse for the Wise Man and the Angel (the Pupils also have some, when they are discoursing with the Wise Man, but remain fundamentally 'prose' characters) means that the familiar contrast, which prevails in the mixed versions of *The Shadowy Waters* and *The King's Threshold*, is established—the contrast between the world of visionary intensity and the imperceptive fashion of the common man. This works very well in the case, for example, of Bridget, when she answers in prose to the Wise Man's verse. But it injures the Fool's part and goes far towards extruding him from the true dramatic action. The play at first was referred to as '*The Wise Man and the Fool*'; the point of the original parable, the 'naïve legend' which Yeats found in Lady Wilde's *Ancient Legends of Ireland*, is that the child (in Lady Wilde) or the Fool (in Yeats) knows by instinct and experience the truth that the Wise Man has hidden or hides from. In the beginning the play was firmly enough built upon this antithesis, while the contrast between the Fool's idiom and the Wise Man's, though they both speak in prose, clearly realized it. In the mixed version, because the Wise Man rejects relationship with the Fool as well as his message, the Fool exists in a half-world between intensity of vision and common blindness; and, because, along with the other commonsensical characters, he still speaks in prose as he always did, he is even forced over, in contradiction of the original theme, to the side of Bridget and the Children. His part at the end of the play retains only a stub of meaning. In the prose version the Fool comes back with a message from the angel and saves the Wise Man in the end by disclosing it:

Once I was alone on the hills, and an angel came by and he said, 'Teigue the Fool, do not forget the Three Fires; the Fire that punishes, the Fire that purifies, and the Fire wherein the soul rejoices for ever!'[4]

Yeats miscalculated when he left the relic of this episode in the new version, and even made it more vivid, but at the same time felt obliged to rob it of its climactic value:

Wise Man. The last hope is gone,
    And now that it's too late I see it all,
    We perish into God and sink away
    Into reality—the rest's a dream.   [*The Fool comes back.*
Fool. There was one there—there by the threshold stone, waiting there; and he said, 'Go in, Teigue, and tell him everything that he asks you. He will give you a penny if you tell him.'
Wise Man. I know enough, that know God's will prevails.
Fool. Waiting till the moment had come—That is what the one out there was saying, but I might tell you what you asked. That is what he was saying.
Wise Man. Be silent. May God's will prevail on the instant,
    Although His will be my eternal pain.   (*Responsibilities*, pp. 177–8)

4. *Plays for an Irish Theatre*, p. 177.

Here the Fool's prose becomes inconsequential, mere chatter punctuating the Wise Man's exaltation; and it is paradoxically odd for the Angel (who after all started the whole thing) to linger about the threshold with the vital message and then to permit his messenger to be thrust away. One general effect of the mixed version, indeed, is to reduce the Fool to not much more than a bit of local decoration. This destroys the dramatically meaningful antithesis between the folly of the wise and the wisdom of the foolish. The play becomes a theophany imposed upon a drama; but Yeats's theatre was not yet ready for Miracle.

In *The Hour-Glass*, as elsewhere, the '*local* mixing' of prose and verse within a single episode sometimes produces that effect of steep contrast, the 'shudder in the rhythm', which is one of its justifications. Dr Donoghue mentions the colloquy with Bridget.[5] Even more striking is the first appearance of verse in the play: when the Wise Man responds in soliloquy ('Were it but true 'twould alter everything') to the intimations, which he and his Pupils have been scornfully dismissing, of the Fool's tale of the Country of the Young. This soliloquy actually takes the form of a poem in two nine-line stanzas, which have some resemblances to the stanza used in 'In Memory of Major Robert Gregory'. The method here anticipates one which is often used in the later plays, where the lyrical irruption of the supernatural, or the alienating and distancing effect of the Noh musicians' songs, forms the steepest of contrasts with 'ordinary' speech, whether in blank verse or prose. (Similarly, though not in close juxtaposition, three rhythms are used in *On Baile's Strand*—prose, chant, and blank verse; *The King's Threshold* and *The Shadowy Waters*, also, set the rhythms of song and rhyming curse against those of blank verse and prose.) But in general, in these early plays, it is blank verse and prose which are juxtaposed; and there are few enough examples even of that mixture, because the plays are contrived, in accordance with Yeats's dualistic habit of thought, in such a way that, except in *The Hour-Glass*, the prose and verse characters do not often meet; instead, they form contrasting patterns of rhythm and sentiment with one another.

5. *The Third Voice* (1959), pp. 46–47.

In this connection a passage in *On Baile's Strand* illustrates some significant virtues and defects—the moments when Cuchulain learns that he has killed his own son:

Blind Man. None knew whose son he was.

Cuchulain. None knew! Did you know, old listener at the doors?

Blind Man. No, no; I knew nothing.

Fool. He said a while ago that he heard Aoife boast that she'd never but the one lover, and he the only man that had overcome her in battle.   [*Pause*

Blind Man. Somebody is trembling, Fool! The bench is shaking. Why are you trembling? Is Cuchulain going to hurt us? It was not I who told you, Cuchulain.

Fool. It is Cuchulain who is trembling. It is Cuchulain who is shaking the bench.

Blind Man. It is his own son he has slain.

Cuchulain. 'Twas they that did it, the pale, windy people.
Where? where? where? My sword against the thunder!
But no, for they have always been my friends;
And though they love to blow a smoking coal
Till it's all flame, the wars they blow aflame
Are full of glory, and heart-uplifting pride,
And not like this. The wars they love awaken
Old fingers and the sleepy strings of harps.
Who did it then? Are you afraid? Speak out!
For I have put you under my protection,
And will reward you well. Dubthach the Chafer?
He'd an old grudge. No, for he is with Maeve.
Laegaire did it! Why do you not speak?
What is this house? [*Pause.*] Now I remember all.
      [*Comes before* Conchubar's *chair, and strikes at it with his sword as if* Conchubar *was sitting upon it.*]
'Twas you who did it—you who sat up there
With your old rod of kingship, like a magpie
Nursing a stolen spoon. No, not a magpie,
A maggot that is eating up the earth!
Yes, but a magpie, for he's flown away.
Where did he fly to?

Blind Man. He is outside the door.

Cuchulain. Outside the door?

Blind Man. Between the door and the sea.

Cuchulain. Conchubar, Conchubar! the sword into your heart!

                                                              [*He rushes out*][6]

6. *Poems 1899–1905*, pp. 133–5.

Lennox Robinson, quoting part of this, called it 'dramatic dialogue at its highest pitch',[7] but he ended his quotation before Cuchulain's switch to verse. The strength of the prose lies in the way in which, itself inexplicit, it points to action and underpins it: the two men on the bench, the shaking bench. If we regret the unnecessariness of 'It is his own son he has slain' (similar words are assigned to Cuchulain himself in the 1903 version), at least the sudden removal into the third person shows effectively how Cuchulain is now rapt, beyond the reach or aid of others. It is the verse, I think, which is barely adequate—too mannered, too allusive, too stale in its rhythms. Its driving idea —'Who did it?'—is good, and gives the speech a kind of unity; it instructs the actor where to move in the search for his enemy's identity—to Conchubar's vacant throne; and it gives him action to underwrite his words—the striking of the throne with the sword; and this action explodes and finishes the meaning of much of *On Baile's Strand*, which has depicted Cuchulain's wild impotence in the face of Conchubar's *imperium*. There is also a suggestion that the physical blindness of the Blind Man has possessed the hero's movements—he does not wholly *see* that Conchubar is not actually sitting in his chair until the realization comes with 'Yes, but a magpie, for he's flown away.' But, as against these merits, Cuchulain's grammar is too careful; the force of the speech is weakened by the passage about the wars, by the languid movement of 'The wars they love awaken / Old fingers and the sleepy strings of harps', by the conscious choice between the similes about magpie and maggot, by the literary wit and high circumlocution that are active here and elsewhere in the passage. They are the author's properties and not his hero's. Both the raising of the pitch by the change to verse and the underpinning of Cuchulain's words by action and gesture are prevented from fully achieving their effects by the very qualities of the verse itself. As often in early Yeats, it is as though having painfully acquired many of the skills of the theatrical writer, he had then insisted on assuming silken robes and playing 'I, the Poet'.

The comparative timidity which Yeats showed in juxtaposing prose and verse, his frequent willingness to tolerate prose which is simply 'melted' verse, the confusions which revision some-

7. *Scattering Branches* (ed. Stephen Gwynn, 1940), p. 100.

times wrought, the restricted understanding of the functions
of prose in drama which his practice indicates, as well as the
occasional triumphs of his dramatic prose when it is seen in
contrast with a blank verse that aspires without achieving—all
these features suggest that a special interest may attach to *The
Green Helmet*, the one play of this period which escapes from
these dilemmas.

I do not think that there can be any doubt that *The Golden
Helmet*, the predecessor in prose of *The Green Helmet*, lacks the
bravura and brilliancy of the later play. The verse is much more
effective in setting the scene and creating the atmosphere;
Yeats breaks up single speeches into dialogues, cuts out the
rather vapid songs for the three wives and concentrates them all
in a fine chant for Emer alone ('It has got some passion in it at
last'),[8] and he manages the climax of the play much better.
Mrs Vendler's limiting judgement that *The Green Helmet* is 'a
fairly trivial comment on . . . literary and political conten-
tiousness',[9] while it does point at one meaning in the play,
applies more to *The Golden Helmet*, which contains specific
references, afterwards eliminated, to the 'quarrels of Ireland',[1]
and it overlooks the degree to which the hero Cuchulain represents the new mask of fiery energy, of 'creative joy separated
from fear', which Yeats, as Ellmann has pointed out,[2] was now
trying to assume in a pose deliberately antithetical to his own
'timidity'. The gesture has the deepest interest for the formation of the style during this transitional period, and *The Green
Helmet* is in some ways the plainest and richest clue to the
transformation.

'I detest the Renaissance because it made the human mind
inorganic', Yeats wrote; 'I adore the Renaissance because it
clarified form and created freedom.'[3] Yeats's ambivalent attitude towards the Renaissance[4] is focused in his uneasiness about
the characteristic Shakespearian measure. It is the measure of the
mid-point of our civilization, which scattered anonymity and the
ancient strengths of epic unity and inclusiveness, and prepared

8. *Letters*, p. 546 (8 January 1910).
9. *Yeats's Vision and the Later Plays* (1963), p. 203.
1. *Collected Works*, iv.77.   2. *Yeats: the Man and the Masks* (1949), pp. 179 ff.
3. *On the Boiler* (1938), p. 27.
4. Most recently discussed in Edward Engelberg, *The Vast Design* (1964), especially
chap. i.

the way for a consciousness of the individual self that thenceforward dwindled into abstraction: 'Shakespeare shattered
the symmetry of verse and of drama that he might fill them
with things and their accidental relations to one another.'[5]
Yeats had succumbed by following his example, not least in
admitting the conjunction of the two harmonies of verse and
prose within the plays; *The Green Helmet*, like the earlier *Wanderings of Oisin*, is an attempt, as I have written elsewhere, to 'get
back beyond the Renaissance into a world of imaginative unities,
heroic or medieval'.[6] It has this in common with other 'Arthur-
ian' literature of our time (Cuchulain's story here of course is
also Gawain's or Perceval's), such as *The Waste Land*. As he said
at the end of his life:

When I wrote in blank verse I was dissatisfied; my vaguely medieval
Countess Cathleen fitted the measure, but our Heroic Age went better,
or so I fancied, in the ballad metre of *The Green Helmet*. There was something in what I felt about Deirdre, about Cuchulain, that rejected the
Renaissance and its characteristic metres, and this was a principal reason
why I created in dance plays the form that varies blank verse with lyric
metres. When I speak blank verse and analyse my feelings, I stand at a
moment of history when instinct, its traditional songs and dances, its
general agreement, is of the past. I have been cast up out of the whale's
belly...[7]

It is the 'general agreement' which Yeats, like Eliot, valued, the
dream of a society 'hooped together, brought / Under a rule'.
Such a dream was to be the object of much disillusioned, tragic,
and finally joyous amplification in the major poems from
'September, 1913' to 'Lapis Lazuli'. Beneath its immediate
reference to the 'quarrels of Ireland', *The Green Helmet* is preoccupied with this larger theme. The hero in this play attempts
to act in the first instance as a reconciling agent; he plans, like
the dreamers of 'Nineteen Hundred and Nineteen', to 'bring
the world under a rule', into a 'semblance of peace'. By combining the two stories which he found in *Cuchulain of Muirthemne*, about 'Bricriu's Feast, and the War of Words' and 'The
Championship of Ulster', Yeats arranged them so as to make
possible the newly invented episode that fills the centre of the

5. 'The Autumn of the Body', *Essays and Introductions* (1961), p. 192.
6. *Yeats* (1963), p. 25.   7. *Essays and Introductions*, pp. 523–4.

play: Cuchulain's attempt to turn the Red Man's helmet (which is a prize designedly offered by him in his Até-like role of Bricriu, maker of discord) into a drinking-cup to be shared by all. The Red Man knows, what Cuchulain cannot know, that this attempt must fail. It must fail because the society depicted in the play is one of 'weasels fighting in a hole', whose precarious balance will always break down into disordered jealousy and frantic recrimination, and which, so far from becoming coherent and united in the face of an unnatural intrusion from the darkness outside, will be driven by it into a fearful distraction. But that is not the only reason for failure. A second reason is that it is the Red Man's business, as it was the dramatist's, to choose a hero. Like Shakespeare, the Red Man brings not 'degree, priority, and place, / Insisture, course, proportion, season, form', not 'the unity and married calm of states', but an 'image of heroic self-possession', a personality that seems but the stronger because the social poppy has seeded, the pea-pod burst—brings, in short, one of those 'sundry magnifications [which] became each in turn the centre of some Elizabethan play'.[8] In Yeats's plays the name of this magnification is Cuchulain. We do not need to go into Yeats's distinction between character and personality to be able to assert that upon Cuchulain attend all the paradoxes and contradictions that associate with the Yeatsian hero. In *The Green Helmet* the Red Man's final speech ranks Cuchulain with those Shakespearian characters who, in Yeats's view, do not 'break up their lines to weep', who are mastered and impregnated by pure joy, and who possess 'an energy so noble, so powerful, that we laugh aloud and mock, in the terror or the sweetness of our exaltation, at death and oblivion'.[9] Cuchulain, who has striven in the play for another kind of unity, is obliged to submit to being chosen:

> And I cho[o]se the laughing lip
> That shall not turn from laughing whatever rise or fall,
> The heart that grows no bitterer although betrayed by all,
> The hand that loves to scatter, the life like a gambler's throw;
> And these things I make prosper . . .[1]

8. The references are to *Autobiographies*, pp. 47, 291, 193, and also of course to *Troilus and Cressida*, i.iii.86 ff.

9. *Essays and Introductions*, pp. 253, 322.

1. *The Green Helmet and other Poems* (1910), p. 33.

So speaks the dramatist, the inventor of Cuchulain. And we are left to infer, within *The Green Helmet* at least, that the hero restores the unity of his shattered society not, as he had designed, by sharing the prize with everyone, but by being acknowledged as everyone's Champion. It is a magnification, but it is also a second best. Cuchulain, impelled by his own courage and the needs of his distracted and deracinated world, has become, however unwillingly, the great Shakespearian personality, the precarious individual whose final role will be the magnificent one of presiding in tragic joy over the destruction of civilization, when 'Hector is dead and there's a light in Troy':

In the spiritual dawn when Raphael painted the Camera della Segnatura, and the Medician Popes dreamed of uniting Christianity and Paganism, all that was sacred with all that was secular, Europe might have made its plan, begun the solution of its problems, but individualism came instead; the egg, instead of hatching, burst.[2]

The Green Helmet is a representation of a moment of this kind. But here it is happening not so much in history (and only marginally in the history of modern Ireland) but because the dramatist, like the Red Man and like Shakespeare, needs a hero. The kind of society the hero is in, in *The Green Helmet*, and the kind of society the dramatist is in, both enforce this need. So also does Yeats's interpretation of the literary history of that society, the world of the Shakespearian drama and the personal lyric, a literature that is, in Yeats's view, still working out the consequences of its choice of individualism instead of unity, of what might almost be termed its submission to Shakespeare. Yeats was too great a writer, and too aware of contemporaneity, to decline to meet this literature on its own ground, at the point in his own time to which it had developed. He could not work anonymously, or write ballads or contrive rituals; he could not, as so many minor writers have done, in his own day and before, compose Arthurian-dream epics which refuse to acknowledge that the Globe was ever built, that Donne was born, that Hobbes, and Newton, and Locke had 'with labour pushd / Oblique the Centric Globe'; like Dryden, he was too sensible to pursue such youthful ambitions as that of 'getting our heroic age into verse'. But in working out the consequences, he also worked continu-

2. *Essays and Introductions*, pp. 467–8.

ally towards a fresh awareness of what had been lost. In the ironies and frustrations attendant upon Cuchulain, in his struggle for unity of being in *At the Hawk's Well*, or his struggle against the supersession of his heroic identity—a thing both glorious and foolish—in the other plays, Yeats traced the fortunes of 'personality' in a manner that would express his reasons for detesting it, and for adoring it. And he contrived a series of plays which acknowledge Shakespeare and the Elizabethans but at the same time incorporate into their forms ritual and ballad and 'those traditional songs and dances' which express not personality but impersonality, the irruption of the supernatural, the overmastering of the individual—all that region of life which blank verse, the supreme speech in Shakespeare's hands for the definition and discrimination of individuality, had, in his view, closed off from the theatre.

It is in relation to this general development that balance and combination of elements may be discerned in *The Green Helmet*. The play represents the initiation of the Cuchulain 'personality', issuing forth from a world that has broken to pieces; but it is written in a 'heroic' line, a measure that escapes from blank verse. It escapes, too, from that other Shakespearian device, the alternation of the two harmonies. There is much in the play that could be fitted to this device: the clownishness of some of the characters, the raucous behaviour of wives and stable-boys, might have been stressed against the terror and the intensity of Cuchulain and the Red Man. Though he had, as we have seen, so far achieved little enough with the device, it is doubtful if he avoided it here because he was dissatisfied with it—he was to use it in the mixed version of *The Hour-Glass* within a couple of years. Rather, he wanted an unbroken heroic measure for his heroic farce because *The Green Helmet* acknowledges, as *On Baile's Strand* had not, his increasing imaginative awareness of the unity and community of his imaginary pre-Renaissance heroic society. Such a society has no business to be drawing a line between the speech of the princes and that of their servants:

It is certain that before the counting-house had created a new class and a new art without breeding and without ancestry, and set this art and this class between the hut and the castle, and between the hut and the cloister, the art of the people was as closely mingled with the art of the coteries as was the speech of the people that delighted in rhythmical animation, in idiom, in images, in words full of far-off suggestion, with the unchanging speech of the poets.[3]

It is a fitting paradox that in *The Green Helmet* the unbroken line is being used to give speech to a society which, through refusing Cuchulain's semblance of peace, discloses that 'personality' whose emergence in the hero signalizes the breakdown of the society; as the old order explodes into whirling fragments, each has the energy, the *vigore* and *virtú*, of the great Renaissance individual; but the fragments of a bursting shell have no inherent power that will keep them in the sky.

In *The Green Helmet*, although all is strain, the explosion has not yet occurred. The heroic line is still a bounding and containing line. It is flexible, a single verse-form 'in which everything can be said that has to be said', and it is the last of Yeats's poetic plays of which this is true—until we come to *Purgatory*, the one play in which, according to Eliot, he 'solved his problem of speech in verse, and laid all his successors under obligation to him'.[4] I do not of course think that this means, in respect of this 'problem' even, that we can ignore all the plays that intervene between *The Green Helmet* and *Purgatory*; and Eliot himself was, in an earlier essay, rather more generous to Yeats.[5] But it is true that in this matter *The Green Helmet* glimpsed a solution which was, for many reasons, to be postponed for a long time. Yeats's fourteener is a line which is closer to modern colloquial speech than most of his blank verse and most of his prose. It only requires to be split into two to look much less 'heroic', even with its rhymes (which of course vanish in *Purgatory*):

> So you too think me in earnest
> In wagering poll for poll!
> A drinking joke and a gibe
> And a juggler's feat, that is all,
> To make the time go quickly—
> For I am the drinker's friend,
> The kindest of all Shape-Changers
> From here to the world's end.

---

3. *Essays and Introductions*, pp. 10–11. 4. *On Poetry and Poets*, pp. 74, 78.
5. *The Permanence of Yeats* (ed. Hall and Steinmann, 1950), pp. 340–1.

Compare these three and four stress lines to *Purgatory*:

> Do not let him touch you! It is not true
> That drunken men can not beget,
> And if he touch he must beget
> And you must bear his murderer.
> Deaf! Both deaf! If I should throw
> A stick or a stone they would not hear;
> And that's a proof my wits are out.[6]

It is, in some ways, a great misfortune for Yeats's reputation as a poetic dramatist in the age of Eliot that his discovery of the Japanese Noh not long after the composition of *The Green Helmet* made it easier for him *not* to follow up what that play had begun: the forging of a measure which would avoid the conflict between two or more harmonies which, Eliot considers, jolts the audience into an awareness that people talking poetry are not real people. Yeats had to choose between running this risk, for which he has paid in full, and forgoing his wish to 'transport the audience violently from one plane of reality to another'[7]—the subject of most of his plays, for which he has not yet been fully judged at all. In *The Green Helmet*, at least, Yeats's irregular fourteener does all that it is required to do. The passage, for example, which depicts Cuchulain's entry into the house modulates effectively from comic bravado to bad temper, from swelling anger to dreaming evocation; it bandies the broken lines about between the speakers of dialogue much more effectively than anything in *The Shadowy Waters*, and, like the prose of *On Baile's Strand*, this verse is underpinned by movement and action upon the stage as Cuchulain thrusts Laegaire aside, and examines the table, and sits down to drink from the un-tasted wine.

It is a final irony, perhaps, that Yeats may have owed this 'heroic', this pre-Renaissance line, more to Morris than to anyone else. A line two or three syllables longer, the line of *Sigurd the Volsung*, is for Yeats, as a passage in *Wheels and Butter-flies* makes clear, inseparably associated with the hero and the heroic act. Yeats used it for Book III of *The Wanderings of Oisin*, that part of the poem where the hero is most himself in his assertion of his identity and most clearly foreshadows similar

6. *The Green Helmet and other Poems*, pp. 16–17; *Collected Plays* (1960), p. 686.
7. Eliot, p. 74.

assertions in the later plays—Cuchulain's 'He comes! Cuchulain, son of Sualtim, comes!' in *At the Hawk's Well*, or Congal's 'I am King Congal . . .' in *The Herne's Egg*. The long line, even when it is modified in *The Green Helmet*, is the heroic line, and the heroic act

as it descends through tradition, is an act done because a man is himself, because, being himself, he can ask nothing of other men but room amid remembered tragedies; a sacrifice of himself to himself, almost, so little may he bargain, of the moment to the moment.[8]

The hero is now 'personality' in full flower, tragic because he is a fragment of the exploding shell; his world contains nothing but himself, his society has vanished in the flare. So, at the end of *The Green Helmet*, those who stand and watch, whether reconciled or unreconciled, are forgotten; the final lines recall 'remembered tragedies' and are focused upon the hero, cast up out of the whale's belly:

The hand that loves to scatter; the life like a gambler's throw;
And these things I make prosper, till a day come that I know,
When heart and mind shall darken that the weak may end the strong,
And the long-remembering harpers have matter for their song.

8. *Wheels and Butterflies* (1934), p. 75.

IO

The hero on the World Tree
Yeats's plays

Yeats's biggest theoretical justification of Poetic Drama related
to his attempt at 'the deliberate creation of a kind of Holy
City in the imagination'. He hoped that his work as a playwright
would return his audience to some source of imaginative coherence—the *Anima Mundi*, the Common Memory—and that
players and spectators could commune in a dance that myster-
iously acted forth his ideal condition of Unity of Culture; and
he had a lot of experiences and arguments which demonstrate
why this ought to happen. T. S. Eliot seems to have insisted on
Poetic Drama for reasons which are not perhaps fundamentally
very different from Yeats's. 'The human soul', he wrote, 'in
intense emotion strives to express itself in verse'; and elsewhere
he argued that the characters on the stage must 'somehow
disclose . . . a deeper reality than that of the plane of most of our
conscious living . . . underneath the vacillating or infirm character, the indomitable unconscious will; and underneath the
resolute purpose of the planning animal, the victim of circumstance and the doomed or sanctified being.' This resembles
Yeats's distinction between 'character' and 'personality', and
Eliot might almost be describing the chief personages of *Deirdre*
or *The Death of Cuchulain*. I do not know about Christopher Fry's
principles; perhaps he wrote his plays in verse for reasons of
decorum—the kind of figurative wit in which his characters indulge would sound odder still if they were speaking
prose.

Yeats, Eliot, and Fry were the only poetic dramatists whose
work at any time looked even faintly like winning a place in the
theatre of prose. And now that whole movement of the first half-
century seems quite dead and done for by what has happened in

First published in *English*, xv, 1965, 169–72.

the last ten years. The Poetic Drama now merits its self-conscious capitals, like Speaking to the Psaltery or Furry Dancing. It seems only too probable that, so far as their plays are concerned, Eliot and Yeats will soon be folded in a single party with Gordon Bottomley. To do Eliot justice, it was not he but his commentators who worried so much about the business of justifying verse on the modern stage: he was more interested in the problems of technique. It was Yeats who did the worrying. An absence of justificatory worry characterizes the behaviour of the modern dramatists. Pinter's works are 'the true poetic drama of our time'. They discover, says Mr John Russell Taylor, 'the strange sublunary poetry which lies in the most ordinary object at the other end of a microscope'. (Is this, I wonder, merely a scientifically up-to-date version of the *anima mundi* once more?) And, after a course of Raymond Williams, Denis Donoghue, Ronald Peacock, and the other commentators who were so laboriously busy about *justification* in the wash of the vessel of Poetic Drama, it is with a cry of relief that one sees John Arden cutting through a multitude of cobwebs:

I think the use of formal verse and straightforward vernacular prose in juxtaposition is quite a good solution even in a modern play. If people are speaking formal verse with lines that rhyme, the audience does not have to worry whether it sounds natural or not. They are talking poetry. It's with the half-and-half thing that one is in trouble.

Certainly *The Happy Haven*, with the verses assigned to James J. Crape and Mrs Phineus, makes Arden's point admirably. The Elizabethans would have understood.

But, Yeats might have asked, can such a device be used in tragedy? In spite of incursions into comedy, tragedy was his real interest—tragedy with the 'joyful' ending, as preferred by his theory, if possible; but otherwise tragedy of desolate reality like *On Baile's Strand* or *Purgatory* (*The Player Queen* and *The Herne's Egg* manage to be desolate and funny at the same time—a considerable achievement). If that suggests the *variety* of his plays, let it be stressed again with a look at the variety of the verse-management too. Yeats used Arden's device; he might almost be said to have begun with it: his first play, *The Countess Cathleen*, relies somewhat on songs, and Yeats took a good deal of trouble with them. So do the later plays of the first Abbey

period (up to about 1906). But in these plays the songs are set not
against 'straightforward vernacular prose' but against a specially
still and purified blank verse that even so constantly afflicts
us with a Jacobean aftertaste. Technically speaking, we could
perhaps plot Yeats's whole career as a playwright as an oscillation between the 'half-and-half thing' and bolder kinds of
management, of which Arden's device is only one. The refine-
ment and self-conscious simplicity of the early plays disappeared
in *The Green Helmet* (1910), a pivotal work, the first play in which
Yeats totally abandoned blank verse for a rhyming 'heroic'
fourteener in which 'everything can be said that has to be said';
there are no abrupt shifts between high tragic style and comic
vernacular; instead, they modulate into one another. Yeats had
discovered one of Eliot's laws thirty years before its time. But
he did not follow up this discovery—Pound came in with the
Japanese Noh instead. Yeats's next plays exploit the *difference*
between 'formal verse with lines that rhyme' and blank verse.
Blank verse, the characteristic Renaissance measure, became for
Yeats the speech of the lonely individuated being who seeks to
realize himself ever more powerfully in a Renaissance and post-
Renaissance society that separates man from man; but lyric song,
often deeply tinged with folksong and ballad, became the 'ghostly voice, an unvariable possibility, an unconscious norm'. It
continually reminds the *dramatis personae* of what they have lost,
cast up out of what Yeats described as the 'whale's belly' of
Unity of Culture, or promises them an amazing transcendence
of their limits. Yet this prosodic theory, which was apparently
applied many years before it was explicitly enunciated at the
end of his life, meant that blank verse had to continue to serve
as a vernacular, and it never did so satisfactorily because Yeats
found it hard, as had all his predecessors, to escape from the
echo of Shakespeare. (It was ironically appropriate that Shakespeare, the greatest of *Renaissance* writers, proved the source of
this frustration.) Only on the margins of *The Resurrection* (1931)
and in the translations of Sophocles did he set plain prose against
lyric speech of thaumaturgic obscurity. Finally, however, in the
late plays of *The Herne's Egg* and *Purgatory*, having largely escaped from the Noh in its turn, he invented a three-and-four-
stress/syllabic line of wide scope and originality. This was the
logical consequence of what he had done in *The Green Helmet*. It

was with *Purgatory* in mind that Eliot spoke of Yeats solving the 'problem of speech in verse, and [laying] all his successors under obligation to him'.

If Arden is right, the 'solution' led nowhere. Yeats himself, in any case, had no time in which to exploit it, and his last play of all, *The Death of Cuchulain*, resurrects blank verse once more. One may be filled with a vast regret that Yeats didn't write his plays in prose and put in lyric measures whenever his Muse instructed him to do so. Even this, presumably, would not have saved his plays from their current neglect on the stage: they are too short, their subjects are recondite, and everybody now agrees with George Moore (though they would hate it to be thought that they were doing *that*): Irish mythology is a bit of a joke. Perhaps a spurt of interest could be induced if it were cogently demonstrated by a competent critic how existentialist the plays are, all depicting what René Wellek has called (not with reference to Yeats) 'agonizing revelations of reality in moments of supreme decisions, in "limiting situations"': Cuchulain and the Witches, Cuchulain and the Hawk Dancer, Emer's renunciation, the Young Man and the Ghost of the Traitors, the Old Man and the Ghost of the Mother.

So Yeats's plays emerge for revaluation during this centenary year (if revaluation they are to be accorded) into a cold climate. Mr J. I. M. Stewart has treated them with indulgent patronization through many pages of his volume in the *Oxford History of English Literature*, writing with all the authority that that sad and unrisen project confers, and Professor Donald Davie has declared himself satisfied. Mrs Helen H. Vendler, the author of one of the most interesting books on Yeats for some years, uses the plays as a quarry for digging out of Yeats's poetic theory, but can hardly find adjectives enough to express her discontent with their literary qualities: negligible, thin, arid, trying, and so on. And Yeats's famous theatre is a ruin. But even if the plays are never performed again, except at the Sligo Summer School, they will continue to be written about because the Yeats scholarly industry is just beginning to encompass them. We may expect many more books on their interpretation, their relation with the lyrics, their texts, and their theatrical history. It may be guessed that these books will arise out of admiration not for Yeats the playwright but for Yeats the poet, and this is as it should be. There is much in them that can illuminate that supreme achievement. I confess for my part that I would much like to have a properly ordered and fully documented study of the Irish literary movement in the days of Synge, Moore, Martyn, Lady Gregory, and the rest, as well as a similar study of the Abbey Theatre. Such works will be written in Ireland by Americans. May they come soon: there is a plethora of criticism and not very much good biography or history. These desires, it may be said, betray a deplorable taste for historicism and factualism at the cost of putting aside true judgement. It is, though, an evaluative act in itself to shrink from advocating the plays for their own sake if there is the slightest risk that such advocacy would distract the general reader of literature from the area on which his interest ought to be centred—on poems like 'Nineteen Hundred and Nineteen' and not on plays like *The Dreaming of the Bones*, on 'Among School Children' and not on *The Hour-Glass*. The plays may safely be left to the scholar whose speciality is Yeats, and there is no danger, so huge are the armies encamped upon that fruitful plain, that they will be overlooked. Probably the real danger comes from somewhere else, and is an aspect of the development of modern criticism: the tendency to turn Yeats into too much of a theoretician and aesthetic philosopher, to transform him into Yeats the Mind and oblige him to contribute all his various wealth to the process of juggling terms and concepts which signalizes the ambition of literary criticism to exalt itself into a general philosophy of life; amidst those fearful symmetries Yeats the poet and Yeats the playwright will alike cease to exist.

Perhaps, though, at whatever risk, Yeats's plays need to be correlated, as his poems are being correlated, with his ambitions for them and with his ways of composing them, and then to be estimated. He was obsessed with the heroic character and the heroic act. 'In literature we need completed things', he wrote; he saw the heroic personages as 'complete arcs' from the vantage-point of the artist, whom he thought doomed to be an uncompleted arc, the unfinished man and his pain. For him, the heroic act was the act that combined the greatest degree of self-sacrifice with the greatest degree of self-realization. His emblematic reference for this was not to Celtic but to Norse mythology, to the Elder Edda: 'the sacrifice of himself to himself' of Odin who, pierced with a spear, hung for nine days and nights on the World Tree, the ash Yggdrasill:

> I know I hung
> on the windswept Tree,
> through nine days and nights.
> I was stuck with a spear
> and given to Odin,
> myself given to myself . . .

That is why Yeats could not accept Jesus, whom Milton held 'most perfect hero', for the voluntary self-sacrifice of Odin is performed not in order to save men but in order to win the knowledge of the secret runes:

> They helped me neither
> by meat nor drink.
> I peered downward,
> I took up the runes,
> screaming, I took them—
> then I fell back.

Yeats's heroes tend towards this condition; their destiny is often to be cheated of, or to refuse, its accomplishment. His tragedies and comedies enact themselves in this region, at the foot of the World Tree.

11

The plays

I

As early as 1900 Yeats was able to express even the past and future history of the drama in terms of widening and contracting gyres. 'The drama', he wrote,

has need of cities that it may find men in sufficient numbers, and cities destroy the emotions to which it appeals, and therefore the days of the drama are brief and come but seldom. It has one day when the emotions of cities still remember the emotions of sailors and husbandmen and shepherds and users of the spear and the bow . . . and it has another day, now beginning, when thought and scholarship discover their desire. In the first day, it is the art of the people; and in the second day . . . it is the preparation of a priesthood. It may be, though the world is not old enough to show us any example, that this priesthood will spread their religion everywhere, and make their Art the Art of the people. (*Essays and Introductions*, 1961, pp. 167–8)

This is an accurate enough sketch of the historical principles that guided Yeats's own practice as a playwright. Playwrights of the great days traditionally selected their locations from the metropolis, where palace, castle, and market jostle for the best sites. The Victorian theatre chose its locations at random; no style seems to have established itself, and certainly nothing that could convey to their inhabitants the real sense of what was happening to their cities. There are records of the absurd labours that sometimes went into making Shakespeare accurate: *The Winter's Tale* with Pyrrhic dances contrived from Nuttall's *Classical and Archaeological Dictionary*, and Mamilius drawing a toy cart based on a terracotta prototype in the British Museum; 'Mr Punch has it upon authority to state that the Bear at present running in Oxford Street in *The Winter's Tale* is an archaeological

First published in *An Honoured Guest: New Essays on W. B. Yeats* (ed. Denis Donoghue and J. R. Mulryne, London, Edward Arnold, 1965), pp. 143–64.

copy from the original bear of Noah's Ark.'[1] When Shaw began *Widowers' Houses*, when, four years later in 1889, Yeats met Maud Gonne at his father's house in Bedford Park and sat down to write *The Countess Cathleen* for her, English playwrights had, for all serious purposes, been for some time locked up in the middle-class drawing-room. Even Shaw did not for some years do much to release them from their bondage. Yeats wrote in 1904 about a performance of Ibsen's *Ghosts*:

All the characters seemed to be less than life-size; the stage . . . seemed larger than I had ever seen it. Little whimpering puppets moved here and there in the middle of that great abyss. Why did they not speak out with louder voices or move with freer gestures? What was it that weighed upon their souls perpetually? Certainly they were all in prison, and yet there was no prison. (*Plays and Controversies*, p. 122)

And two years later he wrote of the elaboration of the scene and technique in the modern theatre in an essay which is full of his suspicion of the *painted* stage, of the kind of thing which Charles Kean had done so successfully at the Oxford Street Theatre to *The Winter's Tale*:

The theatre grows more elaborate, developing the player at the expense of the poet, developing the scenery at the expense of the player, always increasing the importance of whatever has come to it out of the mere mechanism of a building or the interests of a class, specialising more and more, doing whatever is easiest rather than what is most noble, and shaping imaginations before the footlights as behind, that are stirred to excitement that belongs to it and not to life. (*Plays and Controversies*, p. 178)

'Puppets in prison', the 'mechanism of a building or the interests of a class'—clearly, more than one act of liberation was necessary. The first and last and the most important for Yeats was to make the play reach at 'life' by freeing itself more and more from elaboration that only mimicked the surface of life. This, with all its need for definition, for an accurate understanding of what he meant by the 'deeps' and what he meant by the superficies, was the most complex task which Yeats undertook as a playwright, and the one most liable to backfire in unexpected ways, to turn out to be a serpent with its tail in its mouth after

1. Quoted in W. M. Merchant, *Shakespeare and the Artist* (1959), p. 216.

all. If that story could be rightly written, we might have the whole truth about Yeats the playwright. We need only to quote his late confession from 'The Circus Animals' Desertion':

> Players and painted stage took all my love,
> And not those things that they were emblems of,
> (*Collected Poems*, p. 392)

in order to realize that the fascination of 'theatre business, management of men' was something that often distracted him from 'life'. His suspicions of the stage as a place where the single vision of the poet had to master, if it could, the wayward behaviour, the quarrels, and the merely minor accomplishments of fragmentary men and hysterical woman were complicated by the deep appeal which all that fuss and fury made to something histrionic and gregarious in himself. He was far less successful in making his various roles—as Irishman, or theatre director, or mage, or courtly lover—serve his plays than he was in forging them all into the poems' unities of being; and the plays are therefore smaller things by far. Yet there is no doubt that his attempt to discover 'life' by means of a refashioned and liberated drama made abundant calls upon his genius, which was not always unresponsive. The complexities of that particular act of liberation may for the moment, though, be put aside while we examine the simpler matter of the 'interests of a class' and its terrible symbol, that stifling drawing-room.

For Yeats was right in foreseeing, at a time when the Abbey Theatre had only just begun, that the devotion to Irish subject matter, the mere shift of the location from London, with its Anglo-Saxon passion for the abstract and the ideal, its disordered subjection to a kaleidoscope of international, intellectual fashions (as it seemed to him), would solve the problem of the drawing-room. 'Let a man turn his face to us', he wrote, 'and talk of what is near to our hearts, Irish Kings and Irish Legends and Irish Countrymen' (*Plays and Controversies*, p. 111). It was the last of these three that mattered most in practice; there is no doubt that in bringing with them their inevitable ambience of Dublin streets and Mayo cottages the Irish countrymen put an end to the West End drawing-room so far as the real history of the drama is concerned. 'Our opportunity in Ireland', Yeats wrote in 1905, is not that our playwrights have more talent—it is possible that they have less than the workers in an old tradition—but that the necessity of putting a life that has not hitherto been dramatised into their plays excludes all these types which have had their origin in a different social order. (*Plays and Controversies*, p. 143)

The consequential danger—that the plays would become merely propaganda for the Nationalist cause—he foresaw just as acutely and evaded as adroitly. For the time being, at least, it did not happen (though how much of the credit is due to the fact that the Irish theatre was then ultimately overseen by an official of the English government it would be impolitic to inquire). 'The public life of Athens', Yeats reminded *The United Irishman* and kindred spirits, with that touch of resonant arrogance that is one of the glories of his mind,

found its chief celebration in the monstrous caricature of Aristophanes, and the Greek nation was so proud, so free from morbid sensitiveness, that it invited the foreign ambassadors to the spectacle. (*Plays and Controversies*, p. 150)

The greatest of Irish comedies, *The Playboy of the Western World*, and the greatest of Irish tragedies (if tragedy it is), *Juno and the Paycock*, are there to assure us that he was prophetically right on all counts. 'Somebody must teach reality and justice.'[2]

These plays are far finer than any that Yeats could achieve. Yet, within this same context of the discovery of new locations, an interest still attaches to his own drawing-room plays, *Where There Is Nothing* and *The Words upon the Window-Pane*. Both are, of course, attempts to *faire tordre le cou* of the drawing-room, to smash or explode it. Nearly thirty years separate them (1902–30), and they have the additional interest of showing how much Yeats had advanced, by 1930, in the rather complex operation of making a dramatic form turn its sword in its own proper entrails. *Where There Is Nothing* begins, if not in a drawing-room, in the equally dismal setting of a croquet lawn, a setting which the hero endeavours to dismantle as he takes his way out on to the tinkers' roads, seeking to become the 'beggarman of all the ages', to 'express himself in "life"'. But, apart from its other defects, which were sufficiently recognized by its author, the play makes too many concessions to the form which it is trying

2. *Autobiographies* (1955), p. 562.

to destroy; its naturalism strives against the hero's exalted vision and turns it all into a rhetoric which awakens distrust and unbelief. In *The Words upon the Window-Pane*, on the other hand, Yeats momentarily shocks us into suspending our disbelief by, precisely, introducing the Furies into the drawing-room—the device that T. S. Eliot was to repudiate and Yeats continually to desire just because he hoped that it would 'transport the audience violently from one plane of reality to another',[3] or, in his own, and not Eliot's, words, would induce 'the sense of spiritual reality [that] comes . . . from some violent shock', since 'Belief comes from shock and is not desired.'[4] In the centre of a naturalistic problem play about spiritualism he sets an image of discarnate suffering, and unites us violently to that image not by rhetoric but by a single gesture when the medium, Mrs Henderson, cries out in Swift's voice and phrase as the curtain falls. Of all Yeats's plays, for an audience still attuned to the naturalistic tradition as reinforced by Eliot, *The Words upon the Window-Pane* is the one that most deserves to be judged in the theatre and will best serve to give an appetite for working through the *Collected Plays*.

And yet the violence which Yeats had in his fashion wrought upon drawing-room expectations was already by 1930 something of an anachronism. The Abbey had taken the course which he expected, growing ever more 'objective with the objectivity of the office and the workshop' (*Plays and Controversies*, p. 206), its locations chosen from cottage or streets and not from the English house. Synge had produced the perfected form of the 'peasant play', and O'Casey had brought the movement to full maturity by returning it to its megapolitical and Jonsonian centre with the one indisputable masterpiece of the whole repertoire. *Juno and the Paycock* is a great expression of 'the emotions of cities', and the degree of its objectivity, in both the Yeatsian and the ordinary senses, can easily be measured if one consults the appropriate pages in *Inishfallen, Fare Thee Well*. The only play which Yeats set in a city offers a startling contrast to *Juno*, with which it is almost exactly contemporary. Yeats had told Lady Gregory some years earlier, now that the time had come for him to leave the Abbey because the plays had turned

3. T. S. Eliot, *On Poetry and Poets* (1957), p. 74.
4. *Wheels and Butterflies* (1934), p. 110; *A Vision* (1961), p. 53.

towards objectivity, and the players had begun to copy their old grandmothers in Aran, that he sought the theatre's anti-self; and *The Player Queen* may be said to be the anti-self of *Juno*. Its two scenes, an open space at the meeting of streets and the throne-room of a palace, return us to the city of power; but this city is a comic emblem of a civilization which is collapsing, as the gyre expands, in preparation for a second coming and the birth of a new era; the heroine is an actress who plays queens' parts, but would prefer to be a real queen and so have power over the city. In the process of 'mocking his own thought', thought which had by now contrived to crystallize into almost credal pattern, Yeats's intimations of the anti-mask and the gyres (both of which originate in the 1890s), he has produced, as Mrs Vendler has said, something resembling 'a chapter from *A Vision* read with an eyebrow cocked'.[5] From the confusion of allegorical cross-currents Mrs Vendler has teased out those elements in the story which relate to the fortunes of the *poète maudit* Septimus, his wife Decima, and his Daimon of poetic inspiration, the chaste, white Unicorn with whose undying image the poet longs to unite his muse, but never can. The fickle wife cannot, I think, be read, as she is by Mrs Vendler, purely as an allegory of the Muse; the play ends with her union not with the Daimon (whose coming is farcically and vengefully postponed) but with the Prime Minister and with the role of Queen, and the Unicorn is not only an aesthetic symbol but also the immanent beast-deity which was for Yeats a figuration about the character of a new cultural and religious dispensation. If beneath the characters of *The Player Queen* there obscurely lurks a very old story, about the cursed poet whom his Muse rejected, we must not forget that what Maud Gonne rejected him for was Nationalism and John MacBride the politician. As its location in the city suggests, the play is about kingdoms as well as about the poet; the strong elements in it of neo-classical intrigue, appropriate to this location, have savage undertones of tragedy, deriving not only from glimpses of the city's mob (turbulent and murderous as their city shudders towards a new age) but also from the final extrusion of Septimus from his place at the Queen's table and from the final frustration—we might almost say 'punishment'—of Decima. In devising her fate, Yeats

5. H. H. Vendler, *Yeats's Vision and the Later Plays* (1963), p. 128.

strikes almost the note with which, illiberally, he wrote of Eva Gore-Booth:

> I know not what the younger dreams—
> Some vague Utopia—and she seems,
> When withered old and skeleton-gaunt,
> An image of such politics.
>
> (*Collected Poems*, p. 263)

II

These themes remind us, leapfrogging, backwards this time, over the space of another thirty years, of the plays of the earliest period, and perhaps most of all of two that are specially significant, *The Countess Cathleen* and *The King's Threshold*, another play about whether the poet's vision has any place in the kingdom. Aleel, whose unchristened heart the Countess rejects in order that she may succour her people, Seanchan in *The King's Threshold*, who makes out of his rejection by the old world a visionary acceptance, joyful in tragedy, of life-in-death and death-in-life, and Septimus in *The Player Queen*, a comic parody of them both, who recognizes his kinship with the beggars, as Seanchan had, and has to deal with a tricky Muse who turns her face elsewhere —these persons march sufficiently with the process which, in Yeats's poems, transforms the vague speaker of *The Wind Among the Reeds*, a pre-Raphaelite voice in the head, into the seer of 'Byzantium' and the scarecrow of 'Among School Children'. To that series, others could be added: the Stroller/Swineherd of *The King of the Great Clock Tower* and *A Full Moon in March* is the proper issue of the *miraculeuse nuit nuptiale* of Forgael and Dectora in *The Shadowy Waters* so many years earlier. *The King's Threshold* has also to be taken more literally and impersonally, for it has one dimension as a Ruskinian plea for the recognition of a necessary link between the kind of society which is worth living in and the cultivation of approved arts:

> But why were you born crooked?
> What bad poet did your mothers listen to
> That you were born so crooked?
>
> (*Collected Plays*, p. 133)

The problem of how the 'wasteful virtues', heroical as well as

poetical—for the poet's 'book', as in the dedicatory poems to
Responsibilities, affirms his kinship with his chivalrous and reckless forebears—may be integrated into the ordered kingdom,
the cities of power, is a controlling theme in other plays of the
period, most clearly in the first of the Cuchulain series, *On
Baile's Strand*. Cuchulain's and Conchubar's dilemma in this play
is how to be both strong and wasteful, reasonable and poetical,
how to get things into order without losing the impulse to
create; how, in short, does the city attain Unity of Being? It was
Yeats's own personal and aesthetic dilemma, but it was also
interdependently, or so he thought, that of his society. This
should remind us that, when he writes in Berkeley's phrase of
'We Irish', speaks of 'the poems of civilisation', or describes the
ruin and rebirth of cultures in *A Vision*, he is not merely cultivating metaphors for aesthetic experience. In *On Baile's Strand*
Cuchulain's mind is got into disorder by Aoife's evil will; this
is an early intimation of Yeats's Conradian theme of what heroes
have to fight against, 'the breath of unknown powers that shape
our destinies',[6] the ghost, the evil spell, but, for Yeats as not for
Conrad, also a longed-for annulment of human intricacies:

> oblivion
> Even to quench Cuchulain's drouth,
> Even to still that heart.
> (*Collected Plays*, p. 293)

Conchubar unawares helps to do Aoife's work for her, and
Cuchulain's unity breaks down into madness, leaving the city
desolate and unguarded. Perhaps, since it has lost him, it is a
city without poets, too; when last we see it the beggars are running off to steal the chickens from the pot. *On Baile's Strand*
records in its hero a failure of the imagination to accomplish
the task assigned to it (that of recognizing and loving his son);
but the play nearest to it in date, *Deirdre*, though on a famous
tragic theme, is its counter-truth, for it describes in its heroine a
triumph of the loving imagination. Again, a Conrad parallel
suggests itself—the difference between Lord Jim and Axel
Heyst. Deirdre's mind ends in that state of high imaginative
order in which she recreates her self out of a paradigm of possible roles, and attains, for the space of time necessary to triumph

---

6. Conrad, *The Shadow-Line*.

over Conchubar's amorous will and her own fearful horror, unity of being. Of all Yeats's early plays, *Deirdre* is the one in which he came nearest to reaching down to 'life' by contriving a 'ritual of passion' which would, he hoped, induce the condition of tragic reverie where player and spectator draw upon the *anima mundi*, 'that soul which is alike in all men', the dikes between them broken down and drowned—the dikes, that is to say, of 'players and painted stage', the footlights, 'the mere mechanism of a building or the interests of a class'. And, in *Deirdre*, the poets *are* present to commemorate the scene:

> Now strike the wire, and sing to it a while,
> Knowing that all is happy, and that you know
> Within what bride-bed I shall lie this night.
>   (*Collected Plays*, p. 201)

Enough perhaps has been said to show that these early plays are not merely gestures in support of a cultural enterprise, the Irish National Theatre Company or the Abbey players, but central to the history of a great poet's mind. Yet nobody who wished to argue that any of these plays deserve a continued life within a less specialized context than the history of that mind, could possibly be persuasive. The poems in *The Green Helmet* of 1910 are the first that speak out; much more is this true of the plays of the same period. There are powerful fables, a few examples of vigorous words tied to the speaker and responsive to what else is on the stage with him; but all is vitiated by Yeats's very intensity and purity of purpose, which produces guarded and monotonous rhythms, pages of *carefully* organized periods that open out from time to time into figurative writing which curiously adds no extra dimension to the verse—the wallpaper suddenly blazes with a peacock, but it is a flat peacock still, and looks self-conscious amongst the grave arabesques that surround it.

Still, despite their now much-faded appearance, these are plays which were hammered out with a very intent consciousness of the stage at Yeats's command, the things and people on it; they are certainly not just lyrical exercises, and it is sometimes hard to tell, especially when we have in mind the prima-facie evidence of Yeats's continual revision in the light of actual experience in the theatre, how much their failure to survive is due to a change of taste and ideas in the theatre audience, which once took these plays and now, having in the meantime submitted to other masters, cannot take them. It is impossible to arrive at any general rules about what is and is not theatrically viable when audiences of our own day can sit enthralled by the soliloquies of actors buried up to their necks in mounds of earth. (Yeats anticipated this device early in his career when he suggested that barrels with castors on them might be used at rehearsals so that actors could forget their bodies and concentrate on their speech.) The playwright is the audience's master, and as he gives place to his successors they alter the notion of what is truly of the theatre, so that the accolade of 'theatrical craftsman' honorifically accorded to a writer by 'practical men of the theatre' is the most valuable part even of Shakespeare. Yeats's best theatrical effects are often muffled, though, by the literary wit and high circumlocution of his verse; it will not do to dismiss him as merely another lyric poet who wanted to turn the stage into a sounding-board for his own voice and has been suitably punished; but it is true that, while admitting that dramatic action must 'burn up the author's opinions', he found it hard to recognize that it must, in another sense, burn up a concern for purity of diction and articulated syntax. There were several reasons for the failure. His healthy reaction against the meaningless movements of naturalism, the endless 'dressing of the stage', the perpetual fidget, led him to value stillness and absence of gesture and to stress the primacy of speech—but it could not bear the weight of all that devoted concentration and authorial redaction. He wanted the speech, too, to be vivid but remain still and quiet; yet this quietness was not natural to him: did he not confess at the end of his life that 'Synge, Lady Gregory, and I were all instinctively of the school of Talma', which permits an actor 'to throw up an arm calling down the thunderbolts of Heaven' (*Essays and Introductions*, p. 529)? The resistance which he offered, for the sake of his ideology, to the gesture of melodrama resulted in a cautiously constrained and two-dimensional style, a demurely restricted vocabulary resembling the privative arabesques of *The Wind among the Reeds*. Furthermore, he was uneasy about blank verse, the Shakespearian, the Renaissance measure; his wish was to get back behind the Renaissance into a world of imagined heroic unities, away from that mid-point of civilization which he both adored and detested.[7] And yet he was saddled with blank verse, and in retrospect at least tolerated it only when he could 'put [it] out of joint' in *The Countess Cathleen*, for the Countess was 'vaguely medieval' and so could bear blank verse a little better than a character from heroic saga such as Cuchulain (*Essays and Introductions*, pp. 523–5). Always he seemed when writing blank verse to suffer from those varied constraints.

Again, if we apply the criterion of location, the early plays will seem a muddle—but one with some suggestive alleviations. In his settings Yeats has achieved no personal style, no recognizable locale, but shifts about opportunistically 'like some poor Arab tribesman and his tent'. The cottages and castles are simply naturalistic settings, specimens of the genre *cottage* or *castle*, just as the drawing-room in *The Second Mrs Tanqueray* is one of a thousand drawing-rooms. Yeats's later attempts to interfere with these settings in the interests of medieval keepings or bold, primary richness of effect—directing, for example, that the first scene in *The Countess Cathleen* should resemble a missal painting or putting his Fool and Blind Man into masks—do not make any fundamental alteration in the feeling that the location itself contributes nothing to the plays except a more or less appropriate background. In *The Shadowy Waters*, however, there is a more promising arrangement: 'The whole picture', Yeats wrote, 'as it were moves together—sky and sea and cloud are as it were actors' (*Letters*, p. 425). Consider, next, the difference between *On Baile's Strand* and *The King's Threshold*: Baile's strand itself signally fails to contribute anything to the play; but the King's threshold has been turned by Seanchan into an emblem which is also a playing-place; it is central to the inward meaning and the outward action of the play:

> there is a custom,
> An old and foolish custom, that if a man
> Be wronged, or think that he is wronged, and starve
> Upon another's threshold till he die,
> The common people, for all time to come,
> Will raise a heavy cry against that threshold,
> Even though it be the King's. (*Collected Plays*, p. 108)

7. *On the Boiler* (1938), p. 27.

To it everyone must come and towards it all the action of the play flows, and all the local colour, because it is a place where meanings are focused and decisions have to be taken, just as the house in *The Alchemist* is made the centre of a spider's web. There is nothing arbitrary here; place and story interlock. This surely is a great advantage, because a unity of elements which might translate itself into real unity of being must be a criterion for plays on the scale which Yeats normally composed; he had not much time to persuade us into a conviction of the decorum of his scene or to establish by slow gradations that place and people and story cohere, but must present such a conviction highly wrought almost as soon as the curtain rises. Yeats's aesthetic prepossessions, his whole endeavour to convert the vast design into the single image, all suggest that the interlocking of action and location may provide a clue to the presence of that kind of organic unity which his theatre appears naturally to demand. And gradually it becomes clear that one method of distinguishing his more successful plays from the others is to observe that in them the story is *about* the place, or, to put it in another way, that the characters have to come to just this place, and no other anywhere in the world, so that this story may happen. An analogy from the poems may reinforce the point: in those poems which he invests with a sense of the sacred and unique character of the locale—such as 'I walked among the seven woods of Coole' (significantly linked to *The Shadowy Waters* as its dedication), other Coole poems ('The Wild Swans', 'Coole Park, 1929', and so on), 'In Memory of Major Robert Gregory', 'Easter 1916', 'A Prayer for My Daughter', 'In Memory of Eva Gore-Booth', and a number of others up to 'Under Ben Bulben'—it is plain that the location is an actor, too. In these poems, in which the mind is transforming everything into a superhuman dream, it also preserves the places through all that transformation in the first freshness of their nature; Coole, the Tower, the mountains, and the streets of Dublin survive as felt actualities amidst all the reordering imposed upon them by Yeats's convictions, so that they seem freely to play their parts in the great mythology. Having studied that extraordinary Baedeker, we can recognize them if we go to them:

> Not such as are in Newton's metaphor,
> But actual shells of Rosses' level shore.
>
> (*Collected Poems*, p. 278)

Their participation in the total structure of the poems is analogous to the way in which the locations in some of Yeats's later
plays contribute to a unity of all their elements.

III

'The stage is any bare space before a wall . . .' This formula, from
At the Hawk's Well, the first of the plays written under the
influence of the Japanese Noh, is explicit or implicit in most of
those which succeed it. The patterned screen merely and tentatively suggests; the responsibility for evoking the location, its
uniqueness and meaning, is delegated to the characters within
the play:

> I call to the eye of the mind
> A well long choked up and dry
> And boughs long stripped by the wind
> > (*Collected Plays*, p. 208)

or

> The hour before dawn and the moon covered up;
> The little village of Abbey is covered up;
> The little narrow trodden way . . .
> > (*Collected Plays*, p. 434)

We are already caught into the process by which the voice, as an
element inside the work, invites us to see and imagine within a
context which it is actively creating, as Coole is created for us in
the poems by a mind brooding upon analogies and locational
meanings, preserving their freshness and yet organizing them
into a total vision or conviction. The four Plays for Dancers show
this, and show besides most clearly other elements at work,
demanding to be wrought together; and all these are present,
with varying degrees of completeness, in most of the later
plays.

First, in the four Plays for Dancers, there are the Musicians.
Because this is a drama seeking a deep of the mind, they are
charged not only with the task of setting the outward scene and
describing what the protagonists wear and look like and how
(if need be) they are to be dated, but also with enunciating a
theme as they unfold the curtain—woman's beauty in *The Only
Jealousy*, subjectivity and self-absorption in *Calvary*. As Yeats, in

later plays, stylized the superficies more and more, this enunciation became the most of what they have to do:

> *First Attendant.* What do we sing?
> *Second Attendant.* 'Sing anything, sing any old thing', said he.
>   (*Collected Plays*, p. 621)

The conventions adapted from the Noh were eagerly used to deepen and confirm earlier insights and practice. The poets had often been present to enlarge and deepen perspective in the first plays—Aleel in *The Countess Cathleen*, the Musicians in *Deirdre*, even, in their fashion, the Fool and the Blind Man; but now no attempt is made at a logical explanation of their presence in the scene; they come with the confident authority of an un-examined convention (like a rising curtain or the announcement of a theme in music), and like both these devices they withdraw us from everyday consciousness, and achieve what Yeats liked to call an appropriate distance from life. But 'distance' always suggests 'escape', whereas what the Musicians require of us is an act of concentration: the mind is to become 'a dark well, no surface, depth only' (*Autobiographies*, London, 1955, p. 292); we are to plunge down with images which recede from us into a more powerful life, to pass from the superficies to 'life', to 'reality', to the *anima mundi* where masquers and spectators commune in a dance.

The actual dance itself, of which both Yeats and his critics have made so much, is not, as I see it, the most important feature of his plays (many of the later ones, of course, once he had freed himself from the first absorption by the Noh, dispense with it altogether). Nearly all his plays work towards some moment of decision, enlightenment, or revelation, a peripeteia or 'turn'. This, as both Eric Bentley and Ronald Peacock have argued, is the point on which one must insist if one wishes to prove that Yeats is a playwright as well as a poet, and did succeed, as he wanted to, in showing events and not merely talking of them. He understood that his business as a playwright was not to meditate or to soliloquize but to contrive encounters from which a protagonist emerges changed, smitten as by the lightning-flash (the analogy is with artistic experience as Yeats described it),[8] his world or himself revealed to him by new knowledge or the

8. *Essays* (1924), pp. 503–4.

necessity of decision: 'Yeats is not only a dramatist but a classic dramatist'; 'A single, often loose, knot, untied with a single movement—such, for the most part, are his plays.'[9] The Noh plays, with which much of his work has structural affinity, helped Yeats to strengthen and define the climactic moments of revelation and spiritual enlightenment, but such moments are characteristically present in plays written long before he had heard of the Noh; indeed, a list of them would include *all* the early plays—*Cathleen ni Houlihan* itself, long his most famous and popular piece, is one of the best examples. It is these moments, and not the dance, which count, and the dance is not coincident with them, except in a marginal and qualified way. The stress on the dance, which is partly accounted for by Yeats's own emphases, but is more central to his poems and to his symbolist aesthetic than to his work as a playwright, has made these plays seem more remote and inhuman than they are. He scarcely ever, except in *A Full Moon in March*, succeeded in making the dance more than an illustration to the main action of the play; modern producers, chilled at the prospect of having to obtain the services of another Michio Ito or another Ninette de Valois, could well dispense with it altogether, shocking though the suggestion sounds. In *At the Hawk's Well* the dance is more truly vital to the climax than in any of the other plays, but even here it is Cuchulain's decision to *face* the hawk-dancer, in spite of the curse, that leads to his betrayal by his own courage, the ironic point made by the play about the character of the heroic act, 'a sacrifice of himself to himself'.[1] In *The Only Jealousy*, the dance of the Woman of the Sidhe is an accompaniment to a dialogue, and it is in the dialogue that the nature and burden of Cuchulain's choice are made explicit, nor has the dance in this play anything to do with Emer's own moment of decision; indeed it has not much more importance than the Woman's dress or the armour of the Ghost in *Hamlet*. In *The Dreaming of the Bones* and *Calvary* it has become a bit of subordinate styling. The dance is often an amplification of the gesture and appearance of a character and of his recondite meaning (the Woman of the Sidhe is after all a version of the Image), but the responsibility

9. E. Bentley in *The Permanence of Yeats* (ed. Hall and Steinmann, 1950), p. 239; R. Peacock, *The Poet in the Theatre* (1946), p. 99.

1. *Wheels and Butterflies*, p. 75.

for untying the knot rests still with the hero and not with the Ghost.

The moment of revelation, when the play blazes into 'miracle', is found in its purest and most theatrically impressive form in *The Resurrection*, when the masked Figure of Christ enters the room and all the long-calculated and converging lines of the play achieve their resolution. When the Greek touches the wounded side of his Idea, the questions that have been worried at during the play and the irrational intimations that have been throbbing beneath its surface are resolved and confirmed in a moment that has the blank and terrifying authority of the eyes of a Byzantine icon:

The Greek. It is the phantom of our master. Why are you afraid? He has been crucified and buried, but only in semblance, and is among us once more. [*The Hebrew kneels.*] There is nothing here but a phantom, it has no flesh and blood. Because I know the truth I am not afraid. Look, I will touch it. It may be hard under my hand like a statue— I have heard of such things—or my hand may pass through it—but there is no flesh and blood. [*He goes slowly up to the figure and passes his hand over its side.*] The heart of a phantom is beating! The heart of a phantom is beating! [*He screams. The figure of Christ crosses the stage and passes into the inner room.*] (*Collected Plays*, p. 593)

This moment has all the significance that Yeats would have liked to bestow upon the dance in the Noh form, and none of it is lost because the figure of Christ cannot and, of course, need not dance. The purity of the moment here is due to the fact that *The Resurrection* is a play of ideas; the Greek, the Hebrew, and the other characters are representative figures, surrogates for Yeats's insights into the nature of primary and antithetical civilizations and men. (*The Resurrection*, at least, must be taken on a literal and historical level and not translated into assertions about poetry.) It has been made into a play not only by the shown event but by some sufficiently sharp historical actualizations. But it has no hero; nobody is responsible.

But in those plays where the characters are not surrogates in quite the same way as they are in *The Resurrection*—plays, in short, which are not *primarily* plays of ideas but which do incorporate a moment in which not only ideas but sometimes names and destinies are altered or made clear—we encounter the problem of the hero who does possess and validate a name or an individuality. This is specially true of *At the Hawk's Well*, *The Only Jealousy of Emer*, *The Herne's Egg*, *Purgatory*, and *The Death of Cuchulain*. These five works are at the centre of Yeats's achievement as a playwright and probably constitute his chief claim for consideration in that role.

What distinguishes the protagonists in these plays is that each of them has a long personal history and a destiny which is being consciously worked out. Even the young Cuchulain in the first of them, although at the beginning of his history, carries explicitly the burden of its future unfolding. Yeats, of course, was not concerned to create 'character', to discriminate and define individuality, in the way that Shakespeare does; indeed, he valued most those moments in Shakespearian tragedy where character seemed to him to 'sink away', where Cleopatra or Hamlet become exemplars of creative joy and blaze with a noble, powerful, and uncommitted energy, like Chapman's heroes at the moments of their deaths and Herculean apotheoses. A consummation such as that drowns the lines and accidents of individuality, which, from this point of view, belong to those superficies (like the 'wheels and pulleys', footlights, elaborate scenery, the 'mere mechanism of a building or the interests of a class') that it is the play's business to recede from into the more powerful life where we share the 'one lofty emotion' and seem to ourselves most completely alive.[2] Not Rembrandt, therefore, but Michelangelo; not the world-considering eyes of Roman portrait-busts, but the blank eyes of the Phidian statues and the masked face of the Noble Dancer. These plays, however, dramatize the encounter between this condition and the human life and history of the hero. He brings to that encounter sexual desire or defiant courage, love and hatred, ignorance and crime, as these have been written in his history and nature. These passions are simply written, for Yeats, as we would expect from his rejection of highly discriminate characterization, has no wish to distract our attention ('God asks nothing of the highest soul but *attention*') from the vivacity of the encounter by giving the hero much more than a sense of his identity as a human being and the

---

2. This theory is clearly set out in Yeats's most important essay on the drama, 'The Tragic Theatre', written in 1910. There are two versions of it, as the preface to *Plays for an Irish Theatre* (1911) and in *The Cutting of an Agate* (1912), the latter being the version reprinted in *Essays* (1924) and *Essays and Introductions*.

consequently finite nature of his destiny. These are removed from the level of mere generalization enough to make the encounter express in dramatic terms a favourite antithesis between nature and supernature, impermanent and permanent images, artist and saint, the 'soldier's right' and the ascent to Heaven. And so Yeats uses many personages from the heroic cycles, from sagas that do not define and particularize character in post-Renaissance fashion but keep it simple and primary. Yeats's reasoning seems to have been that, if in the greatest moments of the greatest tragedies all the carefully constructed human circumstances and characterizing psychology are burned up or sink away, then, in plays on the scale which he was writing, he could dispense with them almost altogether and proceed in a few strides towards that cherished manifestation. Each of his plays is thus a kind of last act of an Elizabethan play as Elizabethan plays were read by Yeats, and he will borrow from the Greeks the method of incapsulating such history as he needs within the last stride towards the catastrophe. Yeats did not care to notice that in his last acts Shakespeare does preserve the secret traces of individuality in a thousand subtle ways and that his long exposure of his audience to an interpretative rendering of Lear or Othello during the previous acts is, as it were, an invisible asset on which an audience draws in order to modify its experience of the catastrophe. Othello 'roars', Lear's tears scald, Hamlet struggles with Horatio for the poisoned cup, Coriolanus dies in a fit of extremely Marcian rage. Always Shakespeare provides us with something that reminds us of what the heroes are as they become nothing, or prepare for their entrance into the 'condition of fire'. Hamlet and Lear, Yeats said, 'do not break up their lines to weep', but this is just what Shakespeare directs them to do. Yeats forced Shakespeare to fit his own theory, which he fortified with his own highly idiosyncratic experience of Shakespeare, by clapping a conventionalized Greek or Japanese mask on to the deplorably tawdry and real faces of his heroes: conduct perhaps more excusable than Thomas Rymer's, but originating from a not dissimilar suspicion of Shakespeare's vulgar concern with the particular case.

In so far as they stress the antitheses which I have mentioned, these plays are faithful to the way so many of the poems are ordered, and to their manner of both pulling away from and drawing towards the measureless consummation and the undying image: 'Sailing to Byzantium', for example, which represents the sensual music with passionate understanding even while it moves towards the golden artefact, or 'All Souls' Night', which is threaded upon a delight in vivid, human personalities as it passes into

> Such thought, that in it bound
> I need no other thing.
> (*Collected Poems*, p. 259)

In the poems Yeats, being freed from a dramatic theory that had, as he thought, to minimize character for the sake of opening the way into the *anima mundi*, into a 'life' where everything is powerful precisely because it is generalized and archetypal, was able to be much more generous to the human personality. Furthermore, in the poems the antitheses are always more intimate and intense because they pertain to the speaker, the poet in the poem; they do not need ever to be untied or come to an end because they are free from the sequence in time, however short, that plays demand, and are built into the system of stresses and strains that constitute the structure of the poem. This is the ideal unity of the symbolist work, and plays which attempt to imitate it stumble fatally, as Yeats's do, over the need for sequence. A few of Yeats's plays—*Calvary*, especially, and, less rigidly, *The Dreaming of the Bones*—get closest to the symbolist condition, but for that reason have less dramatic power; *Calvary* shows no event. The dilemma is very strange, and Yeats did not solve it. And we might add—since it seems part of the same complex of fatalities—that, because plays have to move on and achieve the resolution of strains, a proof or moral hovers. But it is a contradiction within the form that a work which aspires to the condition of symbolism should be obliged to provide a proof other than the proof of its own existence. A doctrine begins to be offered and asserted outside the work, instead of being protected from scrutiny by safely participating with all the other elements that go to make up the symbolist structure. And one cannot on the whole claim that Yeats's proofs or morals are very useful: if you resist the god you will be reborn as a donkey (*The Herne's Egg*), although it has some respectable antecedents and parallels amongst the religions of the world, is the worst and most obtrusive, unless we are to assume (which is highly probable) that Yeats was here again mocking his own thought.

For, although all the plays represent the heroes' failures of understanding and their consequent exclusion from the condition figured by the springing water in *At the Hawk's Well* or the green tree in *Purgatory*, tragedy is hardly an accurate term for them. To his encounter with the Ghost the hero brings his history of involvement in the crime of death and birth, and that simple tale is seen with mounting irony, until Yeats, when he handles it in *The Herne's Egg*, depicts it as oafish and 'wild'. Neither Cuchulain nor Congal nor the Old Man in *Purgatory* understand the metaphysical aid that offers them changeless beauty or absolution from the 'crime of being born' (and born again). Although we must discriminate between these states when we wish to define Yeats's philosophical mythology, they can, when we are experiencing the plays, be felt simply as the artifice of eternity—a term which is (as Frank Kermode says) reversible. The heroes, therefore, are Blind Men and Fools. They live in a condition of bewilderment and disorder which is described in varying modes, desperate, solemn, and 'heroical-tragical', or brash, energetic, and serio-comic. Like the Artist, they dwell 'in the humility of brutes' and cannot renounce Experience; but, like him, they assert their allegiance to the unfinished man and his pain, to those who love 'in brief longing and deceiving hope' (like the people whom Forgael despised in *The Shadowy Waters*), and to those who, as Cuchulain did in 'The Grey Rock', betray the gods. This is the noblest thing in Yeats's plays, though he is apprehending a tragi-comic dilemma rather than improving a moral. This allegiance the heroes bring to their encounter with the superhuman, as Congal does in *The Herne's Egg*:

> *Congal.* If I should give myself a wound,
>   Let life run away, I'd win the bout.
>   He said I must die at the hands of a Fool
>   And sent you hither. Give me that spit!
>   I put it in this crevice of the rock,
>   That I may fall upon the point.
>   These stones will keep it sticking upright.
>   [*They arrange stones, he puts the spit in.*]

> *Congal* [*almost screaming in his excitement*].
>   Fool! Am I myself a Fool?
>   For if I am a Fool, he wins the bout.
> *Fool.* You are King of Connacht. If you were a Fool
>   They would have chased you with their dogs.
> *Congal.* I am King Congal of Connacht and of Tara,
>   That wise, victorious, voluble, unlucky,
>   Blasphemous, famous, infamous man.
>   Fool, take this spit when red with blood,
>   Show it to the people and get all the pennies;
>   What does it matter what they think?
>   The Great Herne knows that I have won.
>   (*Collected Plays*, pp. 675–6)

Congal has not 'won', and he is a Fool to think so; but he has
brought his name into the lists, the symbol of his history,
uniqueness, and heroic quality; self and name are not easy to
dissever—' 'Tis a spell, you see, of much power!'[3] In *Purgatory*,
which works Yeats's most profound variation on the theme, he
extends it to show us how the Old Man is motivated not by the
sense of himself as 'an image of heroic self-possession'[4]—the
archetypal subjectivity of the hero, making him the proper
object of the desire or malice of the gods who wish, as in *The
Resurrection*, to 'take complete possession'—but instead by a
sense of his degradation and namelessness. This is ambiguously
qualified by his kinship and history, or one part of it—for he is
the son of a fine lady and a drunken beast. This complex of
motives, or, one wants to say, this *character*, drives him to intervene on his mother's behalf in the terrible rationale of a supernatural system. *Purgatory* is as far as Yeats got in modifying his
dislike of character in the interests of a Shakespearian concern
for the particular case. For that reason, and not only because its
verse-line set an example to Eliot,[5] it can be claimed as his best,
though not his most characteristic, achievement in the theatre.

Finally, there is a kind of logic about Yeats's long entangle-
ment with blank verse in a series of plays on the heroic subject.
The first poetic play in which he escaped entirely from blank
verse was *The Green Helmet*, a pivotal and probably underrated

3. *Coriolanus*, v.ii.93.
4. Yeats's description of Hamlet, *Autobiographies*, p. 47.
5. Eliot, *On Poetry and Poets*, p. 78.

work. For it, he chose a 'heroic' pre-Renaissance line. Ironically
enough, it probably owes most to the slightly longer line of
Morris's *Sigurd the Volsung*, a poem which was for Yeats inseparably associated with the heroic subject.[6] In *The Green Helmet*
it is a form of verse in which 'everything can be said that has to
be said'[7] by both the low and the high characters, the prosaic
and the poetical ones, in modes of speech that range from comic
bravado to dreaming evocation. Its irregular fourteeners, when
split in half, greatly resemble the three- and four-stress lines of
the much later plays in which he abandoned blank verse altogether, *The Herne's Egg* and *Purgatory*. Indeed, it might be said
that it was the discovery of the Japanese Noh, which seemed to
him to translate best into blank verse varied with lyric metres,
that prevented for so long any further exploitation of the flexible 'ballad metre' of *The Green Helmet*. It is another irony that this
play, whose metre is an index of Yeats's desire to escape from the
Renaissance and Shakespearian measure in order to depict a
world of imaginative unities that the Renaissance had, he
thought, destroyed, should shadow forth just such an act of
destruction or liberation. In *The Green Helmet* Cuchulain wants to
turn the Red Man's helmet, the prize for valour, into a drinking-
cup to be shared by all; but the society depicted in the play is
one of 'weasels fighting in a hole'; it cannot accept, as the Red
Man very well knows, Cuchulain's vision of a world 'hooped
together / Brought under a rule'; Cuchulain is like the dreamers
of 'Nineteen Hundred and Nineteen' who thought to achieve
a semblance of peace and were cheated by the makers of discord. Although he has striven in the play for another sort of
unity, he is obliged therefore to submit to being chosen, to being
named as the hero, the great personality, the one who will
master his society, take his place as the hero of plays, and enact
the role of one of those 'sundry magnifications' which Yeats
thought of as emerging out of Unity of Culture and 'general
agreement' to flower into the Shakespearian moment. Chaucer's
personages began it:

Chaucer's personages . . . disengaged themselves from Chaucer's crowd,
forgot their common goal and shrine, and after sundry magnifications
became each in turn the centre of some Elizabethan play. (*Autobiographies*, p. 193)

6. See *Wheels and Butterflies*, pp. 75–76.   7. Eliot, p. 74.

Or, as he puts it elsewhere:

In the Spiritual dawn when Raphael painted the Camera della Segnatura, and the Medician Popes dreamed of uniting Christianity and
Paganism, all that was sacred with all that was secular, Europe might
have made its plan, begun the solution of its problems, but individualism came instead; the egg, instead of hatching, burst. (*Essays and
Introductions*, pp. 467–8)

Individualism came instead, 'breaking up the old rhythms of
life' (*Essays and Introductions*, p. 110), and with it 'magnification',
the great Shakespearian personality, who is emphatically *not*
one of Chaucer's crowd, and with him came blank verse. This, as
Yeats put it, was to be 'cast up out of the whale's belly':

When I speak blank verse and analyse my feelings, I stand at a moment
of history when instinct, its traditional songs and dances, its general
agreement, is of the past. I have been cast up out of the whale's belly.
(*Essays and Introductions*, p. 524)

Blank verse, which could express all the subtleties of Shakespearian characterization, superseded the impersonal, chanting
metres of Chaucer's crowd. (Yeats struggling against his fate,
used to try and get his players to speak his blank verse in that
manner, and perhaps the two-dimensional quality on which I
have commented arises from the same compromise.) It is, therefore, oddly fitting that Yeats's own sundry magnifications
should speak in blank verse. The unease that their Shakespearian
and Jacobean rhythms, faintly heard, aroused in their author and
arouse in us is an emblem of their precarious footing and their
individuality. 'Impure and lonely', like the artist, they are
driven to assert their identities and personal histories and pro-
claim the charter of the self; yet all the while they remember
the whale's belly, the peace of an imagined general agreement,
and of a condition where it is the part of the individual to submit
to the god and become the god's artefact and not his own,

> oblivion
> Even to quench Cuchulain's drouth,
> Even to still that heart.
> (*Collected Plays*, p. 293)

The whole development clearly demonstrates the need for

seeing Yeats's aesthetics and his readings of actual history as vitally interdependent guides to his poetic practice.

If Yeats, like the neo-Platonic mages who interested those Medician Popes, had ever devised his City of the Sun, one wonders if it would have contained a theatre. He had certainly hoped that his work as a playwright would deepen the political passion of a nation and would make it more completely alive by returning it to some source of imaginative coherence, creating the 'one mind of enjoyment' to which all things are possible. But as he gradually perceived the sheer unlikelihood of Unity of Culture, there was a change of feeling: 'I did not see', he wrote in 1909, 'until Synge began to write, that we must renounce the deliberate creation of a kind of Holy City in the imagination, and express the individual.' The change freed his poetry and made it possible for it to develop into a supreme accomplishment; but both dramatic theory and dramatic practice lagged behind, looking backwards towards the dream of a great act of imaginative communion between audience, playwright, and player, at the ideal but unreachable shadows of Athens and Urbino behind the crowds in the Abbey and the more restricted group of 'leisured and lettered people' in Lady Cunard's drawing-room. Perhaps the poetry could not have achieved such liberation, had Yeats not been able to maintain the integrity of his artistic endeavour and a continuity with ambitions which he was deeply reluctant to discard by reserving the principal expression of them for the plays. In that way, the weakness of the plays, by comparison with the strength of the poems, might be justified at last.

12

W. B. Yeats and the Shakespearian moment

On W. B. Yeats's attitude towards Shakespeare
as revealed in his criticism and in his work
for the theatre

The nobleness of the Arts is in the mingling of countries.
'Poetry and Tradition'

I

In September 1937 Yeats went to see *Richard II* at the Queen's Theatre, London. He was not specially pleased, complaining that the 'rhythm of all the great passages is abolished. The modern actor . . . has packed his soul in a bag and left it with the bar-attendant.' A surprising judgement, if we remember that Gielgud, whom we still consider our most poetic actor, played the king, and had dazzling support from a cast that included Redgrave as Bolingbroke and Peggy Ashcroft as Queen Isabel.[1] How is it that such a performance failed to satisfy poetically? Because, Yeats said, the modern actor can speak to another actor, but he is incapable of reverie. And he ends with a question: 'Did Shakespeare in *Richard II* discover poetic reverie?'[2]

This question has behind it the whole weight of Yeats's concern with Shakespeare,[3] with playmaking, and with examining the character of the emotional experience afforded him by the theatre. It is the complex formed by these three elements that

A lecture delivered at Queen's University, Belfast, on 27 April 1966, and published by the Institute of Irish Studies, Queen's University, 1969.

1. *Richard II* (ed. J. D. Wilson, 1951), p. xcii.
2. *Letters of W. B. Yeats* (ed. Wade, 1954), p. 899.
3. The question has been discussed in B. L. Reid, *William Butler Yeats: The Lyric of Tragedy* (1961), pp. 256 ff.; Edward Engelberg, *The Vast Design: Patterns in W. B. Yeats's Aesthetic* (1964), pp. 160 ff.; and Leonard E. Nathan, *The Tragic Drama of William Butler Yeats: Figures in a Dance* (1965). I am indebted to all three treatments.

I want to look a little way into in this lecture. I want to use some of Yeats's expressed opinions about his experience of Shakespeare as a lens to bring into focus some portions of his dramatic theory and to see how these relate to his accomplishments as a playwright.

It is not difficult, for instance, to take him up in the matter of *reverie*, poetic and tragic, by tracing out his concern with *Richard II*.

Nearly forty years before he saw Gielgud play in London, Yeats spent a week at Stratford-upon-Avon watching F. R. Benson's production of the whole cycle of history plays. This was one of the most important bits of playgoing he ever did. He enjoyed, too, his little bout of coughing in ink as a fake Shakespeare scholar. He was allowed to use the librarian's private room at the theatre: a letter ends charmingly:

> The boy has just brought me in a translation of Gervinus' Commentaries and I must to work again. I do not even stop for afternoon tea. (*Letters*, p. 349)

Richard II emerged as the major discovery of this encounter with Shakespeare on the banks of the Avon. The essay by Yeats,[4] 'At Stratford-on-Avon', which resulted remains his only purely Shakespearian piece.

The long history behind this essay involves the relations of Yeats and of his father with their eminent friend Professor Edward Dowden of Trinity College, Dublin.[5] It attacks quite

---

4. Actually two essays, first published in the *Speaker*, May 1901, reduced to one in *Ideas of Good and Evil*, 1903. (See Wade, *Bibliography*, 1968 ed., p. 360.) My references are to the text in *Collected Works* (1908), vi.

5. Dowden (1843–1913) was born in Cork and held the chair of English at Trinity from the age of twenty-four until his death. He and J. B. Yeats were friends at Trinity as undergraduates, but we find them disagreeing about literature in 1869 (*Letters of Edward Dowden*, 1914, pp. 43 ff.). Later, in the 1880s, they were neighbours at Rathgar, and J. B. Yeats was painting Dowden's portrait in 1904 (*J. B. Yeats Letters to his Son*, 1944, p. 77). There was a proposal, which came to nothing, that W. B. Yeats should succeed Dowden at Trinity (see Philip Edwards, 'Yeats and the Trinity Chair', *Hermathena*, ci, 1965, 5–11). Dowden was both enthusiastic and exceedingly considerate about this. W. B. Yeats's accounts of J. B. Yeats's feelings about Dowden (*Autobiographies*, pp. 85–89) cannot really be trusted; in the chapter devoted to Dowden he describes the friendship between the two men as an 'antagonism' (p. 88), which is absurd; J. B. Yeats was on occasion sharply critical of Dowden's writing and literary opinions (eg *J. B. Yeats Letters*, p. 160), but he also had to remind W. B. Yeats not to be too hard on him and on his memory: 'I would ask you, indeed beg of you, to remember that he not only was a very old friend, but the best of friends . . . He took the keenest interest in your success . . . it is better to be

brutally Dowden's very influential and characteristic book, *Shakespere: A Critical Study of his Mind and Art*, which reached a twelfth edition in the same year, 1901. Dowden's idea of Shakespearian criticism is to pass in review Shakespeare's characters one by one and award plus or minus marks to them. For Yeats, this is middle-class moralizing, Blake's Accusation of Sin; it comes out of the middle-class movement, which is his legitimate enemy, just as Dowden was an 'intimate enemy'⁶ of his father, who was his first and most important Shakespeare preceptor. There is a fine assault on the Dowden type of approach to Shakespeare in another of the essays:

This character who delights us may commit murder like Macbeth, or fly the battle for his sweetheart as did Antony, or betray his country like Coriolanus, and yet we will rejoice in every happiness that comes to him and sorrow at his death as if it were our own. (*Plays and Controversies*, 1923, p. 104)

---

illogical than INHUMAN' (ibid., p. 168). W. B. Yeats was uncharacteristically apologetic to J. B. Yeats in 1915 about the admittedly 'harsh' chapter on Dowden in *Reveries over Childhood and Youth* (see *Letters*, p. 602), but the apology itself explains why prosperous middle-class Dowden, politically a Unionist and in literature a moralist, insufficiently enthusiastic about Shelley, sceptical about Irish literature, got such prejudiced treatment from W. B. Yeats: '[*Reveries*] is a history of the revolt, which perhaps unconsciously you taught me, against certain Victorian ideals. Dowden is the image of those ideals . . .' W. B. Yeats ended simply by dropping Dowden in the latter's old age in spite of his personal kindness.

The relations with Dowden are also of course an aspect of Yeats's relations with his father. It is not too much to say that the father taught the son Shakespeare: 'I study [Shakespeare] and all other poets exclusively that I may find myself', J. B. Yeats wrote (*J. B. Yeats Letters to his Son*, p. 199). He does his best in numerous other letters to detach Shakespeare from the prevailing moralistic climate of Dowdenian criticism of him: Shakespeare is a Catholic-Agnostic—he reasons with himself but does not judge other people (ibid., p. 95), rather he forgives them because he has much to forgive in himself and is humble and sympathetic; Shakespeare was not strong-willed, as are the moralists who go over 'to the side of the authorities', like Browning and Wordsworth—all literature nowadays has 'gone over to the side of the schoolmaster': but Shakespeare remains one of the boys (pp. 124–5). And J. B. Yeats's understanding of Shakespeare as a poet of dreams not of realism exactly anticipates his son's theory of reverie plunging beneath the surface to a place where we 'find ourselves' (pp. 198–9). J. B. Yeats also had Yeatsian views on the contemporaries of Shakespeare: 'If he was to live he must escape from the surface of life . . .' (p. 189). It is not at all surprising that W. B. Yeats wrote to Lady Gregory: 'My father is delighted with my second article on Shakespeare [the second portion of the Stratford essay in the *Speaker*, May 1901]. He has just written to say that it is "the best article he ever read". . . . The truth is that Dowden has always been one of his "intimate enemies" and chiefly because of Dowden's Shakespeare opinions' (*Letters*, p. 352).

6. *Letters*, pp. 349, 352.

And yet, Yeats goes on, if it were not for the skill of the dramatist, managing to suspend our ordinary moral judgements in favour of a profound imaginative experience, we might go away from the theatre muttering the ten commandments. This is the general position from which he tries to disable Dowden in the Stratford essay. Dowden offended because he gave good marks to the far-seeing and resolute Bolingbroke and sent the slack, voluptuous, and dreamy Richard to the bottom of the class. This is for Yeats a product of the same taste that admired the 'argumentative' George Eliot and the 'malign' Wordsworth.[7] Yeats believes that, like the history of English poetry, Shakespeare's history plays exhibit a series of contrasts between men of rhetoric, energy, and practical ability—*objective* men, as he was later to call them—and men of lyricism, subjectivity, and dreamy, inward abundance. Richard II is the vessel of porcelain to Henry V's vessel of clay. Many other critics before him, he says, had identified these two types; but his sympathy for Richard because he is a man too full of inner wisdom to bother with the trivial externals of life—'as for living our servants will do that for us'—has an immediate progenitor in Walter Pater's essay on the same topic, 'Shakespeare's English kings', first published in 1889.[8] In Yeats's Stratford essay Pater is brought in to redress the balance upset by Professor Dowden.

If we focus the Stratford essay for a moment on the plays of the first Abbey period it is easy to recognize the way the thoughts of the essayist correspond to the practice of the playwright. Thomas Parkinson has summed up the general character of that first batch of plays:

The major subject of Yeats' Abbey dramas was the conflict between the fixed palpable world of human affairs (Guaire, Conchubar) and the world of passion and aspiration, which is beyond reason, system, or office (Seanchan, Cuchulain). The basic split in the plays is that between the institutional world—limited, tame, calculating, interested in the virtue of fixed character—and the personal world—exuberant, carefree, wild, affirming the values of intense personality. (*W. B. Yeats: Self-Critic*, p. 54)

7. *Collected Works*, vi.119; Wordsworth was the poet whom J. B. Yeats and Dowden disagreed about in 1869; for 'malign', see *J. B. Yeats Letters to his Son*, p. 117.

8. See Nathan's admirable study of the subject, *Tragic Drama of William Butler Yeats*, pp. 45 ff.

Thus Yeats's own plays clearly exhibit the vessels of porcelain and of clay. But there is something else as well. Yeats understands that when Shakespeare put king and usurper into *Richard II* he was not passing a judgement, as Professor Dowden was, even one in favour of instead of against the failed king. Yeats knows this because when he himself created the corresponding antitheses—king and poet, king and warrior—he was not passing judgement either. Those *dramatis personae* stand for 'the two halves of the soul separate and face to face'.[9] Unlike Dowden, Shakespeare and Yeats were not involved in the world of moral opinion at all; they were creating myths. Yeats was beginning his long toil on his myth of the objective and subjective man, the lasting dialogue of self and soul. And Shakespeare, Yeats claims, was at work on a similar myth:

Shakespeare's Myth, it may be, describes a wise man who was blind from very wisdom, and an empty man who thrust him from his place, and saw all that could be seen from very emptiness.

This was the story of 'Richard II, that unripened Hamlet, and of Henry V, that ripened Fortinbras'.[1]

We shall never go far in the study of Yeats without coming across examples of this kind of interlocking device. It is perhaps the basic module for all his thought. He finally externalizes it in the diagrams of the widening and contracting gyres in *A Vision*, the two cones, one inverted into the other. It can take a rigid, baffling, and mechanical form, sculpture in wire; or it can lie hidden, nourishing the roots of an inexhaustable poem.

II

After the Stratford essay Yeats never wrote another piece wholly devoted to Shakespeare. But, scattered up and down the other essays and the letters there is much instructive comment.

Yeats uses Shakespeare as a stick with which to beat the naturalists in his long campaign against the naturalistic theatre. He hated this theatre because it was busy only with the surface of life, with the outside of men and things, and never treated these as clues which lead to the different sort of 'life' within. In Yeats's day commercial directors were still staging Shakespeare in an obsessively realistic style, running to the British Museum to

9. *Plays and Controversies*, p. 218.　　1. *Collected Works*, vi.126.

check whether the furniture and clothes were right. He tells of a 1905 production of *The Merchant of Venice* which must have seemed more like *The Gondoliers* than Shakespeare.[2] 'One kept asking oneself "What has brought me to this childish peepshow?"' It is characteristic of Yeats's dialectic that he should cite time and again the same example of Shakespeare's bold use of convention and disregard of the timider realisms—the pitching of Richard's and Richmond's tents side by side on the stage before the Battle of Bosworth in *Richard III*. For Yeats this is an example of the 'seeming irresponsible creative power that is life itself'—a power that considerations of 'external probability or social utility' are out to destroy. 'Logic in the mere circumstance', he says, does not matter in the finest art.[3] It is ironic that at Stratford in 1901 F. R. Benson did *not* pitch the tents side by side, as Shakespeare had directed; Yeats was looking at the text, not at what he actually saw on the still unreformed stage.

'Our drama', he affirms, 'has grown effeminate through the over-development of the picture-making faculty.'[4] This kind of objection is endorsed by a consistent vision of a more austere drama, one of marked rhythms and spare, calculated movement. His choice had metaphysical as well as aesthetic implications. Drama ought to reach at the common life all men share in the depths of the collective soul, the *anima mundi*; a play must recede from the surface of life, where men are separated from one another by character, into the more powerful life, where they come together under the aegis of their archetypes; there we can share the same lofty emotion; there we are most completely alive. Shakespeare's Richard II, for example, like all great dramatic persons, can give us a valuable experience not because he tells us anything about the historical Richard but because he enables us to 'know of something in our minds we had never known of had he never been imagined'.[5] To understand him is an act of self-discovery at that deep level where Shakespeare's mind communes with ours. As old J. B. Yeats said, he read Shakespeare that he might find himself; and Mallarmé, in a phrase that appealed to Joyce, spoke of Hamlet: '*Il se promène, lisant au livre de lui-même.*'[6]

2. *Letters*, pp. 465–6.   3. *Plays and Controversies*, p. 98; *Essays* (1924), p. 346.
4. *Letters*, p. 466.   5. *Plays and Controversies*, p. 93.
6. See above, pp. 205–6, n. 5, Stuart Gilbert, *James Joyce's Ulysses* (1960), p. 24.

To revisit the archetypes in this way was to attain near to Yeats's supreme value, 'unity of being', long sought with despair. Drama seemed to him to yield this experience especially, and the experience validates what he writes about drama. For similar reasons, he stresses the primacy of speech in Shakespeare. He thought, mistakenly, that the Elizabethan playhouse stage was small and so inhibited movement;[7] this confirmed his own belief in bodily stillness and expressive speech. Even the shape of the Elizabethan stage—about which, it is safe to say, Yeats knew very little—seemed to indicate a desire to escape from the surface of life.[8] How are we to get away from the fidgety movements and visual showiness of naturalistic theatre? The art of speech, Yeats explains, is older than all that. We can refresh an art form by going back to a time when it was 'nearer to human life and instinct' and less overlaid with 'mechanical specializations'. The way to achieve renewal for the drama is to concentrate on speech, the centre of Shakespeare's art. Before men could read, they could listen. Listening, enjoying a beautiful rhythm, is a natural human activity.[9]

Yeats was frightened and yet allured by professionalism in the arts, especially in the art of the stage, by organization, technical contrivances. He feared that they might keep him on the surface. When he was an old man he wrote regretfully of an earlier period:

> Players and painted stage took all my love,
> And not those things that they were emblems of.

The painted stage easily becomes a painted toy. Busy on the surface, sporting with the actual shells of Rosses' level shore, men forget about the great ocean of imaginative experience that lies beyond. So Yeats turns to Shakespeare to aid him in resisting the claims of Edwardian professionalism because he thinks of Shakespeare as a bold anti-naturalist and primitivist. He does not think of him, as we incline to, as a sophisticated man of the theatre, always delighted to exploit a new technique; nor does he think of the Elizabethan playhouse, as we do, as a tremendous aesthetic machine for expressing a great urban and courtly art: to Yeats it is something much more half-timbered and folksy—by Norman Shaw out of William Morris.

7. *Letters*, p. 441.   8. *Plays and Controversies*, p. 127.
9. *Plays and Controversies*, pp. 175 ff.

But he also knew perfectly well that Shakespeare belonged to the Renaissance. In one of his stories, the works of Shakespeare are symbolically bound in 'the orange of the glory of the world'.[1] He recognized without reluctance that his art is not so fresh and pastoral as his enlistment in the anti-naturalistic cause might, ideally, demand. Yeats said that he both adored and detested the Renaissance. His attitude to Shakespeare is ambiguous, too. Shakespeare, he says in one place, corrupted literature by his too abounding sentiment.[2] For Yeats, the Renaissance was a great flowering which ought never to have happened. It produced some overwhelming things, especially those 'sundry magnifications', the great dramatic personalities, Lear, Hamlet. Yeats, like the rest of us, put them at the heart of his imaginative experience and selected Shakespeare as the first of the six authors that should suffice a man after forty. He could not hate England because of Shakespeare.[3] But the Renaissance explosion was in itself a disaster; the egg, as Yeats put it, which had been ripening since the time of Chaucer, instead of hatching, burst.[4] A putative unity of culture which had prevailed before, when men were content to be members of a community and share their imaginations rather than toil at them in solitude, was shattered. For a time you had a splendid sight—the sky blazed with the fragments of the bursting shell. But the unity of Europe was gone for ever, and soon the artist was left raging in the dark. Yeats uses many metaphors for this mythical catastrophe. The most expressive, perhaps, and the most relevant to Shakespeare, comes when he speaks of being cast up out of the whale's belly.[5] The whale's belly is the comfortable womb of 'general agreement', a hierarchical society, a period prior to the Lord's invention of the rising middle classes and his abandonment of affairs to the moral leadership of Professor Dowden. Society before this catastrophe was unified by an image; it 'found certainty upon the dreaming air' and was accomplished in inner peace like a great ideal personality. Byzantium became the symbol for this imaginary commonwealth, this Hobbesian or, rather, Blakean, artificial man. He became immortal in the Byzantium poems

1. *The Secret Rose* (1897), p. 223.
2. *The King of the Great Clock Tower* (1934), preface. [Yeats is not saying this in his own person, but quoting Pound—C. J. R.]
3. *Autobiographies* (1955), p. 193; *Letters*, pp. 791, 872.
4. *Essays and Introductions* (1961), p. 468.   5. Ibid., p. 524.

and was recognized in the end as the artifice of eternity, or the
heaven of artefacts.

Shakespeare is extruded from that unity. His world, like
Yeats's own, is 'but a bundle of fragments'. Yet he is within
earshot of it. Pater had given Yeats a most important clue. He
had written about how much the need for organization that a
play demands may undercut its struggle for lyrical unity and
about how this puts drama at a disadvantage compared with the
lyric. Yeats similarly insists that all the organization and planning
that a playwright has to go in for when he is constructing a play
tends to infect the work of art with something abstract and
intellectual that is hostile to its life; its body becomes bruised
by the labour like the bodies of the toiling schoolchildren in the
poem. He read in Pater:

A play attains artistic perfection just in proportion as it approaches that
unity of lyrical effect, as if a song or ballad were still lying at the root
of it. (*Appreciations*, 1890, p. 211)

It was the 'song or ballad . . . lying at the root of it' that Yeats
paid special attention to in Shakespeare. This was the folk-song's
'ghostly voice, an unvariable possibility, an unconscious norm'
that Yeats always heard in great poetry: it was this ghostly voice
that made the imagination dance and, as he put it, carried it
'beyond feeling into the aboriginal ice'.[6] Shakespeare, though
corrupt with warm sentiment, had the necessary coldness too.
For he lived in a time when his groundlings 'could remember
the folk-songs and the imaginative life'.[7] So Yeats lent an atten-
tive ear to Shakespeare's fools and songs because they are the

6. *Essays and Introductions*, pp. 523–4.
7. *Plays and Controversies*, p. 86; cf. *Four Plays for Dancers* (1921) p. 88. The coldness
is also related to Shakespeare's belonging amongst antithetical types to the cold,
brighter, creative artists' side of the moon in the phasal system of *A Vision* (my page
references are to the 1937 edition). Shakespeare belongs also to those phases where
'Unity of Being is no longer possible, for the being is compelled to live in a fragment
of itself and to dramatise that fragment' (p. 148). Shakespeare, in company with
Balzac and Napoleon, is a man of Phase 20, one of those phases during which things
fall apart and 'crumble'. Shakespeare's 'actual personality seemed faint and passion-
less'; he is conceived as projecting all his passions into his art (p. 153). But because
the faculties of his soul (in the special *Vision* sense) are turned towards the 'orange
and the glory of the world', to power and material fact and generalized truths, he
seeks the material for his art in the stories that other people have invented, and in the
outward world. Since this outward world is fragmented as a result of the Renaissance
'catastrophe', the result is the endless fragments which are Shakespeare's characters,
each of them informed with or personifying the dramatist's own passions (including

vestiges of the old world of unity before the Renaissance scatterings. In his own plays, the songs and fools are his most immediately identifiable direct debt to Shakespeare. But more than that—several of the plays—*The Green Helmet, The Hour-Glass*—are actually about the complex of ideas I have just been describing: the bursting of the old unity of culture into the star fragments of 'magnification', the great personality, with Shakespeare animating all, sharing the peacock pride of Renaissance man, yet continually murmuring in the old ghostly voice.

Yet another accent in which Shakespeare murmurs is of course not the impersonal ballad of the folk, but blank verse, a speech invented in order that character, inward and outward, and the most subtle relationships between characters, may be defined and discriminated with the greatest imaginable complexity and exactitude. Yeats saw this Shakespeare, too. He held both

---

that of ambition). Yeats does not seem, beneath the blanket of visionary terminology, to be achieving more than a fairly commonplace statement that Shakespeare's characters are historical or pseudohistorical persons animated by passions which Shakespeare found in himself or understood through his own experience. Shakespeare's art is conceived as an achievement in balance, with the relations between inward and outward satisfactorily poised; and it is an art specially concerned with characterization though Yeats as usual prefers to call it personification. This is correct, perhaps, but certainly not wildly original: Shakespeare, says A. G. Stock reporting Yeats's view, 'neither copies fact, nor creates independently of it' (*W. B. Yeats: His Poetry and Thought*, 1961, p. 129); and H. H. Vendler similarly expounds it: 'It is by preserving the delicate balance between creative intuition and factual reality that drama exists at all' (*Yeats's Vision and the Later Plays*, 1963, p. 43). In discussing the men of Phase 23, Yeats adds that Shakespeare's interest in the concrete, in the accidents of the visible world, did not go as far as that of Synge or Rembrandt. His mind is less receptive than theirs and more powerfully subjective, so that he shapes the outside world more strongly according to his own inner needs. Since style is a personal matter, Shakespeare's style partakes of this powerful 'shaping joy' and reflects his own energetic delight in artistic creation: 'Shakespeare showed, through a style full of joy, a melancholy vision . . .; a style at play, a mind that served' (p. 166). The last phrase means, I think, 'served the external world': like the 'faculties' of all the souls belonging to these phases, Shakespeare's 'faculties' seek and serve the external world; and its externalities constitute the nature's *mask*, or, the opposite which, according to Yeats's system, it endlessly desires and pursues (see 'The Phases of the Moon', *Collected Poems*, 1950, p. 187). Shakespeare's tragic vision, therefore, is inseparable from joy and a self-delighting creative energy and fulfilment. He resembles his own heroes in this; they reconcile their tragic fates with a joyous life-style. There is also close kinship with Yeats's own last aim: 'To me the supreme aim is an act of faith and reason to make one rejoice in the midst of tragedy' (*Letters on Poetry to Dorothy Wellesley*, p. 12). Much earlier (*Essays*, 1924, p. 312), he wrote that 'only when we are gay over a thing, and can play with it, do we show ourselves its master'. Essentially, then, the Shakespeare described in *A Vision* masters the world by means of a 'style at play'.

Shakespeares in his mind when he contemplated the essence of his adorable, detestable art. He himself wrote in blank verse, varying it with lyric measures, in Shakespeare's manner. He knew, too, that Shakespeare's audience was not just a collection of groundling peasants vaguely recollecting an Edenic past. If they had once dwelt in Arcadia, they were now 'all but as clever as an Athenian audience'[8] and were ready to welcome great literature; they were interested in emotion and intellect at their moment of union and at their greatest intensity; they were able to see that Shakespeare's great characters personified spiritual power. For this reason they watched his princely personages 'in terrified sympathy' and not merely with the social envy of the modern working man.[9]

Yeats was generally ready to recognize that Shakespeare's art and the audience's relation to it had more dimensions than are ever likely to be successfully computed. Shakespeare leans 'upon the general fate of men and nations', upon vast sentiments and generalizations;[1] he depends upon the interplay between main plot and underplot for echoing richness and variety of appeal.[2] He induces from all quarters the imaginative participation of his audience; 'emotion of multitude' is the name for what we experience in the enjoyment of his multi-dimensional art. Another aspect of his multi-dimensionality connects with Yeats's insistence that Shakespeare was always the author of tragi-comedy.[3] Yeats is obviously quite unaware of what may be called the official theory of tragi-comedy: the notion of it as the expression of a 'middle mood' and Guarini's view that it decorously joins together selected elements from its two tributary modes. Yeats's view that Shakespeare writes tragi-comedy derives directly from his need to keep intact his own theory that the definition of character and individuality pertains to the surface of life; being in itself a kind of 'mechanical specialization', it often hinders access to the archetypal 'life' beneath. Tragedy, which supremely in his experience communicated with the deeps of the mind, cannot therefore be an art of character; comedy, on the other hand, being an art of the surface, may be cheerfully permitted its concern with the definition of character,

8. *Plays and Controversies*, p. 101.   9. Ibid., p. 201.
1. *Autobiographies*, p. 313; *Letters*, p. 853.   2. *Essays* (1924), pp. 266–7.
3. *Autobiographies*, pp. 470–1; *Essays*, p. 297; *Letters*, p. 548.

which is continuously present, Yeats thinks, only in comedy. He ends up in an awkward posture, obliged to imply that Falstaff is more of a 'character' than Cleopatra or Hamlet. The view that Shakespeare is a 'tragic comedian' is, as it were, Yeats's device for explaining the powerful characterological element in Shakespeare without abandoning his theory that tragedy does not define and sharpen character. For Yeats, then, tragi-comedy is a form which manifests one function of tragedy (decharacterizing) and one function of comedy (characterizing) in the same play. Whether such a play is either a coherent or a credible form his concern with the moment and momentary experience absolves him from seriously considering.[4] But at least the whole manoeuvre is a reluctant tribute to two of the many dimensions in Shakespeare.[5]

III

One of the functions of the great Shakespearian personality, therefore, is to express not what divides men in terms of the moral life but what unites them in terms of the imaginative life. Yeats makes a concomitant distinction between *thought* and *reverie*. Thought is for him shaping energy, obstinate questioning, a busyness over abstract and external matters. Reverie is the attribute of Shakespeare himself and of the people he made.[6] Yeats was to call it nothing less than the 'condition of tragic pleasure'.[7] It is the chief means for inducing those sensations in the theatre, intense and momentary, which Yeats most valued. It works in terms of moments and not of constructions. For artistic activity generally Yeats preferred the metaphor of the lightning-flash; it manifests uncommitted energy, blinds through its very fullness, and leaps from an unknown region, from the boundless and unforeseen. The most complete account of what

4. See below, p. 216, and n. 8.
5. I am unable to accept Nathan's view (*Tragic Drama of William Butler Yeats*, chap. iii) that the plays of the first Abbey period are themselves tragi-comedies. To suppose this entails assuming that a theory that won't work for Shakespeare will work for Yeats; even though it is Yeats's own theory, it is not a good assumption. Yeats's only 'true' tragi-comedy is perhaps *The Player Queen*, but it has to be classified as one for non-Yeatsian reasons.
6. *Plays and Controversies*, p. 87.
7. *Plays for an Irish Theatre* (1911), p. ix. The Wordsworthian phrases in the description of 'thought' are naturally meant to have a derogatory force.

Yeats took to be the essence of tragic pleasure comes in his essay on 'The Tragic Theatre', 1910–11. In graceful compliment to the dead shepherd, Yeats makes the cornerstone of this essay an account of what he felt during the performance of the last Act of Synge's *Deirdre of the Sorrows*:

'Is it not a hard thing that we should miss the safety of the grave and we trampling its edge?' That is Deirdre's cry at the outset of a reverie of passion that mounts and mounts till grief itself has carried her beyond grief into pure contemplation . . . I listened breathless to sentences that may never pass away, and as they filled or dwindled in their civility of sorrow, the player, whose art had seemed clumsy and incomplete, like the writing itself, ascended into that tragic ecstasy which is the best that art—perhaps that life—can give. And at last . . . we knew that the player had become, if but for a moment, the creature of that noble mind which had gathered its art in waste islands, and we too were carried beyond time and persons to where passion, living through its thousand purgatorial years, as in the wink of an eye, becomes wisdom; and it was as though we too had touched and felt and seen a disembodied thing.[8]

Poetic reverie induces a trancelike state, a 'twilight between sleep and waking'; it is a 'perilous path as on the edge of a sword' and can easily be ruined in the theatre by a clumsy gesture or an ill-placed property.[9] It does not augment our sense of the speaker's character but diminishes it; but we share down at the root of life, in the *anima mundi*, in his activity of soul.

8. *Essays*, pp. 295–6. Most of the rest of the esssay is relevant, too. The final sentence of the passage quoted relates to the moment of revelation in *The Resurrection* when the Greek touches the side of the resurrected Christ (for more about the significance of this see p. 223 below and n. 2). A somewhat similar gesture seems to have caused a good deal of Yeats's excitement on the *Deirdre of the Sorrows* occasion. Many years later in *A Vision* (p. 167), describing what is obviously the same episode, he tells how the actress playing Deirdre, 'moving like a somnambulist . . . touched Concubar upon the arm, a gesture full of gentleness and compassion, as though she had said, "You also live"'. This was putting all the pity, an important constituent of Synge's art and temperament, into a gesture. On the momentary and ecstatic character of artistic experience in Yeats see especially the unpublished dialogue *The Poet and the Actress* (quoted by Ellmann, *The Identity of Yeats*, 1954, p. 105): 'The end of art is ecstasy and that cannot exist without pain. It is a sudden sense of power and of peace that comes when we have before our mind's eye a group of images which obeys us, which leaves us free, and which satisfies the needs of our soul.' There are many similar testimonies to the sudden descent of the experiences, but it plainly lasted some time during the *Deirdre of the Sorrows* evening, and on another occasion an hour's duration is mentioned: see especially the 'Anima Hominis' section of *Per Amica Silentia Lunae*, sections xi and xii, and Vendler, pp. 28–29.

9. *Plays for an Irish Theatre*, p. ix.

In the passage about *Deirdre of the Sorrows* Yeats described the reverie in terms of the listener's experience. But he also often spoke of it in terms of the experience of the *persona*; then it is the joy and self-fulfilment which he preferred to stress. Hence his famous assertion that in the midst of disaster Hamlet and Lear are gay. 'Shakespeare's persons', he writes,

when the last darkness has gathered about them, speak out of an ecstasy that is one half the self-surrender of sorrow, and one half the last playing and mockery of the victorious sword, before the defeated world.[1]

He cites Timon and Cleopatra also. As he completes his life and consummates his image, 'shaping joy' is what a great tragic character has in common with a creative artist; he *becomes* such an artist, but his artefact is his own life, his sorrow is 'pure', that is, free from self-pity and gloom. Each one masters his sufferings and is born anew into the state of a permanent image, as though he were the golden bird of Byzantium itself. Indeed, the first Byzantium poem mimes and describes this very transformation.

It is all this, then, which piles up behind that question which we may now recall—'Did Shakespeare in *Richard II* discover poetic reverie?'

We can guess what passage from the play Yeats might have been thinking of when he asked Dorothy Wellesley this question. The year before he had quoted a couple of lines from *Richard II* and asked, 'Do you not feel there the wide-open eyes?'[2]—the eyes, that is, of the 'wise man who was blind from very wisdom'. The lines come from the speech that goes:

> For God's sake let us sit upon the ground
> And tell sad stories of the death of kings;
> How some have been deposed, some slain in war,
> Some haunted by the ghosts they have deposed,
> Some poisoned by their wives, some sleeping killed.
> All murthered . . .

The strong, incantatory rhythms, Yeats might have argued, depersonalize Richard as he moves towards the vast generalization

1. *Essays*, p. 314. For 'style at play' compare pp. 212–13, n. 7 above, *A Vision* (1937), p. 166, and *Essays*, p. 312.
2. *Letters*, p. 853.

supported by tradition; this ever-expanding tragic rhythm rubs out the marks of individuality; the face becomes a lamenting, stylized Byzantine or Japanese mask; we commune with the falling king in an experience shaped by sorrow at our common mortality. This speech, and others in the play, including John of Gaunt's, communicate primarily as artefacts, only secondarily, if at all, as expressions of character. Certainly it is true that Gaunt is an artfully arranged cluster of tropes and commonplaces rather than an individual (at least when the play is only being read and not acted). Yeats has a good chance of finding in the text of *Richard II* the impersonal reverie which belongs to a more powerful and more generalized life than that of the individual.

IV

I would like now to try and focus what has been exhibited so far upon Yeats's own plays.

We shall not, it seems, find that the tragic reverie has been successfully given life in the plays that Yeats had written up to the date of the 'Tragic Theatre' essay, 1910–11—not even, or not quite, in his own *Deirdre*. Deirdre's rhythms never achieve, nor does her situation ever permit, the incantatory, depersonalizing reverie of passion. There is too much pathos, and too much sheer strength of character, too abounding a personal accent, fluttering and quickening through everything.[3] This judgement could be argued about; there is certainly every sign that since his earliest plays Yeats had been striving towards effects of tragic reverie; it is possible, indeed, that by dint of actor's voice and stance the right combination of marmoreal stillness and turbulent energy[4] was accomplished in Abbey performances now lost to us of *Deirdre*, *The King's Threshold*, *The Shadowy Waters*. But we should remember that it would have been difficult for Yeats to have produced persons exactly conforming to a theory that had not yet been clearly formulated. There are surely no clear instances, at least, of those joyous consummations of the artefact that Yeats observed in the Shakespearian moment. Those are enacted in the later poems, but not in the earlier plays.

3. For argument, see chap. iii of my *Yeats the Playwright* (1963). Yeats did claim the effect for his own *Deirdre* in *Plays for an Irish Theatre*, p. ix.
4. *Essays*, p. 316.

On the other hand, if we look at the later plays—those written after 1915—some of them seem designed to do everything that the reverie does. It is not so much a case of the characters within the plays aspiring to reverie as of the plays themselves so aspiring. They try to induce the great Shakespearian moment of tragic ecstasy; they try to enact in their own persons, as it were, the lyricism, the unmixed passion and integrity of fire which Yeats attributed to Hamlet or Lear at the moments when they compose their last symbolic attitudes. The plays themselves become great personalities in their own right; having acquired unity of being and heroic self-possession, like Hamlet himself, their dramatic form strives, in Pater's words, to approach the 'unity of a lyrical ballad . . . a single strain of music'.[5]

All this may sound obscure and excessively metaphorical. But it is only a way of saying that many of the later plays aspire to resemble as closely as possible the later symbolist poems. It is not improper to think of those poems as the equivalents of the poetic reveries of Richard II or Timon, as Yeats expounds them. Their speaker is very often a great dramatic *persona*, whose name is usually but not always the same as the poet's. The compliments paid by Yeats to Synge's Deirdre fit his own poems better.

I do not of course make the same claims for the plays, but the aspiration is there. The devices by which the plays are brought close to the nature of the symbolist poems—the self-dependent structure, the use of the dance, chorus, masks, music, and so on —have often been described. We may locate the reverie, which is supposed to transcend individuality and draw us down into the more powerful life, in some of these devices, especially perhaps in the dance. The strong rhythms, the masked face, the mysterious conjunction of life and artefact, dancer and dance—all these are, *mutatis mutandis*, the bodily equivalent of something like Richard II's lament. And we can find in the later work the verbal equivalents, too, of those wide-eyed tragic rhythms; they have a power that appears nowhere in the earlier plays:

> In pity for man's darkening thought
> He walked that room and issued thence
> In Galilean turbulence;
> The Babylonian starlight brought

5. *Appreciations*, p. 211.

A fabulous, formless darkness in;
Odour of blood when Christ was slain
Made all Platonic tolerance vain
And vain all Doric discipline
                    (*The Resurrection, ad fin.*)

'Into the unity of a choric song', Walter Pater wrote, 'the perfect drama ever tends to return, its intellectual scope deepened . . . but still with an unmistakable singleness, or identity, in its impression on the mind.'[6]

> *Second Attendant.* Why must those holy, haughty feet descend
>   From emblematic niches, and what hand
>   Ran that delicate raddle through their white?
>   My heart is broken, yet must understand.
>   What do they seek for? Why must they descend?
> *First Attendant.* For desecration and the lover's night.
> *Second Attendant.* I cannot face that emblem of the moon
>   Nor eyelids that the unmixed heavens dart,
>   Nor stand upon my feet, so great a fright
>   Descends upon my savage, sunlit heart.
>   What can she lack whose emblem is the moon?
> *First Attendant.* But desecration and the lover's night.
>   (*A Full Moon in March, ad fin.*)

Does all this finally mean, then, that Yeats tried to validate his idea of the Shakespearian moment (which is both a historical and an aesthetic moment) by embodying it in the composition of the later plays? Something of the sort may be admitted, but there are serious and interesting qualifications to be made.

V

In one of his letters Yeats expressed the hope that when Ben Jonson put the praise of Virgil into Horace's mouth in *The Poetaster*, he was really writing about Shakespeare. Yeats often quoted:

> And for his *poesie*, 'tis so ramm'd with life,
> That it shall gather strength of life, with being,
> And liue hereafter, more admir'd, then now.[7]

6. Ibid., p. 211.
7. *Letters*, p. 479; cf. *Autobiographies*, p. 480, and *Per Amica Silentia Lunae*, in *Essays*, p. 528. From *The Poetaster*, v.i.136–8.

In the Yeatsian contexts we have been concerned with, 'life' is in the depths below the naturalistic surface; reverie grants access to that world. At the archetypal level, what is powerful is so because it is generalized and shared; individuality, that separates man from man, is lost. In the primordial depths Cuchulain, Othello, Job, and the Ancient Mariner are folded in a single party. It is the realm of the Mothers, at the roots of the World Ash. If we get our mythologies mixed up down there, there is some excuse for us. And yet if Jonson *was* thinking of Shakespeare when he wrote of the life with which Virgil's poetry is rammed, he can hardly have been thinking of life in that sense.

Shakespeare's concern with individuality, with the unique case, has always been something of a stumbling-block. Thomas Rymer thought it vulgar and unphilosophical; and Yeats seems constantly to evade the facts; he seems even to have made the mistake of confusing Jonsonian humour with Shakespearian character.[8] The subject of (Shakespearian) drama, he affirms, is not man himself, but purified passion.[9] This is really the point where Yeats attaches himself not to what Shakespearian drama really is but to what he would like it to be—something more akin to heroic drama, to the plays, for example, of Dryden, where men tend to be merely surrogates for passions. 'Life' in Shakespeare, more often than not, enforces a sharp awareness of individuality. Characters in Shakespearian drama are commonly engaged in expressing their dissatisfaction with any Yeatsian definition of them that would lump them all together as 'eddies of momentary breath'. Love defines, hatred defines, and men ask each other or the gods the most resonant of all Shakespearian questions: 'Who is it that can tell me who I am?' Lear does not want to know what species he belongs to.

Is this kind of question, then, excluded from Yeats's plays because of the primacy of the depersonalizing reverie? I think not. Since Yeats's accounts of his experiences directs us to think so much in terms of fragile and momentary enlightenments, it seems only fair to approach this question too with the same scale to hand. There are other kinds of Shakespearian moment besides the ones that allure to reverie; there are those which clarify unique dilemmas and illuminate the fate of the individual.

8. *Autobiographies*, pp. 191–2.   9. *Plays and Controversies*, p. 105.

Some of Yeats's later plays are primarily plays of ideas. *The Resurrection* and *Calvary* are both recognizable as continuations of the old myth about subjective and objective men which, in the old Abbey period, had helped Yeats to get Shakespeare's history plays and his own legendary plays into some kind of imaginative relation with one another. But neither *Calvary* nor *The Resurrection* characterize their persons strongly enough to awaken our interest in them instead of in the author's ideas. *The Words upon the Window-Pane* is a play of ideas exploded from inside by a 'magnification', a great personality; it has something in common with *The Green Helmet* in being a paradigm of that mythical catastrophe, a little before Shakespeare's birth, when personification yielded to characterization,[1] when the 'great man' appeared, cast out of the whale's belly. But Swift, the central figure, is in so very strange a position in relation to the audience that its normal responses to dramatic characterization are somewhat inhibited.

There are, however, four or five plays in which the individuating characteristics of hero or heroine are, if not themselves at all complex or particularized, none the less the mainsprings of the movement. In *At the Hawk's Well*, for example, our attention is elaborately invited for Cuchulain's courage, both as the quality that distinguishes him from others and that determines the course and the results of the play's action. In *The Only Jealousy of Emer*, it is a self-effacing love that distinguishes the heroine from the other woman in the play; it gives her her rank; and upon it pivots the encounter of natural and supernatural which the play tells about. More and more we begin to feel that at the centre of these plays is some distinguished creature of this sort, quite simple and grand, out of the sagas, but at the same time quite sharply individuated. Their task is not to reach towards the 'pure contemplation' of tragic reverie, but to make severe and exciting decisions. It is an urgent moment when Emer, with a single renunciatory phrase, cancels the bond that draws Cuchulain away into the lunar world—a moment as different as possible from Deirdre's rapture of grief.

The Herne's Egg is also concerned with the ambiguity of the gifts the gods provide. The gods offer, or threaten, transcendence; but the hero, out of some stubborn preference for the

1. *Autobiographies*, p. 191.

blind man's ditch, some conviction, or old allegiance of his own, fails or refuses. One remembers Aoife's question in 'The Grey Rock'—

> Why must the lasting love what passes,
> Why are the gods by men betrayed?

Men betray the gods because they prefer each other, or themselves. There is a great—perhaps a truly Shakespearian—moment in *The Herne's Egg* when the hero, alone on the mountain-top about to die, really does ask who he is, and, like his Shakespearian prototype, has a Fool to help him to an answer. The excitement for the audience here is, in its way, of an intellectual sort—will the hero comprehend his dilemma in time? It matches the excitement of the moment in *The Resurrection*—a supremely thrilling moment—when the Greek touches the beating heart in the phantom's side—and that particular idea, at least, is made clear for ever. Again the kind of involvement proposed here seems some distance from the tragic reverie; the lightning-flash helps us to see rather than submit; it illuminates the features of the situation and of the persons. There should be a point even in a problem-play (as Shakespeare at any rate realized) where things are cleared up.[2]

Constantly in these final plays one feels the working out of the ancient dialogue of self and soul, and the intention to dramatize the moment when the self chooses to 'commit the crime once more', or when the woman young and old chooses the 'horror of daybreak' for her lot. *Purgatory*, the greatest of them, is filled with the central character's continual brooding over his mixed nature; the spirits in the play, like the Self in the last stanza of 'A Dialogue of Self and Soul', are living through 'in exact detail' the circumstances of their vanished lives:

2. It is doubtful, however, if Yeats would have accepted the distinction drawn here. He writes in the 'Tragic Theatre' essay, still with reference to the reverie, that in the supreme moment of tragic art there comes upon one that strange sensation as though the hair of one's head stood up' (*Essays*, p. 301). In *The Words upon the Window-Pane* Miss Mackenna uses the same physical metaphor about experiences at séances (*Wheels and Butterflies*, p. 49) and this in its turn connects with Yeats's description of what he felt when he came across the original incidents which inspired the beating heart (in *The Resurrection*) in Crookes's *Studies in Psychical Research* (*Wheels and Butterflies*, p. 109). The audience itself is meant to feel the 'terror of the supernatural' rather than to have its ideas clarified (perhaps there is a bit of both), and Yeats would probably not have been interested in distinguishing between the sensations accompanying that terror and those accompanying 'the supreme moment of tragic art'.

> I am content to follow to its source
> Every event in action or in thought,

declares the Self. Such is the condition of purgatory. Although it is, in the philosophical mythology, a condition which is to be followed by release and transcendence, the drama, like the poem, is centred upon the torturing process of self-examination and self-definition. What has happened to that rapturous smoothing away of the lines of selfhood which marks the poetic reverie? It seems that in *purgatory* and *reverie* we have discovered yet another Yeatsian myth of antithesis.

It should be added, too, that the speech-rhythms of both *The Herne's Egg* and *Purgatory* are, more than any of Yeats's other verse, invented to allow full play to accents wild and clownish, subtly alert, unfigurative—at any rate a long way from the anonymous voice of the ballad-singer or the strong enchantments of Elizabethan rhetoric. At their root lies not the ghostly voice, but the conversabilities of the modern novel, the conversational idiom that Eliot borrowed for *The Cocktail Party*.

As a playwright Yeats never relaxed his principles enough to admit the individual into his plays as freely and generously as he admitted him into his poems. That is one reason why the poems are so much more Shakespearian, so much more dramatic, than the plays. But it is possible to believe that from toiling with Cuchulain and his other characters through fifty years of playmaking Yeats did learn something. He said himself that even Shakespeare learnt from his characters. There is a letter of 1928 to Sean O'Casey[3] which ought to be famous in the history of modern drama: my last quotation shall be of part of it:

Dramatic action is a fire that must burn up everything but itself; there should be no room in a play for anything that does not belong to it; the whole history of the world must be reduced to wallpaper in front of which the characters must pose and speak.

Among the things that dramatic action must burn up are the author's opinions; while he is writing he has no business to know anything that is not a portion of that action. Do you suppose for one moment that Shakespeare educated Hamlet and King Lear by telling them what he thought and believed? As I see it, Hamlet and Lear educated Shakespeare, and I have no doubt that in the process of that education he found out that he was an altogether different man to what he thought himself, and had altogether different beliefs.

PART III

CONTEMPORARIES

13

Character and imagination
in Conrad

He loved these dreams and the success of his
imaginary achievements. They were the best
parts of life, its secret truth, its hidden reality.

Imagination, the enemy of men, the father of all
terrors.   *Lord Jim*

I

'A man of great sensibilities; of exalted and dreamy temperament; with a terrible gift of irony and of gloomy disposition'—
Conrad's description of Apollinary Korzeniowski fits his son. As
we read through the letters in Jean-Aubry's collection, parallels
of another kind may be perceived, *ébauches* of the fiction,
dissolving views of the Conrad hero in a crisis of mistrust, a poet
of the sea and of human honour

> qu'un Dieu moqueur
> Condamne à peindre, hélas! sur les ténèbres.

Conrad was, at times, his own hollow man:

My head feels as if full of sawdust. Of course many people's heads are
full of sawdust—the tragic part of the business is in my being aware
of it. The man who finds out that apparently innocent truth about himself is henceforth of no use to mankind . . . I am like a tight-rope dancer
who, in the midst of his performance, should suddenly discover that he
knows nothing about tight-rope dancing (i.247).[1]

Conrad's desperate struggles with finished or unfinished work
form an intriguing commentary on the adventures and despairs

First published in *Cambridge Journal*, iii, 1950, 727–40.

1. References preceded by a volume number are to *Joseph Conrad. Life and
Letters* by G. Jean-Aubry (London, 1927).

of a Nostromo or a Lord Jim, the height of their aspirings as well as the trajectory of their falls: 'The last shred of honour is gone—also the last penny' (on his inability to finish *The Rescue*); 'The end of [*Lord Jim*] has been pulled off with a steady drag of 21 hours. I sent wife and child out of the house (to London) and sat down at 9 a.m. with a desperate resolve to be done with it' (i.295). The mood echoes Nostromo's: 'I am going to make it the most famous and desperate affair of my life—wind or no wind.' And then there is the punishment of despair:

I've been satanically ambitious, but there's nothing of a devil in me, worse luck. The *Outcast* is a heap of sand, the *Nigger* a splash of water, *Jim* a lump of clay. A stone, I suppose, will be my next gift to impatient mankind—before I get drowned in mud to which even my supreme struggles won't give a simulacrum of life (i.299).

His occupation as a writer of imaginative prose made demands upon Conrad's nature which he faced with equivocation and a kind of terror. Perhaps he felt that the exercise of the imaginative power itself threatened to melt his 'blessed stiffness before the inward and the outward terrors'. Such dissolution was a cause of Jim's ἁμάρτημα, his deadly mistake in his progress towards virtue. The writing of fiction for bread was an invitation to those phantasms of the dead and living which throng the pages of *Nostromo* and *Under Western Eyes* to irrupt into the mind, hungry spectres to which one must, like Captain Whalley (in *The End of the Tether*), give up 'something of one's truth and dignity in order to live':

It is strange [Conrad wrote to E. L. Sanderson]. The unreality of it seems to enter one's real life, penetrate into the bones, make the very heart-beats pulse illusions through the arteries. One's will becomes the slave of hallucinations, responds only to shadowy impulses, waits on imagination alone. A strange state, a trying experience, a kind of fiery trial of untruthfulness. And one goes through it with an exaltation as false as all the rest of it (i.283).

It was the chamber of Phantastes in *The Faerie Queene*, a place of 'idle thoughts and fantasies, / Devices, dreames, opinions unsound', which was occupied by a hollow-browed and melancholy individual:

> one by his vew
> Mote deeme him borne with ill-disposed skyes,
> When oblique *Saturne* sate in the house of agonyes,

and Conrad lingered, appalled and fascinated, on the enigmatic threshold. Yet he trod it often, and often underwent the trial. The imagination, he said in a letter of advice to a young writer,

should be used to create human souls: to disclose human hearts . . . To accomplish it you must cultivate your poetic faculty,—you must give yourself up to emotions (no easy task). You must squeeze out of yourself every sensation, every thought, every image,—mercilessly, without reserve and without remorse: you must search the darkest corners of your heart, the most remote recesses of your brain . . . And you must do it sincerely, at any cost: you must do it so that at the end of your day's work you should feel exhausted, emptied of every sensation and every thought, with a blank mind and an aching heart, with the notion that there is nothing,—nothing left in you (i.183).

These images of violence, this searching of the cranks and caverns of the brain, show the efforts the process demanded of Conrad himself. Yet he wrote, years later, 'to be a great magician one must surrender oneself to occult and irresponsible powers, either outside or within one's breast'. The writing of imaginative literature appears to him in the light of a Faustian bargain, and 'I have a positive horror of losing even for one moving moment that full possession of myself which is the first condition of good service'. Only the conscience of the writer, that which enables him to maintain an 'exact notion of sincerity', can preserve his selfhood:

In that interior world where [the artist's] thought and his emotions go seeking for the experience of imagined adventures, there are no policemen, no law, no pressure of circumstance or dread of opinion to keep him within bounds. Who then is going to say Nay to his temptations if not his conscience? (A Familiar Preface to *A Personal Record*)

The reluctance and equivocations of Conrad in the face of his self-imposed imaginative task are some help in explaining the nature of his heroes, and the movements of his own mind provide a key to distinctions that may be made between one fiction and another. Conrad's heroes, partly fashioned in his own image, are sometimes highly imaginative men, and yet at the same time men who can be punished by what may be described as a degeneration of the imaginative faculty. Or their imagination in a state of decay becomes the symbol for their loss of selfhood, the point where Spenser's idle fantasies, 'Infernall Hags, Centaurs, feendes, Hippodames', swarm in to encumber eyes and ears. Conrad's double vision of the dangers as well as the achievements of the imaginative life accounts for his creation of types who are antithetical to one another, heroes who refuse, for 'conscience' sake, to be imaginative, and heroes whose triumphs are substantially imaginative in nature. And perhaps it was his own consciousness of the Faustian bargain that endows with such an intensity of despair and horror those of his figures who are haunted by irresponsible powers. Conrad recognized that imaginative achievement of any kind involved a risk—the churned-up sea might disclose all Topsell's kingdom craftily rapacious beneath its surface. And yet that inwardness which he advised Noble to write from very often implied an exploration of the inward life of his characters too, an attempt to show how their passion for prestige, for honour, or for a woman's love, can be transformed into imaginative activity as fine-grained as the Henry James conscience.

II

A description of a part of Conrad's work with these antitheses in mind is also a method of discerning the characteristic powers and weaknesses of Conrad's heroes in relation to each other and their whole context. It is, for example, in *Typhoon* (1902) and *The Shadow Line* (1916) that we find Conrad handling the theme of mere, blank resistance to those potencies in and outside a man which threaten to destroy his capacity for service. The strength of MacWhirr in *Typhoon* is made in perfect dullness; he is *not* 'one of your fancy skippers': 'Having just enough imagination to carry him through each successive day, and no more, he was tranquilly sure of himself.' It is this 'blessed stiffness' which saves the *Nan-Shan* and raises his seaman's honour to a kind of sublimity with his laconic: 'Can't have fighting aboard the ship.' 'The instinct of primitive man . . . is awakened again in the breast' of the civilized by the troubled sea. 'One seems to have known gales as enemies', wrote Conrad in *The Mirror of the Sea*, but such personalization of the hostile storm is not for Mac-Whirr; like the steamship, he is engaged in a slogging match—he receives smashing blows, but he advances. The climax of the story deflects us from the spectacular behaviour of the China seas to that of the crew stretching life-lines across the hold for the fighting coolies: the task, as conceived in MacWhirr's dutiful mind, has an imperial simplicity, legendary in its grandeur, yet professional and didactic also. MacWhirr's triumph is the triumph of doggedness, of the 'few simple notions' that Lord Jim was able to include within a larger field and to some degree displace as irrelevant to his own accomplishment.

The narrator-hero of *The Shadow Line*, too, succeeds in the face of subtle dangers, in preserving his force. The peril here proceeds from another man's thick-coming fancies: Mr Burns, the chief mate, unhinged by fever, believes that the ship is haunted by the ghost of her dead captain; she becomes bound in 'an evil spell' of sickness and calm. When the narrator (the new captain) first hears from the mate of the old captain's intention 'to have gone wandering about the world till he lost [the ship] with all hands', he is 'profoundly shocked':

That man had been in all essentials but his age just such another man as myself. Yet the end of his life was a complete act of treason . . . It appeared that even at sea a man could become the victim of evil spirits. I felt on my face the breath of unknown powers that shape our destinies.

The dead captain's frightening wickedness is seen only in its effect on the mind of Burns and in the way the eerie travail of the frustrated schooner, the ship without a crew, begins to help the mate's sick fancies to make their inroads on the mind of the commander himself: the crew are ghosts, by thrusting one's hand over the side of the ship 'one could touch some unearthly substance'. Yet the whole task of the narrator is to resist the pressure of these feverish imaginings, 'the seamen's instinct alone survived whole in my moral dissolution'. And the ship is finally brought home, yet not without Conrad's having told us something of what it is, within themselves, that men have to resist. When Captain Giles, the solid man of conscience, the kind of man Jim failed to be and Captain Whalley began by being, meets the narrator on his return, he tells him 'with his air of conscious virtue':

'A man should stand up to his bad luck, to his mistakes, to his conscience, and all that sort of thing. Why—what else would you have to fight against?'
     I kept silent. I don't know what he saw in my face, but he asked abruptly:
     'Why—you aren't faint-hearted?'
     'God only knows, Captain Giles,' was my sincere answer.

What do men have to fight against? A disordered imagination
may be a weak place—what happens if the breach is made? *The
Nigger of the Narcissus* is in many ways complementary to *The
Shadow Line*, not least in that it further explicates the answer
Captain Giles could not get. Here, instead of mere resistance, we
have a study of a whole crew of merchant seamen who become
the victims of a disorder of heart and mind. Conrad's merchant
seamen are not heroized creatures—his comment on Marcus
Aurelius' precept, 'Let all thy words have the accent of heroic
truth' (*A Personal Record*) is relevant here. For the accent of
heroic truth transmits itself unmistakably in MacWhirr's 'Can't
have fighting' or Podmore's 'Galley . . . my business'; yet it
does so with a marked obliquity because it is the result of obedi-
ence to a conscience deliberately 'humble' rather than fine-
grained or 'romantic'. But James Wait, the Nigger, has, like
Kurtz in the *Heart of Darkness*, a 'haze of meaning' whose
bringing out is the factor which destroys that direct simplicity
of a seaman's yarn—and a seaman's conscience—that Marlow's
tales so constantly refined upon.[2] Wait's spectral nimbus is
'brought out' by the very detachment and irony with which
the man at its centre is presented. As a 'coloured gentleman'
with an inextinguishable baritone, who likes to think of himself
as malingering when he is, in fact, dying, Wait has a substantial
reality and appeal. The tyrannous seductions of this 'prince' and
'emperor' induce a curdled devotion in the hearts of his subjects
the crew, not unlike the relationship of the Russian and the
'Intended' to that aboundingly eloquent 'universal genius'
Kurtz. Beyond this, Wait has a larger imaginative force, but it is
a force which requires no *verbalisme* to make it convincing:[3] we
can watch it operative in the lives of his fellows. Wait becomes
the gap in nature through which break 'occult and irresponsible
powers'. It is his unsettling presence that sets Donkin thieving,
accentuates Podmore's mania, starts the men fighting, and
brings the whole crew to the edge of mutiny; everyone loses,
for several moving moments, 'that full possession of [them-

2. To Marlow 'the meaning of an episode was not inside like a kernel but
outside, enveloping the tale which brought it out only as a glow brings out a
haze . . .' (*Heart of Darkness*).

3. On Conrad's *verbalisme* see the excellent work by Professor Raymond Las
Vergnas, *Joseph Conrad* (Paris, 1938), pp. 62 ff. This is the best general study of
Conrad. Cf. also F. R. Leavis, *The Great Tradition* (London, 1948), pp. 177 ff.

selves] which is the first condition of good service'. It is a replica of that situation ('We have all heard of simple men selling their souls for love or power to some grotesque devil', *A Personal Record*) of which Conrad had a 'positive horror', and there is a certain horror about Wait in his phantasmal aspect: we can hypo-statize Death only from our knowledge of the dying, and Wait becomes, in his decline into a skeleton, gradually assimilated to the mysterious figure at his side, while the superstition that he is delaying the progress of the ship by refusing to die forms another ray of his spectral illumination. Within the Nigger's orbit wholesale deterioration of all the conditions for good service is perilously near; the superstition, the mutinous dis-order, the generosity clouded by malice and mania, are the equivocal and burlesque subtleties of the irresponsible powers which invalidate the conscience. Here, as in the *Heart of Darkness*, is something from which Conrad normally shrank, a recognition that man is the object of weird and uncontrollable solicitations, that 'the mind of man is capable of anything' (*Heart of Darkness*) when 'to the negation of the habitual, which is safe, there is added the affirmation of the unusual, which is dangerous' (*An Outpost of Progress*).

Conrad was not, however, content merely to issue a call for resistance or to document strange states and trying experiences analogous to those of the writer of fiction who feels his blood and bone interpenetrated by the shadowy creatures of Phantastes' chamber. His first two novels, *Almayer's Folly* and *An Outcast of the Islands*, may be read as preparatives for the third and greater, *Lord Jim*. The organization of a novel is more complex than that of 'vision' or fable, and it is profitable here to note Conrad's attempts to endow his heroes not only with a sense of stability threatened but with something more positive—with passions, with *raison d'être*, and with the wish to transform such passions into achievement, to realize dreams of love and power. Such transformation, in that it is an expression and ordering of emo-tion, is itself imaginative; and expenditure of spirit upon it, whether successful or wishful, is an index of imaginative energy in the character concerned. This energy may, however, be cor-rupted at its source by a pervasive weakness, by very incompe-tence of soul; the images that it produces will then be false even to the passions that nourish it.

Almayer is a man of this kind: his ἁμαρτία has taken on the
proportions of an unfailingly apposite irony. He sketches with
some completeness the fate that might have befallen Jim: his
original 'mistake'—his marriage to Lingard's protegée—is not
lived down but becomes a debility which eats away the substance
of his life. His love for his daughter is presented merely as a constituent of his dream of grandeur, and what little imaginative
energy he has left takes perverted forms, fallacious hope and
nightmare. In *An Outcast of the Islands* Willems's life can be seen
as a struggle to find a means of imaginative expression in his love
for Aïssa, which is designedly contrasted with his relationship
with his wife, whom he has acquired, in Almayer's fashion, as the
price to be paid for his career. But Willems is defeated in this
struggle, just as he had failed in those relationships of trust which
demand a conscience. His love for Aïssa appears to him as a
mésalliance, a 'surrendering to a wild creature the unstained
purity of his life, of his race, of his civilization'; but Willems's
final failure with Aïssa is also a failure in imagination, an inability to respond to the demands that Aïssa makes (for she has
the right) upon his courage and single-mindedness. In the final
scene, the poverty of his imaginative response has become a
corruption which indulges him with nightmare images reminiscent of Almayer's at a similar crisis. Willems, with his failure to
fuse his impoverished imagination with his conscienceless
respect for himself and his white civilization, is a *persona* more
subtle and ambitious than any in *Almayer's Folly*; that it is obfus-
cated may be due to the reader's feeling that Conrad's own
disapproval of such *mésalliances* has interfered with his use of
Aïssa to demonstrate Willems's failure in imaginative activity.
When Lord Jim fell in love, he did so with someone conveniently
white.

Lord Jim is, indeed, the touchstone of our theme. For this novel
displays with a bewildering largeness of ambiguity all Conrad's
ambivalence in the face of an imaginative nature, all his recognition of the perils it must undergo in order to enjoy a prize
markedly Hesperidean. Jim 'wouldn't let me forget how
imaginative he was':

Ever since he had been 'so high' . . . he had been preparing himself . . .
had been elaborating dangers and defences, expecting the worst, re-
hearsing his best. He must have led a most exalted existence . . . A

succession of adventures, so much glory, such a victorious progress! and the deep sense of his sagacity crowning every day of his inner life. He forgot himself; his eyes shone . . .

Jim lives, the 'imaginative beggar', in a 'fanciful realm of reck-lessly heroic aspirations'. Yet this imagination, in its other aspect as the breach for evil solicitations is—twice—his downfall. Jim deserted the *Patna* because his 'confounded imagination' evoked for him all the horrors of the seemingly inevitable disaster; 'gifted poor devil with the faculty of swift and fore-stalling vision', he could depict to himself too clearly what pain it would be to drown. The act of desertion itself still retains a penumbra of mystery, for it proceeds, with a sufficient decorum, from the atmosphere of metaphysical evil which surrounds the conduct and persons of the other white officers and the last events on board the *Patna*, an atmosphere burlesqued and mean, 'planned by the tremendous disdain of the Dark Powers'. The irruption of Gentleman Brown and his gang into Patusan is another of Fate's grim jokes. Brown slackens the τόνος of Jim's soul by his undesigned play upon the former mistake—'it was as if a demon had been whispering advice in [Brown's] ear'. To such solicitation the man endowed with an interior world 'where his thought and his emotions go seeking for the ex-perience of imagined adventures', the man who is, like Lord Jim, 'a finished artist in that peculiar way', lends a ready ear. 'Who then is going to say Nay to his temptations if not his conscience?'

Should Jim merely have 'resisted'? Conrad's reply is ambigu-ous, too. Jim is a 'gentleman'; 'he came', says Marlow, 'from the right place; he was one of us', and Marlow at first ascribes to Jim a ἁμαρτία of the Almayer kind, an act of treason to a con-ditioning modest but absolute in its claims. Nor does the author ever allow Marlow to encourage in Jim the development of a conscience 'fine-grained' in the sense of being sufficiently nice to admit of politic compromises. Conscience is real, that 'heir-loom of the ages, of the race, of the group, of the family', that 'deeper sense of things, lawful and unlawful', as Conrad des-cribed it in *A Personal Record*; honour is real; the dignity of the service is to be maintained: Marlow never condones Jim's act of criminal weakness. Jim has to recover the 'unthinking and blessed stiffness' and he does succeed in doing this in the long and silent struggle in Marlow's room; thenceforward he is permitted to embark, a Stoic προκόπτων on the path of virtue, upon his 'period of probation' as a ship-chandler's clerk. And yet there is a sense in which mere resistance, the rehabilitation of that inward and outward toughness, is irrelevant or inadequate to Jim as he is given us. Obliquely the story leads us to realize this. For, in answering the question 'What should Jim do next?' both Captain Brierly and the lieutenant of the French gunboat that salvaged the *Patna* bring 'those few simple notions that you must cling to if you want to live decently and would like to die easy' to bear upon the situation. Brierly wants Jim to 'clear out', to 'creep twenty feet underground': 'The fellow's a gentleman if he ain't fit to be touched—he will understand. He must! This infernal publicity is too shocking', and, on Marlow's refusal to co-operate in the business of getting the embarrassing criminal off the scene: 'The worst of it . . . is that all you fellows have no sense of dignity; you don't think enough of what you are supposed to be', an ironical echo of the remark already made by Jones in his speculations upon the causes of Brierly's own suicide, 'Neither you nor I, sir, had ever thought so much of ourselves.' The French lieutenant is aware that there is a limit to the bravest man's fortitude, but, if disaster occurs and in the process honour is lost, he is ready to deliver the stern, if makeshift, judgement of 'us'. The lieutenant's *honneur*, defined for us in all its majesty in de Vigny's *La Canne de Jonc*, a work which Conrad probably knew well, closes up the gap between human nature and society in a way that is admirable, but irrelevant to the imaginative events already set in train. Brierly's own fate, his verdict on himself of 'unmitigated guilt' due to the invasion of his life by 'one of those trifles that awaken ideas', combined with our perception that what he, in fact, does is to try to bribe Jim to run away like the unspeakable skipper of the *Patna*, bear suggestively on Jim's refusal to creep twenty feet underground.

For both Brierly and the lieutenant are enemies of the story, enemies of the imagination. Jim is not vulnerable to the ideas that destroy Brierly; he is to be seen in the context of his imaginative life as the sagacious Stein at once perceives, a context that can hardly be spoken of except in Stein's language of 'impalpable poesy'. Jim's real strength lies not in his ability to survive his disgrace, which in itself would not prevent him from becoming, as Marlow realizes, another Almayer or Willems. His strength lies in his power of reorganizing his life and actions on the imaginative and 'romantic' level which has always been the condition of his existence, and must be made to remain so if he is to continue to live and 'live it down'. Ideas of guilt and disgrace, even 'artful dodges to escape from the grim shadow of self-knowledge', any justification for the 'commonplace fears' that Marlow had felt about Jim's future—these cease to appear in the latter part of the book which becomes 'a heroic tale' of the 'conquest of love, honour, men's confidence'. Jim is making the effort to put his criminal act in the perspective of his whole imaginative achievement, which does not mean to condone it, but literally to live it down, to see it not as the sign of a pervasive ἁμαρτία, but as a ἁμάρτημα, in Stoic language 'a missing of the mark at which virtue aims'. He succeeds, and has the opportunity to become in his crowning moment, which, as with his prototypes, is coincident with his death, a hero of antique splendour, the saviour of Patusan, 'alone of his own superior kind'—a kind of Hercules, indeed, 'illum quem hominum fama, beneficiorum memor, in concilio caelestium collocavit', whose last moments of 'extraordinary success' are an abundant gratification of the visions of his boyish imagination. 'I affirm he had achieved greatness,' says Marlow, 'but the thing would be dwarfed in the telling, or rather in the hearing ... I could be eloquent were I not afraid you fellows had starved your imaginations to feed your bodies.' Jim's end, like Heyst's, is a kind of suicide and a kind of apotheosis, substantially Stoic in derivation. 'Hercules', Cicero observed, 'has gone to join the gods; but he would never have done so had he not paved the way for himself while he was still a man among men.' That might be a sufficiently relevant gloss on the part played by a conscience 'romantic' rather than 'humble' in the achievement of an imaginative triumph such as Jim's (for conscience has changed its meaning and function with the change in the hero's character) were it not for the final ambiguity, which must be seen in relation to Marlow's many refusals to 'affirm', of Jim's colloquy with Gentleman Brown. For Jim's achieved stability of imagination is not, it seems, proof against the demons that can still be nourished by it—'your imaginative people swing farther in any direction'. And yet, in the mechanism of the novel, it is Brown who enables that 'spirit so utterly out of reach' to proceed to his extraordinary success.[4]

Perhaps Conrad never attained again such a willing and ex-alted acceptance of the restless paradoxes of living as Stein des-cribes them: 'A man that is born falls into a dream like a man who falls into the sea', and yet his nature demands that he should follow the dream, immerse himself in that destructive element, the wish-created world of the romantic imagination. *Lord Jim* is a recognition, qualified enough, that success is possible; it implies that there are spots of time of a nature renovating to the poet 'in the endless and inspiring game of pursuing from day to day the ever-receding future'. The quotation is from Conrad's note on Turgenev, and Lord Jim does attain something of the precarious felicity of Lemm, the musician in *A House of Gentle-folk*, Turgenev's most potent objectification of the depths from which an artist's honours proceed. But—how cold is the shock of awakening! It was this theme, the human tragedy that attends upon the discovery that one is not such a fine fellow after all, that occupied Conrad in *Nostromo*, that recognition of Stein's that: 'It is not good for you to find you cannot make your dream come true, for the reason that you are not strong enough, or not clever enough.'

For in *Nostromo* the ambiguity is deeply integrated with the lives of the major characters, the Goulds and Nostromo. These are three studies in the imaginative attachments which men form, the 'spiritual value which everyone discovers in his own form of activity'. Gould, morally bound to make a success of the silver mine which had debauched the imagination of his father, is really accomplishing an ethical task which becomes his and his wife's means of imaginative expression: the Gould 'fairy-tale', as Decoud calls it, is an activity of the imagination which includes and transcends the mere *officia*:

[Mrs Gould] had laid her unmercenary hands, with an eagerness that made them tremble, upon the first silver ingot turned out still warm from the mould; and by her imaginative estimate of its power she en-

4. It will be seen from this analysis that Miss Bradbrook's opinion that *Lord Jim* tails off badly seems to me, like her view that that interesting little *fabliau* 'The Secret Sharer', is the 'perfected version' of *Lord Jim*, a misreading of Conrad's intention and Marlow's affirmations (*Joseph Conrad*, Cambridge, 1941, p. 25).

dowed that lump of metal with a justificative conception, as though it were not a mere fact, but something far-reaching and impalpable, like the true expression of an emotion or the emergence of a principle.

But for Gould the original justificative act is widely and obsessionally extended, the 'strange idea of justice' which Gould, with utter incongruity in Decoud's eyes, attaches to the mine, enlarges its meaning until the mine becomes 'symbolic of abstract justice' in Costaguana, and Gould is haunted by his *idée fixe* to the point of insanity. It turns into a fetish, and destroys his marriage: the mine is 'a wall of silver-bricks, erected by the silent work of evil spirits, between Mrs Gould and her husband'. The enterprise is a 'terrible success', yet it began as an act of moral justification seeking its expression 'in the experience of imagined adventures'.

For Nostromo, 'that man [with] a peculiar talent when anything striking to the imagination has to be done', the central incident of the novel, the attempt to rescue the lighter of silver, can be read as a last and desperate attempt to express and gratify the passion for being well spoken of which is the mainspring of his whole existence. It fails, and it is Nostromo's sense that he has failed in the expression, by means of the successful fulfilment of an absolute trust, of his inward passion, that contributes—together with Teresa's curse acting upon the mind of a 'romantic mouthpiece of the "people"',[5] Dr Monygham's lack of understanding and the tempting compulsions of the silver—to his feeling that his individuality has been betrayed. The mere presence of Decoud, the Parisian intellectual, on board the lighter appears to him one way in which this betrayal has been organized, for he had been commanded, against his own wish, to take him. Otherwise, Nostromo would probably have sunk the silver and gone down with it 'round his neck', his glory untarnished. From his sense of betrayal proceeds his crime and tragedy.

It is dangerous, for the sake of economy of statement, to offer this summary account of characters firmly planted in a context of such uncommon complexity. But, if we make every allowance for Gould's reaction against corrupt *politicos*, and for the distortions induced in Nostromo by silver and curses, it can still be said that the terrible failure of the one, and the terrible

5. Conrad's own description of Nostromo (Jean-Aubry, i.338).

success of the other, are, in their true inwardness, tragedies of men who are self-betrayed by the ambiguity of their most expressive and valuable impulses. Gould's idealizations breed strange compulsions, Nostromo's quest for an inviolable reputation is thwarted by an egoism that declines all but an unattainable garland. This, Conrad seems to say, is what happens to men who live beyond their strength, to 'artists' who attempt to transcend normal morality and the code of 'us', for the sake of an imagined rightness, a fantasy of perfect justice or perfect trust. Such men, in his words to Garnett, are satanically ambitious, though there's nothing of the devil in them. 'It is not good for you to find that you cannot make your dream come true.' And, indeed, in *Nostromo* the characters are not free of the devil that haunts the imaginative; the silver mine which they have chosen as their means to the sweet fruition of a heavenly crown is itself the centre, darkened with symbolism, of many solicitations to evil. It is guarded, subtly enough, by the 'legendary inhabitants of Azuera', the two gringos spectral and alive, 'dwelling to this day amongst the rocks, under the fatal spell of their success'. Their condition and their fate—to be 'rich and hungry and thirsty'—is constantly associated with that of the Goulds and Nostromo. As in the earlier stories, Conrad here enriches his theme with Fate and metaphysical aid withal, with the buzzing flies of Phantastes' chamber that are evidence of imagination become the victim of its own thaumaturgy.

III

Nostromo plumbs the depths of Conrad's pessimism. It would not be sensible to make too sharp a division between the writings I have discussed and the novels of the middle period, but it is plain that in the later works Conrad has refocused his theme. He puts in the centre of his compositions not the ambiguity of the imaginative nature but its capacity for devotion and its response to love. Dr Monygham, with his 'imaginative exaggeration of a correct feeling', finds in his devotion to Mrs Gould a means of rehabilitation: 'The doctor's soul, withered and shrunk by the shame of a moral disgrace, became implacable in the expansion of its tenderness.' Monygham, although he foreshadows the central preoccupations of *Under Western Eyes* and

Victory, is still ambiguous—for his tenderness saves Mrs Gould, it is true, but his implacability helps to destroy Nostromo. Love, loyalty, and devotion are not yet at the centre of the human scheme; in the earlier works they had always suffered displacement in favour of dreams, wishes, triumphs, all those sinkings or struggles in the destructive element within and without a single *persona* which seemed to Stein the last truth about human life. At first, *Under Western Eyes* seems to be yet another study in the decay of the imagination (of Razumov), a mere ghost story: 'The dead can live only with the exact intensity and quality of the life imparted to them by the living', and throughout the book Razumov is struggling with the phantom of the man he had betrayed; he is, literally, haunted by Haldin's shade; the 'ghost of that night [of Haldin's betrayal] pursued him', a phantom which he constantly thinks his contempt has vanquished and which as constantly reappears. Perhaps this emphasis deflects us too widely from Conrad's new purpose, and it is certain that the scenicized depiction of revolutionary *mœurs* throws the book out of shape. For Razumov is considerably more than a Russian version of Mr Burns: it is his love for Miss Haldin which saves him from ultimate undoing at the moment when he has done with life. More 'centred' is, in *The Secret Agent*, Mrs Verloc's love for Stevie, but it is in *Victory* that we are most able to plot the distance Conrad has travelled.

The movement of the book is like that of *Lord Jim*, but it is one of far greater range and power. Heyst begins as a man almost without personality, a figure so detached from life, except in his pity for the living, that he can be given any label—Enchanted Heyst, Hard Facts Heyst, the Spider, the Utopist, the Enemy, or the 'genuine gentleman'. His story is concerned with his deliberate plunge into the destructive element, but not that of fantasies of his own strength or cleverness: love is its unfamiliar name. Heyst almost creates Lena, just as Stevie's existence in *The Secret Agent* was one 'created by Mrs Verloc's genius'; 'Do you know,' says Lena to Heyst, 'it seems to me, somehow, that if you were to stop thinking of me I shouldn't be in the world at all!' Heyst's greatest achievement is not in any gratification of boyish visions, for he had none and retains to the end his fastidious mistrust of life, but in making possible the conditions for Lena's victory, 'capturing the very sting of death in the service of love'. The struggle in the book is not between love and the haunting phantoms of a corrupted imagination (as in *Under Western Eyes*), nor is it concerned with the effort to re-create the conditions for an imaginative existence (as in *Lord Jim*); it is a pitched battle between love and inhuman evil incarnate in Ricardo and his gang. This evil is represented not as the fantasia of a clouded imagination but with the objectivity of the great and little devils in *Dr Faustus*. The struggle, therefore, takes on a sharpness of drawing which is almost theological in character: 'I will play them for their souls', says Ricardo. Yet this world, which is not one of the terrors and exaltations of the ambiguous imagination but of Good and Evil, Holiness and Sin, is conceived with a verisimilitude which checks incredulity. There is, indeed, plenty of evidence in *Victory* that love has its own ambiguities. But in centring this theme in his work Conrad is more able to order and dispose Phantastes's warming familiars. The Faustian bargain is objectified into a morality, and if, because of that, it loses some of its cloudy intensity, it acquires a tightness of dramatic structure and a freedom from *verbalisme* which is all to the good.

It is not the full story, nor, certainly, the end of the story: 'I am always trying for freedom—within my limits', Conrad wrote in 1918 (ii.204). But it is a part of Conrad's journey: from Lord Jim, that lofty and solitary existence, to the creative and interacting duality, Heyst–Lena. It is a progress from the epic to the drama, and from the 'noble Stoicism' of de Vigny to Turgenev's bringing of 'all . . . problems and characters to the test of love' (*Notes on Life and Letters*). Conrad has sometimes been compared to the Elizabethan dramatists: he moves, indeed, from Chapman's celebration of the glories and corruptions attendant upon the *mens adepta* of the Herculean man to the fabulous symmetries of *The Tempest*:

> All thy vexations
> Were but my trials of thy love, and thou
> Hast strangely stood the test.

14
George Moore
as historian of consciences

It was in 1900, sitting in Dublin under his celebrated apple-trees, that George Moore was overcome by a feeling of his own goodness. 'An extraordinarily clear and inflexible moral sense rose up and confronted me', he wrote in *Salve*, '. . . I had never been able to do anything that I thought wrong, and my conscience had inspired my books.' The passage comes immediately after one which advocates polygamy; it is plain that Moore, lodged in the Catholic puritan city, is at his exercise again. Conscience, he seems to be saying, is a process by which the individual's 'ideas' or 'thought' will shape his deeds; if they fail to, 'if our deeds go down one set of lines and our ideas go down another', a life is wasted. For a novelist, this implies the possibility of tragedy or comedy according to which kind of story he chooses. In either case, a study in conscience is a study in the relation between 'ideas' and deeds. Moore claims to detect this interest as early as his first novel, *A Modern Lover* (1883). Most of us would probably think of this book, better known in its revised version *Lewis Seymour and Some Women* (1917), as a study in consciencelessness and an early example of the room-at-the-top syndrome; but it is comedy because there is no split in Lewis between what he does and his 'ideas' for himself. Plainly 'ideas' in this context is as tricky a word as 'conscience', for it does not mean simply notions or opinions but seems to include ambition, appetite, *amour propre*, and above all perhaps what Nature whispers to polygamous man.

The passage in *Salve* continues the tale of Moore's early novels:

First published in *Imagined Worlds: Essays on some English Novels and Novelists in Honour of John Butt* (ed. Maynard Mack and Ian Gregor, London, Methuen, 1968), pp. 257–76.

The Mummer's Wife declines, for she is without sufficient personal conscience to detach herself from the conventions in which she has been brought up. Alice Barton in *Muslin* is a preparatory study, a prevision of *Esther Waters*; both represent the personal conscience striving against the communal, and, feeling that I had learnt to know myself at last, I rose from the seat, and looked round, thinking that in Æ as in myself thought and action are at one. Alike, I said, in essentials, though to the casual observer regions apart . . . But everybody in Dublin thinks that he is like Æ as everybody in the world thinks he is like Hamlet. (*Salve*, reprint, 1947, pp. 23–24)

Æ and Hamlet have this in common: they stand, like E. M. Forster's singular Greek gentleman, at an angle to their universes, Mr Balfour's Ireland and Claudius's Denmark. Moore is choosing his ground. He is reminding us that while we may think of Hamlet as primarily a fine conscience whose ideas are not rightly related to his deeds, he is also—and is it secondarily? —one whose conscience strives against the rotten state. That latter theme is at least as important in Moore as it is unimportant in Henry James. He is on his mettle as Zola's ricochet in England; a primary impulse may have been the wish to infuriate the members of his own class by questioning their privileges and attitudes, but beneath the aesthetic foolery there is anger about Ireland and the poor. Nailing Claudius's guilt interests Moore as much in those three early novels as does imparting a fine grain to the characterization of their heroines. My purpose is chiefly to compare the three protagonists in the light of what Moore wrote in *Salve* about them; but no one is likely to find the books of great interest who imagines that sympathy for the victims of social injustice is separable from hatred for those who profit by it.

Any assessment is complicated by the existence of more than one version of each of the three works. It is characteristic of the whole Moorini mix-up that when Moore wrote in 1911 the passage just quoted from a late reprint of *Salve* there was no such book in existence as *Muslin*, which was first published in 1915.* There was only *A Drama in Muslin* (1886), a work whose enormous difference from its descendant requires exploration. But the primary task is to consider how the novels relate to

---

* Actually, the first edition of *Salve* (1912), pp. 32–33, reads slightly differently, and speaks not of *Muslin* but of *A Drama in Muslin*—C.J.R.

one another in the light of facts which do seem clear: that *A Mummer's Wife* (1884, radically revised in 1917) and *A Drama in Muslin* are now in a much worse state than the half-forgotten one to which Moore consigned *A Modern Lover* in *Salve*. They are unlikely to have been read by anybody, except dedicated specialists in Moore, under the age of forty; whereas *Esther Waters* (1894, and never revised so radically as the other two)[1] is still a famous book widely read in the 1960s, if we may judge by the place which it holds in various popular series.[2] The contrast between its fortunes and those of its two predecessors is a steep one. That putative reader sinking into the infirmity of age who has considered all three may be surprised and puzzled by it. It is true that the period covered by them is a long one, a decade during which Moore's artistic fortunes oscillated a good deal—he could little bear in later years to speak of the other novels which he wrote during it, nor shall we. It is true also that the assessment of these books can be and has been satisfactorily managed in terms of a movement from Zola to Balzac by way of Gautier and Huysmans.[3] Such evolutions are radical; yet the conviction may remain that a comparative study of the novels of the kind that the author himself sketched beneath the apple-tree in Ely Place will show that they share a deep-lying similarity of construction and design, and that there is something odd about the way in which the third has prospered at the expense of the other two.

The traveller who is determined to reach Moore Hall will eventually, after wandering far from the Ballinrobe road, come upon the reed-choked lake and the steep foursquare shell of the Georgian mansion, its defiant chimneystacks rising up into

1. This revision has been described by R. A. Gettmann in 'George Moore's revisions of *The Lake, The Wild Goose,* and *Esther Waters*', PMLA, lix, 1944, 540–55. It should be noted that Gettmann omits all mention of Moore's biggest reduction: the cut of seven pages in the 1894 edition from the story of the ruin of Sarah Tucker, entailing the omission of the original's 34th chapter and part of the 35th (see *Esther Waters*, 1894, pp. 271–7); Moore is obviously trying to get under control what remains in the final version a digressive disturbance to the structure.

2. The version used in these series is that of 1920. In 1936 *Esther Waters* was one of the first inclusions in the Penguin series (no. 23 in that history-making list); it is in Dent's Everyman and in 1964 was included in the Oxford World's Classics.

3. See the series of articles by M. Chaikin, in particular '*A Mummer's Wife* and Zola' and 'Balzac, Zola and George Moore's *A Drama in Muslin*', *Revue de littérature comparée*, xxxi, 1957, 85–88, and xxix, 1955, 540–3; and Enid Starkie, *From Gautier to Eliot* (1960), pp. 73–77.

the desolate beauty of the Mayo plain. More evocative than Lissadell even, the ruin would be a perfect setting for the performance of Yeats's greatest ghost-play, but *A Mummer's Wife* is a strange, hot, and alien book to have been composed in so silent a place. The contrast suggests Moore's perverse or virtuoso determination to turn himself into a European (that is to say, a Zolaesque) novelist by fleeing as far as possible from the natural source of his art. Yet the novel itself is not weak from flight but vigorous with ambition. It is a study in the corruption of a conscience inherited from the community and the ruin of the individual who embodies it. Kate Ede, married to a pathetic, shop-bound husband crippled by asthma, runs in association with her husband and his mother a dressmaker's business in Hanley in the Potteries. A liaison with her lodger, Dick Lennox, the manager of a company of actors touring the industrial North, is followed by an elopement. Kate, who is discovered to possess a good singing voice, joins the company and becomes one of its stars. As its fortunes fail in strike-bound towns, her Bovaryesque nature (her soul rises to her lips at a sentimental word and her eyes become 'liquid with love') grows sour with jealousy. The strain of a life that is no longer rooted in one narrow place is hard for her to endure; almost insensibly she begins the slide into alcoholism. The real disaster is the loss of her baby, who dies of cold in her cradle because Kate is in a brandy daze. Her new husband Lennox is, after his fashion, loyal and kind, but his habits, social and sexual, even his table-manners, are not those of Hanley, and he cannot check her insane bouts of jealous violence, which are compounded by drink and unemployability. The last third of the novel is set in London where 'Sentimental Kate', as the prostitutes call her, finally dies of drink and exhaustion.

The apparent contradiction in this story is: how could anyone on whom Bohemianism (as it is frequently called, in the manner of the times) has such a destructive effect have brought herself to leave the narrow path of provincial virtue? As becomes a realist, Moore is volubly anxious to tag every effect with its cause (an anxiety which notably diminishes in the revised version), and the problem gives him a great deal of difficulty. In scene after scene in the first half of the novel we are offered a heroine whose behaviour does not make sense to herself (p.

145),[4] who is disgusted by the animality of the theatrical life and yet enthralled by its sensual melodies (p. 153), who longs to escape from Hanley as a 'horrible place' and yet can't help regarding it as home (pp. 158-9), who hates the present and fears the future (pp. 162 ff.). Moore has to create a character who is to break free from seven years of conditioning (her marriage to Ralph Ede and the dreary mother-in-law whose own conscience enacts itself in her inhibitory cry of 'I'm a Christian woman') and yet to prove unable to adapt herself to her new life precisely because that conditioning has been so thorough. Moore's solution seems to be to stress not so much the passion for Dick Lennox as the sentimentality which earns Kate her sobriquet from the whores: her tendency to abandon herself to slack-bodied and indiscriminate reverie (pp. 29 ff., 59 ff.) even, or especially, in church (pp. 109 ff.). There is a long passage at the beginning of chapter viii in the unrevised version—it was later much reduced—which describes her return to the senti-mental literature of her girlhood before she married Ralph Ede. In the face of the new horizon of experience opening before her in her liaison with the actor, Kate's impulse is to *go back*, and this is in character. She drifts, as it were, through the narrow barriers of her religion and conditioning 'without internal struggle or analysis of mind' (p. 111) on a stream of sentiment, reverie, and vague longing for a sweeter life; but when she has dropped below stream from them, those barriers cast a dreadful shadow over all the rest of her journey, which does not, however, change its essential character of self-indulgent drifting.

In the second half of the book Kate at first blooms, for her dream had its element of actuality; but the languorous process by which she has arrived in this new world has its fatal counter-part in her failure to see the life which she now lives as wholly real. There are idyllic breakfasts (pp. 199 ff.) and hazy evenings (pp. 229 ff.) and in the end a disastrously sentimental and dreamy approach to looking after the baby (pp. 319 ff.). Kate, therefore, does not suffer from 'pangs of conscience' in the ordinary sense—'nothing beyond the mechanical conviction that she was a very wicked woman and deserved to be punished' (p. 199). There are other mechanical convictions which count

4. Page references are to the unrevised version. I have used the second edition (1885).

for even less: the actors live by their wits, cheating landladies and defrauding railway companies when they get the chance, and Kate soon ceases to be shocked by this. But if nearly all the 'conventions of her upbringing' drop from her, there is one cluster of inhibitions, that concerned with sexual behaviour, which remains. In choosing it, Moore showed some insight into the pathology of conscience. Kate's inappropriate strait-lacedness, her absurd (in the context) fastidiousness about the 'moral [i.e., the sexual] question', is the tell-tale sign:

> Anecdotes of clever swindles no longer wounded her feelings . . . The middle-class woman, in a word, had disappeared, and the Bohemian taken her place; and had it not been for the anger with which she repulsed all levity of conversation, and the cold way she frowned upon the spicy little stories, the delight of theatrical supper-tables, the closest scrutiny might have failed to find a clue wherewith to trace her back to her origin. But regarding the moral question she seemed to grow daily more severe, and many were the disputes Kate and Dick had on the subject. For the smallest thing said in her presence she would challenge him with not respecting her. (pp. 243–4)[5]

The rest of *A Mummer's Wife* is essentially a study of how this element of her conscience, having bitten too deep, destroys its possessor by assuming the diseased form of jealousy. Kate's nervousness about 'impropriety' perverts into psychotic anxiety about Dick's inevitable (because professional) association with other women: from jealousy to offended *amour propre*, rage, brandy for calm and comfort and dreaming, the death of the baby, the wish to punish herself for that (p. 328)—the sequence is clear and plausible enough. In other ways, Kate's failure is of course a failure to adapt herself to the way she lives now: the collapse of the touring company worries her as it might worry any middle-class, unbohemian wife (p. 290), but it is hardly such worries that are going to destroy her.

This record of the falling to pieces in an alien atmosphere of a piece of 'cheap Tottenham Court Road furniture', as Moore puts it with the studied cruelty of an aesthete or of a practitioner of the scientific novel, has at its heart, therefore, a reversal of the conventional patterns. Consciences such as Kate's neither humanize nor act as the agents for some divine strategy of punishment or reformation. The fault for which Kate suffers is,

5. This passage does not appear in the revised version.

if anything, the wish to be punished. If she disapproves of herself it is not because of rectitude but because of habit—a 'mechanical conviction'—and the obverse of this is her drifting and
dreaming and drinking. These are aspects of a personality which
is habituated to using its dreams to cheat its inhibitions and vice
versa; if this process is identified we can glimpse the coherence
that informs the apparent contradictions of her story.

There is something comically gallant in the spectacle of Moore
returning to his pastoral and lacustrine solitudes in order to
compose a book so foreign in material, if not in final moral
insight, to the manners of County Mayo. But his next novel, *A
Drama in Muslin*, came straight out of the drawing-room and
demesne at Moore Hall. Whatever else it is, this book, as A. N.
Jeffares has sufficiently indicated,[6] is one of the prime documents
of the last phases of Anglo-Irishry, belonging to the group of
which *The Real Charlotte*, some of Yeats's tragic poems, or Lennox Robinson's *The Big House* are worthy members. In his
anxiety to avoid 'telling', and to reduce the elements of hysteria,
melodrama, and sexuality, Moore revised *A Drama in Muslin*
much more destructively than even *A Mummer's Wife*, totally
remaking it in the image of his 1915 self.[7] The effect is to insu-
late nerves which in the earlier version, as in its companion-
piece *Parnell and his Island* (1887), were nakedly and offensively
exposed. The articulations of *Muslin* flow so smoothly as to produce an effect of bonelessness. Its predecessor, without being at
all inefficiently constructed, has raw patches on its surface which
remind us of Moore's need to torment a community that was
still living and blundering on. Another major result of his
excisions is almost to demote Alice Barton from being the central awareness to merely acting as another participant, if the
most important, in its social kaleidoscope.

A Drama in Muslin dramatizes the fortunes of a group of
Galway Ascendancy families during two Dublin Castle seasons.
The family central to the pattern is that of the Bartons of Brookfield, who are Catholics: two daughters, Alice the intellectual
and Olive the prettier of the two, a dominant mother whose
whole life is concentrated on disposing properly of her girls in
the Dublin marriage-market, and a dilettante father who spends

6. *Essays Presented to Amy G. Stock* (ed. R. K. Kaul, 1965), pp. 137–54.
7. See Appendix, pp. 258–60.

his idle, landlordly time in painting large and foolish historical pictures. Their neighbours are the Cullens: Lord Dungory, a perpetual guest at Brookfield, takes refuge there in the ambiguous ministrations of Mrs Barton from the bullying of his two fanatical Protestant daughters. His third daughter, the crippled Cecilia, is Alice Barton's passionately attached friend. Then there are the Scullys, who are despised because their forebears kept a grocer's shop in Gort. The son, Fred, is a horse-riding lout of the kind described in *Parnell and his Island*, while the daughter, Violet, is Olive Barton's chief competitor in the marriage-stakes, especially for the person and fortune of the 'little Marquis', Lord Kilcarney. Olive romps affectionately with another 'hard-riding country gentleman', Captain Edward Hibbert; but he has no money, is compromised with a mistress, and is soon ordered out of the house by Mrs Barton. After five months in a countryside shaken by the Land League campaign, these groups and one or two others go up to Dublin for the season. Here Alice Barton encounters an English intellectual or 'literary shopboy', John Harding, who encourages her attempts to write. She learns to know her own mind better and to detach herself from an Ireland that continually enforces a painful contrast between the peasant's cabin and the big house, Dublin Castle and the Dublin slums. Her emancipation is signalized especially in the episode towards the end of the novel when she rescues her old schoolfellow May Gould from despair after she has become pregnant by Fred Scully and secretly helps her through her confinement with money which she has earned from writing stories for magazines. In her own sister she has an example of the harm wrought by the communal conscience and its institutions (such as the marriage-market): for Olive, after losing Lord Kilcarney to Violet Scully despite Mrs Barton's frantic campaigns on her daughter's behalf, tries to elope with Captain Hibbert, is stopped by his mistress, and, after a serious illness, ends the book still on the market. Alice herself, in the face of her mother's bitter enmity, marries the unpretentious English doctor who attends Olive; as they leave Ireland for Kensington their last sight of the country is of an eviction accompanied by all the traditional stigmata of brutality (a scene greatly modified in *Muslin*).

Although it is a hundred pages shorter than *A Mummer's Wife*, this novel is a work of greater and more numerous dimensions. In that one of its aspects which is most imperilled by the revision, it deals with the emotional and intellectual growth of Alice, that is to say, with the formation of her personal conscience. This puts it in the same category as other works concerned with a young girl's education, such as *The Tempest*, *Mrs Warren's Profession*, *Saint Joan*, or *Roots*. This conscience is formed chiefly by what it sees, although for the ideas to come to life in confident action it requires the timely catalyst John Harding, who is the one educator who comes from outside to help. Moore does not discipline his own tongue and manages point of view but laxly; yet what Alice sees is more or less the entire contents of the novel, which thus contribute to Alice's slowly accumulating resistance to the values of her society. When we look back from the vantage point of the final chapters we can see that Alice's total repudiation of her milieu is explained by all that has been described in the novel—from Mrs Barton's syrupy manoeuvres to the disastrous tale of Olive, from Cecilia's Lesbian sickness (an education in the horrors of emotional disablement) to May Gould's incurably frivolous femininity (a lesson in woman's underrating of herself). Moore does not need, in the quest for a supposedly scientific explanation of the sort favoured in naturalistic theory, to draw upon half-baked notions, concocted outside the novel, about middle-class womanhood, as he does in *A Mummer's Wife*; instead, he can point to his whole story as the necessary cause of Alice's turning out as she does. Except in its final actions (the secret protection of May Gould, and the open defiance of her mother) Alice's conscience does not simply strive against the communal one—it is educated by it to reject it. In the same way, in the year of *Esther Waters*, Shaw was to make Vivie's role in *Mrs Warren's Profession* one of both repudiating and being educated into awareness by her wicked mother, who is the emblem of the communal conscience as it decays. Vivie and Alice have other things in common. While Vivie is brisk and Alice spiritual and pre-Raphaelite (p. 296),[8] both have a certain aura of coldness. Although her author constantly assures us of the warmth of her temperament and her longing for marriage, Alice's union with the stout Dr Reed and her retreat to a house adorned with yellow porcelain by William Morris is satirically handled in a way that reminds us of Paula

8. My reference is to the unrevised version (1886).

De Stancy's remarks at the end of Hardy's *A Laodicean* as she contemplates a similar fate:

'And be a perfect representative of "the modern spirit"?' she inquired; 'representing neither the senses and understanding, nor the heart and imagination; but what a finished writer calls "the imaginative reason"?'. (*A Laodicean*, reprint, 1926, p. 499)

Alice's is a rescue operation limited to herself; she cannot drag anyone else out of the pit that is Ireland. To this extent her conscientious resistance takes on a probably unintended air of selfishness. Even her work for May Gould does not much modify this; and in the final pages she can offer her sister Olive, who seems virtually broken by her experience, only cold comfort and the promise of a long stay in Kensington.

As we approach the task of setting *Esther Waters* in the light of the other two, it seems that the much greater fame of the third is not easily to be accounted for by proportionate superiorities in construction and style. Here again is a book over which the ruined shell in County Mayo conspicuously broods, for Woodview is plainly Moore Hall transplanted to the Sussex downs. The horse-racing element which centres on Woodview and the King's Head has its counterpart in the *mœurs* depicted in the other novels—play-acting in the industrial North and marrying and giving in marriage amongst the Ascendancy families. The formula is the same: a heroine confronting a destiny affected by a social phenomenon of a fairly recondite sort. *Esther Waters* disturbs us much less than the others with passages which are coldly assertive or melodramatically crude; but if the revised versions of the first two (which are presumably the ones commonly read, if read at all) were to be compared with the (naturally much less revised) third, it would be hard to prove that the advantage lies with *Esther Waters*, in respect at any rate of quality of composition and texture.

It is only common justice to Moore to observe that he does not resemble those novelists who are the realists' legacy to our own day—those who merely exploit recondite manners for their own sake, contentedly furnishing them with character stereotypes in order to convert what is really history or sociology into instant fiction. Here, if anywhere, the advantage lies with the first two books. There is much in the King's Head betting

scenes and the famous study of Derby Day that looks like
ballast, whereas in *A Drama in Muslin*, as we have seen, Moore
has contrived that everything that he shows us constitutes in
the end the substance of the 'ideas' by which Alice acts and
judges. In *A Mummer's Wife*, despite the Zolaesque high relief
in which much of the detail is drawn, there is surprisingly little
feeling that the characters are merely stalking-horses for the
manners. Though Moore may think of his characters as typical
and sometimes lectures us on the middle-class woman and
similar topics with the prescribed objectivity, their social roles
are countervailed by their individualities. The individualities do
not range very widely. There is a Moore's heroine of whom Kate,
Alice, and Esther are only avatars. But this heroine, although
partly begotten by Moore's French masters, is an invention and
not just a stereotype.

Moore also seems from the first to have been accomplished
at *pace*, at the achievement of a large and satisfying movement,
or rhythm, through his books. They conform at least to his own
criteria, formulated about this time, for the 'avoidance of any
disruptive sense of finality at the end of each episode or chapter'
and for 'rhythmical progression of events, rhythm and inevit-
ableness (two words for one and the same thing)'.[9] Rhythm
entails iterative devices, a trick Moore often overworked (as in
the numerous, repetitive descriptions, many of them excised
for *Muslin*, of Mrs Barton's appearance and gestures); but
Esther's recurrent mental images of the racehorses at Woodview, or the stress in *A Mummer's Wife* on Dick's gluttony, are
more successful examples. Rhythm also entails the reader's
being carried forward through a larger movement, and here
Moore's continuities of story help. We are kept always at
Kate's elbow, and, although her story covers four years, there
are no apparent breaks in it; Esther's lasts eighteen, and the
same techniques are used. In *A Drama in Muslin* we note (more
clearly than in *A Mummer's Wife*) the device of a central turning-
point or watershed that is to be used also in *Esther Waters*.
This occurs when the family groups go up to Dublin for the
Lord Lieutenant's season, when Alice meets Harding, her sister
fails with Kilcarney, and the lavish colours and contrasts of life

9. Quoted in Kenneth Graham, *English Criticism of the Novel 1865–1900* (1965),
p. 118.

in Dublin are shaped against the country scenes that precede and follow (in both books there is a deliberate rhythmic and symbolic interplay between town and country). In *Esther Waters* the novel reaches its crest when, after William's and Esther's chance meeting in London, Esther finally takes her decision to throw in her lot with her old lover and not with Fred Parsons, and changes from a servant-girl into a publican's wife.

The final maturity of this heroine's 'idea' is, however, given expression in a later colloquy with Fred:

'You used to be a good religious woman. Do you remember how we used to speak when we used to go for walks together, when you were in service in the Avondale Road? I remember you agreeing with me that much good could be done by those who were determined to do it. You seem to have changed very much since those days.'

For a moment Esther seemed affected by these remembrances. Then she said in a low musical voice—

'No, I've not changed, Fred, but things has turned out different. One doesn't do the good that one would like to in the world; one has to do the good that comes to one to do. I've my husband and my boy to look to. Them's my good. At least that's how I sees things.'[1]

'Them's my good' is one of those crystallizing moments, like 'Nelly, I *am* Heathcliff' or Madame Merle's 'Everything!', that the novel achieves less frequently than Elizabethan drama. It deserves to be written in the forefront of any criticism of *Esther Waters*, although its effects are perhaps muffled, as are many things in *Esther Waters*, by Moore's somehow unconvincing attempts at English demotic. This affirmation of the personal conscience is echoed in the structure of the book, which might otherwise be mistaken for an example of the moral duality which Brian Nicholas thinks it is.[2]

1. p. 289; references are to the unrevised (1894) edition of *Esther Waters*.
2. Nicholas's severe account (chap. iv of Ian Gregor and Brian Nicholas, *The Moral and the Story*, 1962), is the most important critique of *Esther Waters* known to me. A good deal of it is unarguable, but, if I understand it rightly, it appears to derive from three main ideas which do not seem to be fully supported by the text as I read it:

(i) That there is an 'extreme contrast between [Esther's] known character and [her] behaviour'. Esther's is a divided self at the beginning of the book, not unlike Kate Ede's. She is a good, 'religious' girl but at the same time a Moore heroine with a strongly sensual side, a sensuous feeling for the world around her, and a fiery temper. There is more than one passage which tries to realize Esther's feeling

Esther does at first seem paradoxical enough. Her character combines puritanism with a vivid responsiveness to nature and man and a fiery *amour propre*. After her child is born, the book sets her on the lowest rung of her community, in a posture of perpetual struggle against the selfishness and lack of conscience of those above her, employers, baby-farmer, and the rest. Her own fiery moral sense, which is never primarily abstract but directly expressed in her cherishing of Jackie against all the odds, is seen in her actions on his behalf and in an occasional outburst:

> Two innocent children murdered so that a rich woman's child may be brought up. I'm not afraid of saying it, it's the truth; I'd like every one to know it. (p. 142)

---

for 'Aprille with his shoures soote' (eg, pp. 31 ff., the opening of chap. vi). 'Above [her] Protestantism', says Moore, 'was human nature.' This *double* self is her 'known character'. Her puritanism is therefore, for good characterological reasons, in abeyance when William seduces her; but the episode brings it out again overwhelmingly, together with her capacity for sullen fury (p. 71). She recovers from this, but remains extraordinarily scrupulous about admitting responsibility (p. 84) and at the same time is in love with William (p. 73). None of this is especially paradoxical or extraordinary.

(ii) That Esther is represented as both a victor over life and a victim of it, and is therefore a psychological illogicality. It is true that Esther displays a strong will and purpose and at the same time has a tendency to claim at crises that 'life' is too much for her. For Nicholas, it is chiefly this, if I understand him rightly, that vitiates the scenes in which she chooses William instead of Fred. He appears to exaggerate here: for example, the passage which he quotes on p. 105 shows Esther worrying about the danger of Fred encountering William and cursing her rotten luck at the possible upset to her plans for a life with Fred: she is not excusing herself for yielding, as life's victim, to William once more because she is at this point in time quite determined to have Fred. It seems doubtful if Esther's practice of saying that life's too much for her (when in another sense it obviously isn't) is more than an idiom or characterizing device—'What rotten luck I have!' It is of course the case that Esther, in eventually choosing William, is actuated by a mixture of rational prudential motives and irrational ones; she asks herself what is best for Jackie while at the same time experiencing her old sensations about William. Any bit of the dialogue with Fred (pp. 228–31) shows the two sets of motives at work in a way that reads like a convincing transcript of muddle and strain. Anyone who acts and talks in this way could be said both to choose and to succumb—but not in Esther's case to an external blameable 'life' (though she often complains of this) so much as to a rooted predilection (as the story insists) springing out of a part of her nature.

(iii) That Moore presents Esther's religious principles as the source and sign of her virtue, or integrity, the true self which gives her ultimate validity as a pure woman and virtuous sufferer, and relies on this continued presentation in the hope that the reader will continue to take her virtue for granted despite her readiness to compromise (eg, with racing, pubs, and sex). As I have tried to indicate below (pp. 256–7), the sense of Esther's integrity is, I think, mediated to us in quite a different way.

When she does attain a kind of equilibrium with Fred and Miss Rice, chance unbalances it[3] (the accidental meeting with William). Her decision to go to William emerges out of a muddle of motives, some rational, some purely affective; it is by no means certain whether Jackie's welfare is any more important than what Nature, through its various avatars, whispers to the suffering Esther. Once she has joined William at the King's Head, Esther's posture towards her social milieu—the pub, the racecourse, Soho—becomes one of acquiescence instead of resistance. She makes an occasional protest and an occasional prayer, in character, just as her counterpart Mrs Barfield once did down at Woodview, but 'them's my good' does become her guide in everything.

'Them's my good'—this is the clear and inflexible moral sense, the conscience which inspires Esther's actions. Although her attitudes to society (both that part of it which is deeply implicated with her own religion and the hostile ranks of the proud and careless) shift about, there is no inconsistency in her motives. She takes whatever action she deems must be, in order to accomplish an objective which is always the same. There is no split in Esther between her idea and her deed. Wrong is what may harm her good; she is resolute enough never to *do* anything which she *thinks* wrong. Because 'them's my good' comes completely to override the conventions of her upbringing—her religious faith and duties—it is the very consistency of the motive that is pointed by the two conflicting postures of resistance and acquiescence. The means alter, but the end remains the same. It is not Esther's business to struggle against her society for the sake of her principles of religion; she does so only when 'them's my good' requires it. And when 'them's my good' so prescribes it is her business to compromise with those very principles which, measuring her society, tell her it is wicked and should be resisted. Esther must be one of the first characters in fiction to make so clearly Huck's choice—to put friends first and 'virtue' second. That this choice has incremental gifts of the spirit for the chooser is suggested perhaps by the otherwise over-long case of Sarah Tucker at the end of the King's Head portion—Esther's

3. Moore's willingness to admit chance may have been one of the features that distinguish his work from pure naturalistic theory: see William Newton, 'Chance as employed by Hardy and the naturalists', *Philological Quarterly*, xxx, 1951, 154–75.

charity begins to extend its range, just as that of the 'Saint' enfolded all in her besotted house. It is the actions that follow from this choice that do of course in the eyes of most readers constitute Esther's virtue, although they might commonly choose a less regal word, such as integrity. The novel is none the less a mighty quibble on the idea of virtue as defined by Esther's puritanism and as defined by some term such as Wordsworth's 'strength of love'.

Esther Waters may be marginally a better work of art than *A Mummer's Wife* or *A Drama in Muslin*. But the margin would be established on rather negative grounds; most of these Moore wiped away when, in revising the first two novels, he reduced the number of brash lecturettes and toned down the over-explicit. Even so, it seems likely that *A Drama in Muslin*, at least, would have done better if it had been left alone. The notion that Moore greatly improved the actual texture of his work, his style of writing, by his frequent recasting of sentences and rewording does not survive a thorough comparison of the various versions—the process was not radical enough for that, and may be best summed up as a mild, schoolmasterly attention to mistakes and inelegancies in the originals rather than to the imposition of the freshly woven (and altogether later) manner.

Perhaps the criticism of fiction will be able to evolve absolutely convincing techniques for demonstrating that *Esther Waters* deserves its pre-eminence just as much as the other two merit the relative oblivion to which they have been consigned. It does not appear to have done so yet. No doubt the reflex actions of the publishing business may account for much—a book once singled out tends to retain its place. It is even possible that, for a majority of those readers who can take a realist novel any way, one about London and Epsom seems necessarily more real than one about Galway and Dublin or Hanley and Blackpool. The factors are external and social rather than autonomous and internal. Is it, then, much too rough to say that *Esther Waters* is a world classic primarily because its heroine seems to us so much nicer than Kate Ede or Alice Barton? Esther acts nobly, as we think, Kate ignobly, and Alice merely sensibly. It is not possible to withhold approval from the strength of love when it is expressed in the mother's determination to save the child or the wife's loyalty to the ailing husband. Approval is very easily transferred from the fictive being to the fiction itself. There is no other literary genre where it is so easy to control our approach to the artefact by manipulating our attitudes to the behaviour of the artificial character. It is the novel's privilege, or burden, that it will very often be singled out for popular approval in proportion to the liking accorded to its *personae*. The happy ending is not important in itself but only as a corollary of this.[4]

In writing *Esther Waters* Moore set out to enlarge his audience after he had been brought low by several failures.[5] Although he agreed that the novel had assured his reputation for his lifetime, he was full of doubt in later years. He is reported to have said that *Esther Waters* radiated goodness and had 'done more good than any novel in my generation'; at other times he claimed to regard it as 'worthless', a 'bad' book. A moral and social 'good' and a literary-critical 'bad' are involved here. In his usual frivolous way Moore was putting a perfectly sober question to his posterity.

Appendix

Muslin and *A Drama in Muslin*

A note on the revision

1. The part of Alice is very considerably reduced. In every contact which she makes with other characters there is a tendency to diminish the depths, variety, and intensity of the relationship. (My page references are to the Vizetelly 1st edition of *A Drama in Muslin*, London, 1886.) Thus in the description of the first night at Brookfield, Alice's long reverie at the end of chapter ii (pp. 30 ff.) and the description of the contrasts in the room shared by the two sisters disappear; the contrast between Olive and Alice is consequently underplayed, and this contrast is generally less explicit in the 1915 version. Similarly, Alice's

---

4. Herbert Howarth is the only writer I have come across who considers that the ending of *Esther Waters* is an unhappy one, 'a story of pointless courage and devotion': see *The Irish Writers 1880–1940* (1958), pp. 46–47. Probably the determination of readers and critics that fictive personages whom they admire should end happily has led them to overlook the many clues that give a very gloomy and foreboding character to the last pages of the book: see, for example, Graham Hough's reading, introduction to the World's Classics edition (1964), p. xi.

5. See Malcolm Brown *George Moore: A Reconsideration* (1955), pp. 127 ff.

relationship with John Harding is greatly reduced (pp. 145 ff., 196 ff.). Alice's isolation and difference from her family get less emphasis, and especially diminished is her half-successful understanding of her father (pp. 38 ff.). The most dramatic reduction of this kind is in her friendship with Cecilia, from which the explicit note of sexual repression on Cecilia's part virtually disappears; this entails, amongst many minor tonings-down, the removal of a whole chapter of Cecilia's passionate distraction (book III, chap. vi). Many of Alice's reflections on her experiences and on life in general vanish. She no lónger reads Scott or compares herself to Amy Robsart (p. 53); the development of her religious scepticism is much less starkly described (pp. 66–67), her hostile meditations on the Catholic ceremony of the Mass disappear (p. 70)—indeed, the whole scale of the church-going episode is altered, as are many of those involving Irish manners. The intensity of her feelings after the ball in chapter vi of book I goes, as do her loneliness and despair (pp. 203 ff.), her writings, her room and books (pp. 255 ff.), her resentment over her own spinsterish state after the May Gould episode (p. 263), her feelings after Dr Reed proposes (p. 312). The result of all this is virtually to demote Alice from being the consciousness that broods over the novel, in both its aspects as a family story and an account of Ireland in the 1880s.

2. Moore obviously desires to reduce the element of hysteria and melodrama and baleful political anger. Often in *A Drama in Muslin* he goes over the edge into the ridiculous in his attempts to describe intense feelings—not only those of Alice, but also of Cecilia. A striking example here is the complete excision of the meditations of the Marquis of Kilcarney (pp. 217–20) as he wanders through the streets of Dublin. No doubt another motive, apart from removing a passage of high excess, was the wish to avoid giving undue emphasis to a minor character. Much of the content of Kilcarney's meditations is political, and this connects with another major feature of the revision.

3. After the reduction of Alice Barton the most striking series of cuts affects the rendering of political and social conditions in Galway and Dublin. These are far less vividly rendered in *Muslin* and there seems little doubt that the removal or drastic modification of many passages of this sort constitutes a major loss to the novel. Thus the vivid contrast between the 'big

house' life and the barren countryside (p. 51) is lost; the stress on the squalor of the peasantry during the church-going episode (and Alice's sympathetic reaction) is greatly weakened (pp. 70 ff.); more suitable for excision was the description of Land League troubles and the Irish scene (pp. 94–102, the biggest cut of all except for the removal of book III, chap. vi), which, unlike the scene in the chapel, is little more than rather inert journalism. There are big cuts in the description of social life in Dublin (pp. 156 ff.), its poverty and ignorance and the shallowness of its tea-party view of political crisis; the well-known description of the aspect of the slums as seen by the Lord Lieutenant's guests proceeding in their carriages to the Castle is greatly modified; a long passage on the state of Ireland mixed up with the excitement aroused in ascendancy circles by Violet Scully's impending marriage (pp. 264 ff.) is cut out and, as has already been mentioned, the eviction which Alice and Dr Reed encounter as they leave Ireland is much cut and altered (pp. 322 ff.).

4. This by no means exhausts the tale of revision. For example, Mrs Barton is throughout much rehandled, and when she is first introduced the cuts in the presentation of her (pp. 22 ff.) give a probably unintended prominence to Lord Dungory. Moore tried to 'tell' less by making many reductions in his renderings of settings, landscape, rooms, and so on. There is some rewriting and rearrangement of whole scenes (for example, the picnic, the eviction), but on the whole Moore's chief activity in 1915 was large-scale reducing and minor rewording. Of 343 pages in the 1915 *Muslin*, only 93 pages have escaped unaltered from *A Drama in Muslin*.

15

Master and pupil
in Bernard Shaw

I

Because they make up a sort of diapason, I have chosen four of Shaw's plays, *Caesar and Cleopatra* (1898), *Major Barbara* (1905), *Pygmalion* (1912), and *Heartbreak House* (1913–16) to illustrate Shaw's uses of the relationship between master and pupil. I am interested in the formal implications, the contribution it makes to the fashioning of Shaw's kind of comedy, as much as in the way the subject expresses and clarifies Shaw's ideas about life and history.

Shaw is not the only dramatist to use it. Two important specimens from either end of the time-spectrum are Shakespeare's *Tempest* and Wesker's *Roots*. In both these, and in all the Shaw plays, the pupil is a young girl and the master a somewhat older man. Shaw resembles Shakespeare in that, in all the examples that I am going to discuss, the master has mysterious powers and is isolated from his society; there is also an absence of any sexual bond between the couple.

They could be called the Prospero and Miranda figures; but I shall call them instead the Cheiron and the Epigone. Cheiron, it will be recalled, was the kindly centaur (differing from the other brutish members of his species) whose pupils in his cave on Mount Pelion included the physician Aesculapius, the culture-bearer Jason, and the hero Achilles. The other centaurs were ill-conditioned mountaineers, but Cheiron was accomplished in music and medicine. Finally, having been accidentally wounded by one of Hercules' poisoned arrows, he was unable to die, despite his pain, until he had given up his immortality to Prometheus, an arrangement retrospectively approved by Zeus. The other centaurs were the offspring of Ixion's vain embracements

First published in *Essays in Criticism*, xix, 1969, 118–39.

of Cloud; but Cheiron was the son of a nymph ravished by Cronos in the form of a horse.

II

There are three key sentences in the Ra Prologue of _Caesar and Cleopatra_ (which was written in 1912, long after the rest of the play). The first is: 'The minds of the Romans remained the same size whilst their dominion spread over the earth.' This is an underlying assumption throughout. The Egyptians are children, but the Romans themselves are not much better. In human stature Caesar is as far removed from his own Romans as the Romans, compared with the Egyptians, appear disciplined, courageous, rational, and efficient. The collision between Eastern and Western cultures is used only to isolate Caesar and to exalt him above them both.

The second key sentence is: '. . . Men twenty centuries ago were already just such as you [the modern audience], and spoke and lived as ye speak and live, no worse and no better, no wiser and no sillier.' Martin Meisel, in his excellent book on _Shaw and the Nineteenth-Century Theater_ (1963), has pointed out how Shaw deliberately introduces into his history plays reminders of his own time; this is his way of enacting the permanency of the issues. His chief stylistic method for reminding us is wittily to clash elevated diction against modern idiom. A tiny example:

Who pronounces the name of Ftatateeta, the Queen's chief nurse?
Nobody can pronounce it, Tota, except yourself.

There are several sorts of diction in the play, often used more subtly than this. Shaw believes, with Scott and most great composers of historical fictions, that history will give up its 'lessons' only after it has been embodied in a contemporary grammar. Shaw, therefore, as Eric Bentley says, when it comes to exactitude in the representation of the past, 'retains his right to be absurd in everything except psychology'.

The third key sentence is: 'It is in the nature of a god to struggle for ever with the dust and the darkness, and to drag from them, by the force of his longing for the divine, more life and more light.' Caesar assumes the role of a god in history; he is a saviour and light-bearer. He is contrasted with the cruel, evil, and childish divinities that throng the play. Much of its poetic value comes from this contrast. For the Egyptians, the gods are animals and playthings ('a dear little kitten of a Sphinx'), or ministers of private vengeance and superstition; but Caesar says to the Sphinx at the beginning of the play: 'I am he of whose genius you are the symbol: part brute, part woman, and part god.'

Caesar is a Cheiron figure partly because he is isolated. There is a great deal of imagery at the beginning centred on animal gods and personages descended from animals. Even the voice of the Roman army seems to make a noise which is compared to the 'bellow of a Minotaur', a 'terrible bellowing note'. In this kingdom where gross darkness covers the people, a place where humanity has not yet acquired its proper shape, and Caesar himself is thought of by its cat-queen as a monster out of a fairy-tale ('His father was a tiger and his mother a burning mountain; and his nose is like an elephant's trunk'), he begins his task of 'making a woman' out of her. He must assume at first a 'sorcerer's' role:

Cleopatra [*trembling*]. And will he eat *me*?
Caesar. Yes; unless you make him believe that you are a woman.
Cleopatra. Oh, you must get a sorcerer to make a woman of me. Are you a sorcerer?
Caesar. Perhaps. But it will take a long time; and this very night you must stand face to face with Caesar in the palace of your fathers. (p. 259)[1]

He turns her into enough of a 'woman' and a 'queen' for her to be able to face Caesar from her throne at the end of the act. But who is 'Caesar'? Caesar is of course himself. This is an agreeable *coup de théâtre*; but it also has its importance as a paradigm: the educator's first task is to protect his pupil against himself: the true Cheiron does not wish the Epigone to reproduce his own monstrous form but to find her own form.

The first act achieves chiefly a strong poetical resonance. What it leaves us with is the parable of the Cheiron, whose own nature is ambiguous and frightening, beginning his luci-ferent task in a darkness inhabited by animal-gods and the mysterious voices of Minotaur and Sphinx. As the darkness fades and the shapes become clearer, the daylight part of the

1. All page references are to *The Complete Plays of Bernard Shaw* (London, 1931).

play ensues (though night is to fall once more in the fourth
act); and these processes are paradigmatic also—of the Cheiron
who brings out of darkness the light which may be overwhelmed
again. The first act is amongst the finest of Shaw's scenes of this
poetical kind, and perhaps nothing else in the daylight part of
the play quite lives up to it.

Cleopatra learns her first lesson without too much difficulty:
if she is to be a queen she must no longer permit herself to be
babied and bullied by her servants; but of course she is only a
child still in most matters, as she shows by her many tantrums
and misunderstandings.

During the next two acts Caesar's historical situation and adventures are defined and dramatized, but not much is added
to his relationship with Cleopatra. We see what has happened
to this at the beginning of Act IV, which is much the most important act for my topic. It begins, indeed, with a point or two
about how we learn things, but the passage is also worth quoting
because in it we hear Cleopatra talking unmistakably in the
voice of Caesar:

Cleopatra [*to the old musician*]. I want to learn to play the harp with my
    own hands. Caesar loves music. Can you teach me?
Musician. Assuredly I and no one else can teach the queen. Have I not
    discovered the lost method of the ancient Egyptians, who could
    make a pyramid tremble by touching a bass string? All the other
    teachers are quacks: I have exposed them repeatedly.
Cleopatra. Good: you shall teach me. How long will it take?
Musician. Not very long: only four years. Your Majesty must first be-
    come proficient in the philosophy of Pythagoras.
Cleopatra. Has she [*indicating the slave*] become proficient in the philoso-
    phy of Pythagoras?
Musician. Oh, she is but a slave. She learns as a dog learns.
Cleopatra. Well, then, I will learn as a dog learns; for she plays better
    than you. You shall give me a lesson every day for a fortnight. [*The
    musician hastily scrambles to his feet and bows profoundly.*] After that,
    whenever I strike a false note you shall be flogged; and if I strike so
    many that there is not time to flog you, you shall be thrown into the
    Nile to feed the crocodiles. (p. 282)

As Charmian remarks, 'You try to imitate Caesar in everything.' Cleopatra's demonstrable ability to talk with the voice
of Caesar results from being shut up with him and his Romans

for six months on the besieged island. But it is plain that she has absorbed little of Caesar's spirit, only some of the tricks and shrewdness of the ruler: 'Now that Caesar has made me wise, it is no use my liking or disliking: I do what must be done, and have no time to attend to myself' (p. 284). Yet only a few minutes earlier she had been explaining that she is 'as cruel at heart as my father', but ashamed to admit it. She has learnt enough sense to see that the Egyptians are in Caesar's hands—'And she who is wise enough to know this will reign when Caesar departs.' She is clever enough, therefore, to reject Pothinus's move to invite her to betray Caesar now, but reacts as the cat-queen when Pothinus in his turn betrays her plan to Caesar, and screams to Ftatateeta: 'Strike his life out as I strike his name from your lips. Dash him down from the wall. Break him on the stones. Kill, kill, *kill* him' (p. 288). This is not the voice of Caesar. And it is still not the voice of Caesar even when we remember that Caesar is compromised in the world of gods-like-animals because he is himself the 'slayer of Vercingetorix'. The 'grown-up' Cleopatra who orders the killing of Pothinus, if not in the full sense ineducable, is yet a person who uses the arts of command that she has learnt from Caesar to gratify her unregenerate passions. It is true, after all, that she has learnt 'as a dog learns'. She has become great, or, as Shaw might say, Shakespearian. The rest of the act demonstrates the rest of the deadly little syllogism—Ftatateeta kills Pothinus, the mob rise at the news of his death, Rufio (*a Roman*) cuts Ftatateeta's throat; only Caesar's cool head and military genius save the situation. On the vengeances, Caesar's well-known speech (pp. 291-2) is sufficient comment.

The irony of the play is that it describes merely how Cleopatra grew up into Shakespeare's heroine, awaiting, in the last act, the arrival of Antony. The note of the whole *is* ironic and not tragic, depending on the contrast between what Cleopatra, with Caesar as her teacher, *could* have become and what she does become. Shaw perhaps could never be sufficiently engaged by the imaginative reality of the past to make tragedy out of the ineducability of people such as Cleopatra, although men and nations have paid bitterly enough for it. Caesar himself—the slayer of Vercingetorix—can in his agony just reach something of the tragic note, but Shaw slurs it over, and does not adequately relate the compromised element in Caesar to the ineducable element in Cleopatra. Amongst many other reasons for the predominance of irony over tragedy should be mentioned the marked detachment of Cheiron from Epigone: there is no sexual bond. As Cleopatra says: 'Caesar loves no one . . . *He* has no hatred in him: he makes friends with everyone as he does with dogs and children. His kindness to me is a wonder . . .' And eventually she confesses that she cannot love a god, but prefers Antony. This detachment is to be a mark of all Shaw's treatments of the subject. Eventually one begins to regard the trait with some suspicion. Here, it helps him to avoid anything resembling an air of tragic consequence. The brightness of the play is a 'puritan' brightness: to get involved, to die as Ftatateeta and Pothinus do, is what belongs to the passionate, old-fashioned beings, the Egyptian part, the land of the dark gods. (We know that Cleopatra will die in the 'next' play, the one by Shakespeare.) Of that land Cleopatra remains an inhabitant. Her education has not 'taken', except in a superficial way; but we hardly feel this as a sorrow, though Shaw is doubtless saying that the Caesars can teach their contemporaries nothing (the gods labour in vain amongst us)—a sombre enough generalization, but not really sombrely enacted in the play's personages.

The Cheiron relationship has therefore shaped the play, bringing it from darkness into light and allowing it to curve back towards darkness again. But the last pages of the play only underline the sanative detachment that protects us from the tragedy and the horror. The departing Caesar (who has at first 'forgotten' about Cleopatra) commends the 'natural slaying' of Ftatateeta, but if this is meant to be a last instalment of Cleopatra's lessons, there is no real sign that Caesar wants or expects her to learn it, and it is oddly coupled with his promise to send her a really beautiful present from Rome in the shape of Mark Antony. 'As much a child as ever, Cleopatra! Have I not made a woman of you after all?' (p. 296). The phrase there is steeped in all the irony of which Shaw is capable, totally reductive of great tragedy-queens and immortal lovers.

III

Major Barbara belongs to Shaw's most fruitful period—between *Man and Superman* (1903) and *Pygmalion* (1912). The former is the best of the discussion-plays, the latter the best of the comedies of manners. *Major Barbara* is formally a more ambitious work than *Man and Superman*, but a less perfect one than *Pygmalion*.

In *Caesar and Cleopatra* it would be inaccurate to say that Caesar has any specific lesson to teach. It is what he *is* that counts. One learns from watching the Cheiron figure as he plays out his role as a man of destiny. This is one way of learning, perhaps the most civil, and at any rate the one long favoured as suitable for the education of a gentleman. It is obvious that in any performance of the play a great deal depends upon the quality of life that an actor is able to convey from behind an unassuming appearance (as C. B. Purdom has remarked). But *Major Barbara*, in contrast with this, *has* a definable social and moral doctrine, and it is this rather than the life-quality of the individual that the play attempts to put across.

The doctrine may be extrapolated in this way: man is a creature in society, and you cannot, therefore, save his soul without saving his society. Barbara, who begins the play under the illusion that souls can be saved apart, learns that this is nonsense in the course of it. She is the Epigone, and Andrew Undershaft is the Cheiron figure. We recognize in him some of the traditional stigmata: he is, in Melvillian terminology, an isolato, a foundling (his birth is therefore mysterious), and he is credited with supernatural powers; he is constantly referred to by Cusins, the Professor of Greek (who may be expected to recognize a god when he sees one) as the devil, the Prince of Darkness, demon, and Machiavelli. His relation with his Epigone is warmer than Cheiron's usually is with his pupil:

Cusins. Have you, too, fallen in love with Barbara?
Undershaft. Yes, with a father's love.
Cusins. A father's love for a grown-up daughter is the most dangerous of all infatuations. I apologize for mentioning my own pale, coy, mistrustful fancy in the same breath with it. (p. 479)

But, dangerous though it may be, it is also quite 'safe', with no sex in it in the ordinary sense. Considered only as a variant on the relationship of this father and daughter, Cusins is very interesting. Towards Undershaft himself he certainly plays the part of a second Epigone—he, too, has to learn what Undershaft's power really implies; but, as Barbara's lover he can to some extent mediate between Cheiron and Epigone, and his presence subtly alters the combination. All the rest of the characters in the play are supernumeraries grouped around this 2/1 trio.

The educative process in the play is, much more clearly than in *Caesar and Cleopatra*, a clinical demonstration of the truthfulness of the doctrine being implanted. All the rest of the play is used to set up the right conditions for this demonstration and then, after it is over, to draw the moral from it. The clinical demonstration is the episode, towards the end of the second act, when Undershaft, by giving the £5,000 cheque to the Salvation Army, shows that it is his and Bodger's millions that really have the power, and that they use it for keeping both the souls and the Salvationists at their mercy. It is after this episode that Barbara in despair uses the words of Jesus on the Cross, and discards the uniform of salvation. In order to be educated out of your illusions, you must be broken down in the mould, and recast; it is an Ibsen moment.

Undershaft's motto is repeated many times; he holds fast by it and it will save society and its souls in the end. It is— 'Money and Gunpowder'. This phrase is not easy to get into focus; but in a key-passage it is decoded into plainer language: '. . . money and gunpowder. Freedom and power.' Even this needs some further unfolding: *freedom* means explicitly 'freedom-from-poverty', and, in the scene in the Salvation Army shelter and elsewhere, the play enacts the definition of poverty as the monstrous evil, for both the individual and society, that blocks all the roads to self-realization and salvation.

One of the objections to Shaw's arrangement is that gunpowder is a badly chosen emblem for power, especially since power, as we learn in the course of *Major Barbara*, and especially from the understanding that grows up between Cusins and Undershaft, really means 'power-in-the-hands-of-the-right-people'. The final solution of the problem is Undershaft's: 'Plato says, my friend, that society cannot be saved until either the professors of Greek take to making gunpowder, or else the makers of gunpowder become professors of Greek' (p. 500). But this comes after we have been bewildered for a long time by having our noses rubbed in all the details of the destructiveness and immoralism of the armaments firm, the gunpowder

business. Shaw might have chosen a less distracting emblem
for the power that is to save society by giving it freedom from
poverty. As it is, it is very difficult to apprehend imaginatively
how the qualities that Cusins is going to bring to the gunpowder
business can make any difference to its selfish philanthropy and
cold enlightenment. And this is because Shaw, delighted with
the characterological neatness of his solution, has not himself
troubled to apprehend what really lies beyond it. Shaw and his
audience seem to be trapped together in the theatrical literaliza-
tion of what was only intended to be parabolic, and theatrical
opportunism of various kinds (there is obviously a certain *zing*
about an explosives shed which wouldn't obtain in the case of,
say, a bank) tends to make the central idea—the 'Platonic'
idea—seem false, or unimaginable.

Against this must be set something nearer to my main topic:
the supernumeraries, whom I mentioned earlier only to dismiss.
These—the other members of Undershaft's family—present an
extremely agreeable comic underplot of the ineducable. It is a
brilliant example of Shaw's habit of offering such material in
the form of a witty comment on his major theme. Lady Brito-
mart is a fundamentally helpless old battleaxe who thinks that
society is there to be managed for the sake of herself and her
group; she represents the top people with whom we are so
drearily familiar today, or 'society is there for what I can get out
of it'. Shaw treats her indulgently because he believes that power
has left this group, although in this belief he was unfortunately
mistaken. The scene—extremely amusing and accurate—at
the end of which Undershaft decides that the proper place for
his ineducable son Stephen is employment on a 'high-toned
weekly review', enforces the role of Cheiron as Shaw's mouthpiece; we see that this is a way of describing his customary
relationship with his own audience: he may have believed that
they were all more or less educable, and hoped to teach them
even through his comedies of the ineducable, but the Cheiron
can, like Undershaft, rebuke and scold those whom he despairs
of improving.

IV

I approach *Pygmalion* with anxious respect. It is simply one of the
very greatest of English comedies. The idea is surpassingly

brilliant, its execution superbly theatrical; it is Shaw's most precious gift to the Edwardian middle-class audience, which was the audience to whom he spoke most truly.

The relationship between Cheiron and Epigone is here presented at its fullest and richest. But this fullness and richness offer their own problems of interpretation. Desmond McCarthy's 1914 review of the first English production (with Mrs Patrick Campbell as Liza) asked the right question, though it did not stay to answer it: 'Has it an idea or does it simply bristle?'

The main Cheiron figure need not be laboriously identified. Although he is the progeny of a kind of mother-goddess, considerably wiser than her son, we cannot say that Professor Higgins's birth is exactly mysterious; but he possesses mysterious powers. These are demonstrated in the first act in the form of his seemingly miraculous ability to spot where people come from by analysing their speech. This gives him the essentially Cheironic authority. His casual gifts twice transform the recipients: first, Liza's whole life is changed by his benevolent disposal of excess cash into her flower-basket, and, secondly, Alfred Doolittle's is transformed in a somewhat similar, though less direct manner.

When Liza turns up again in the second act, with the money for her lessons all ready, Higgins takes her on in a quite arbitrary and godlike way, partly as an experiment, partly as a result of his wager with Pickering. There is no need to stress what it is that Shaw exhibits as defective in Higgins's relation with his pupil, for it is quite obvious throughout the whole of the first part of the play, reaching its climax at the end of the fourth act. Absorbed in the technical aspect of the job, Higgins cannot see Eliza as a person at all. It is plain from the beginning, for example, that she has a good deal of pride—possibly misplaced pride, but this hardly matters; she has a sense of what is due to her as a 'pore gel', and a respectable one. Higgins cannot see this pride and continually offends against it; but her pride, and its sullen or fiery expression, are what individuate Liza; Higgins's disregard of it is therefore a sign of his disregard of what she *is*.

That Shaw wants us to be well aware that something is wrong, and that the Cheironic role is itself and for the first time in his plays (since its introduction as far back as *Mrs Warren's Profession*) coming in for internal criticism and modification, is indicated also by the presence of an important variant on the role, which is not to be found in either Caesar's or Undershaft's understanding of it. This is the topic of the educator who is himself educated by, and in the course of, his intercourse with his Epigone. It had not been suggested, by either Caesar or Undershaft, that they have anything to learn themselves: both are bringers of light and sons of Cronos—they can teach, but nobody thinks that they have anything to learn. We would not now regard this as a very enlightened version of the bond between pupil and teacher. In *Pygmalion* Shaw appears to be going in for a substantial change: the notion that every educative process is, or ought to be, a two-way one. When Liza is to live at 27A Wimpole Street, Mrs Pearce, Higgins's housekeeper, tells him that he will have to mend his manners: not come down to breakfast in his dressing-gown any more, and stop swearing in front of Liza. Then, in Act III, his mother tells Higgins that he must start to think seriously about the girl's future and what he is doing to it; but he shrugs off this advice in a way that seems intended to demonstrate his own ineducability. The ineducability of the Cheiron figure himself is a sufficiently startling variant. Thirdly, Colonel Pickering, by the difference in his daily attitudes towards Liza, his courtesy and so on (which she herself comments on), is setting an implicit example to Higgins—which again he disregards. Rightly, all the commentators quote from the conversation in Mrs Higgins's house:

Liza. . . . You never took off your boots in the dining room when I was there.
Pickering. You mustn't mind that. Higgins takes off his boots all over the place.
Liza. I know. I am not blaming him. It is his way, isn't it? But it made *such* a difference to me that you didn't do it. You see, really and truly, apart from the things anyone can pick up (the dressing and the proper way of speaking, and so on), the difference between a lady and a flower girl is not how she behaves, but how she's treated. I shall always be a flower girl to Professor Higgins, because he always treats me as a flower girl, and always will; but I know I can be a lady to you because you always treat me as a lady, and always will. (pp. 746–7)

Higgins, preoccupied with 'the things that anyone can pick up' (emphatically *not* the kinds of thing taught by Caesar or Undershaft, or even by Mrs Warren), is deliberately presented

as offering a very narrow version of the Cheiron/Epigone relationship. One might expect that the dialectic of the drama would
proceed towards showing us how Higgins will manoeuvre himself out of this restricted condition into a more noble one. But
is this at all what happens in *Pygmalion*?

I think not; for in the fifth act Shaw puts up a barrier across
the road into which his play seems to be moving in the fourth
act.

Before that fifth act is reached, he has deliberately surrounded
his Cheiron figure with characters who are wiser than he is,
who see deeper into the relationship with the Epigone than he
sees himself, and who know in general much more than he does
about making a woman of somebody. Alfred Doolittle himself
belongs to this select band, which, though select, comprises all
the other major characters in the play. The Epigone herself
takes a hand in this process. She makes several attempts to *get
through* to Higgins, to *make* him see her as a person in her own
right; and it looks as though she may have succeeded at the end
of the fourth act. He is, according to successive stage-directions
(p. 741), *shocked and hurt, deeply wounded, very sulky*, and when he
dashes the ring in the fireplace:

Liza. . . . Don't you hit me.
Higgins. Hit you! You infamous creature, how dare you accuse me of
  such a thing? It is you who have hit me. You have wounded me to the
  heart. (p. 742)

The phrases and the behaviour are still ambiguous; Higgins
has certainly (as he admits) lost his temper, but 'You have
wounded me to the heart' and the other exaggerated gestures
and excess of rhetoric that he goes in for, during the short
remainder of the scene, perhaps conceal as much as they reveal;
Shaw is already beginning to cover his tracks. None the less, the
episode does justify the silent pantomime of triumph by Liza
on which the act-curtain descends. We realize that we have for a
long time been trembling on the edge of a reversal of the roles;
that it is, after all, Higgins who may be the Epigone and Liza
the Cheiron. The possibility accounts for the richness (up to this
point) of *Pygmalion*, compared with the other plays I have discussed. Here, our central ideas about the disposition of the main

characters are Shavianistically open-ended and reversible. And, at the least, the Cheiron is a figure having an ironic element in his substance—an element which, in the case of both Caesar and Undershaft, is much more externally applied. Caesar and Undershaft are both made fun of, rather as Mr Pickwick is, but their basic authority is never questioned; Higgins's is.

But then Shaw seems to backtrack. For Higgins really to see Liza as a person, or to continue to do so (if it is true that he has already begun), and thus for Higgins to be educated himself, would have entailed a breach of the normal postulates of the Cheiron/Epigone relationship. And the simplest way to breach them in this particular case would have been to show Higgins genuinely falling in love with Liza. This is what everybody expects and longs for, and what Shaw ultimately permitted in the film version of the play. This would also have earned him the approval of those who speak of the education of the heart. Yet Shaw will not do it. He seems suddenly to raise across the path the most privative (for a comic dramatist) of the old defining elements: between Cheiron and Epigone there can be no sexual bond.

Before we criticize Shaw for not bringing the educational process to the ultimate point of being concluded in bed, we can look at what actually happens in the fifth act. It is very hard to take a great deal of what Higgins says seriously, yet Shaw appears to want us to: the fresh-air hot gospelling, the caring for 'life and humanity', the appeal to 'good fellowship' (p. 749), when balanced against Liza's 'every girl has a right to be loved' and 'I only want to be natural', seem to invite a reading heavily charged with sardonic amusement at Higgins's expense— until, that is, they modulate into Higgins's description of the self-indulgent sexual way of life of the 'sentimental hog':

Oh, it's a fine life, the life of the gutter. It's real: it's warm: it's violent: you can feel it through the thickest skin: you can taste and smell it without any training or any work. Not like Science and Literature and Classical Music and Philosophy and Art. You find me cold, unfeeling, selfish, don't you? Very well: be off with you to the sort of people you like. Marry some sentimental hog or other with lots of money, and a thick pair of lips to kiss you with and a thick pair of boots to kick you with. If you can't appreciate what you've got, you'd better get what you can appreciate. (p. 750)

There are no ironic reservations about *that* passage; down to the capital letters it appears to be served to us straight. While not directly addressing itself to the possibility and expectation that Liza and Higgins might become lovers, its force and the emotion packed into it may be accounted for by its being a charge expressly designed to blow that possibility and expectation sky-high. Liza says that it is the speech of a tyrant and a bully, and from thinking that she has no resources left soars inexplicably into independence and defiance. The discovery that she can sell Higgins's secrets to his rival—another comic Professor of Phonetics—and so live, is a bit of comic fudging, not an honest teasing-out of growth and motivation. But it serves, because we now explicitly recognize what we have really known all along, that Liza does not *need* growth to 'make a woman' of herself; her pride and self-reliance have always been her individuating mark: the girl who now defies Higgins is in all essentials the same girl who knew her rights in the portico in the rain at Covent Garden and who came along to Wimpole Street with the money to 'make a lady' of herself. In this sense Liza hangs together; but what of Higgins?

Liza's 'strong' speech is given to us so that Higgins may have his 'triumph' too:

Liza. . . . Oh, when I think of myself crawling under your feet and being trampled on and called names, when all the time I had only to lift up my finger to be as good as you, I could just kick myself.

Higgins [*wondering at her*]. You damned impudent slut, you! But it's better than snivelling; better than fetching slippers and finding spectacles, isn't it? [*Rising.*] By George, Eliza, I said I'd make a woman of you; and I have. I like you like this.

Liza. Yes: you turn round and make up to me now that I'm not afraid of you, and can do without you.

Higgins. Of course I do, you little fool. Five minutes ago you were like a millstone round my neck. Now you're a tower of strength: a consort battleship. You and I and Pickering will be three old bachelors together instead of only two men and a silly girl. (p. 751)

Much of this rings hollow; the vision of the three old bachelors, the consort battleship, and all the rest, is upsetting. We are in the presence of a Shavian kind of 'sentimentality', which is desperately confirmed by the postlude to the play, in which Shaw writes too innocently of Liza's marriage to Freddy and of

Higgins's attachment to his mother. Shaw's readiness to remove all sexuality from our final view of the relationship between Cheiron and Epigone seems in these pages to become an anxiety.

But the more immediate issue is: How are we to take the terms in which Higgins claims his victory? 'By George, Eliza, I said I'd make a woman of you . . .' It is his biggest claim, and his least well-founded. In the sense of which Higgins is speaking—a woman as someone who stands on her own feet instead of crawling under those of others—it is only partially true. Liza was *never* just a sniveller. The course of the play seems to show that Higgins took an originally independent creature—though perhaps one who was disposed to snivel—and reduced her to a kind of dependence from which she has now unshackled herself by recovering her old spiritedness (to some extent, admittedly, in the process of being made to fight *him*). Higgins's claim is therefore qualified by the irony that arises from our perception of its too bold and rashly comprehensive nature and also by our awareness (which the dictionary confirms) that the phrase 'make a woman' of somebody often has a sexual connotation; and this qualifying is in line with those earlier modifications of the unassailable serenity of the Cheiron figure which specially characterize *Pygmalion*. Yet this effect is oddly muffled and doubtful, simply because there is still so much in Higgins that Shaw wanted us uncritically to underwrite: all that part of his character which culminates in the vision of the three old bachelors. Shaw is using the Cheiron/Epigone relationship in two perhaps incompatible ways: the figure it makes is mocked and qualified and stood on its head—hence the richness of the drama, as compared with those that treat it without irony; but, on the other hand, it is also used as a means of warding off that marriage comedy-ending which seems to stimulate all Shaw's facility for proposing his own 'cold and unfeeling' versions of sentimentality—hence the poverties of *Pygmalion*, the feeling that Shaw, like his protagonist, in the end settles too evasively for the 'things that anyone can pick up'—and indeed for the things that Liza already *has*, as the major concern of Cheiron and Epigone together. He is content that Liza has been made a lady of—or a new woman; which is not quite the same thing as a woman. And this choice is seen without any irony. His willingness to criticize the Cheiron figure is clear, dramatic gain; but his

refusal to alter or extend the terms of the bond looks like timidity. For the 'problem' of *Pygmalion* is in reality as much that of
making a man out of Higgins as of making a woman out of
Liza. It is true, of course, that the sexual life of centaurs is not a
subject for high comedy, and it may well be, since we deal with
the Cheironic version of that sort of comedy, that it is all a self-
indulgence to long for the traditional ending of comedy, which
is marriage. Is this perhaps why Shakespeare was so reticent about
the marriage which may or may not take place at the end of
Measure for Measure?

V

The relationship between Ellie Dunn and Captain Shotover is
the clew or thread through the labyrinth of *Heartbreak House*.
Like all the Epigone figures, and like Miranda herself, Ellie of
course learns not only from her Master himself, but directly
and indirectly from most of the other personages in her play.
But their lives, richly deployed though they are and considerable
as are the parts which they offer to their actors, are all, by the
dramatist, directed towards *her*. Despite the elaborate writing
for the supernumary figures, the play, though it has the superficial appearance of a jigsaw-puzzle in which all the pieces have
much the same value, is essentially the story of Ellie's education.
(C. B. Purdom's idea in *A Guide to the Plays of Bernard Shaw* that
the whole play is Ellie's dream hardly seems to work out, even
if it directs the right amount of attention to her centrality.)
Captain Shotover is clearly identifiable as Cheiron. He is
rumoured to have sold his soul to the devil in Zanzibar, and
is the inventor of mysterious rays and other instruments of
destruction and preservation. His message to cultivated, leisured
England is the very celebrated one that it must learn to navigate.
But his message for the individual, for Ellie, is 'life with a
blessing':

Captain Shotover. I tell you happiness is no good. You can be happy when
    you are only half alive. I am happier now I am half dead than ever
    I was in my prime. But there is no blessing on my happiness.
Ellie [*her face lighting up*]. Life with a blessing! that is what I want. Now
    I know the real reason why I couldn't marry Mr Mangan: there would
    be no blessing on our marriage. There is a blessing on my broken

heart. There is a blessing on your beauty, Hesione. There is a blessing
on your father's spirit. Even on the lies of Marcus there is a blessing;
but on Mr Mangan's money there is none.
Mangan. I don't understand a word of that.
Ellie. Neither do I. But I know it means something. (p. 798)

The last interchange may seem cheap, or it may be taken as a
sign that Shaw knows that he has (unexpectedly) wandered into
the Yeats country. (It is no doubt historically explainable that
he should be using the language of 'A Dialogue of Self and
Soul'.) The passage does 'mean something', for both it and the
scene in which it occurs have their defining antecedent in Captain
Shotover's great speech in the previous act ('. . . I looked for
hardship, danger, horror, and death, that I might feel the life
in me more intensely . . .' [p. 790]). This is Shaw's version of
Yeats's 'fascination of what's difficult'.

Ellie's education up to this point has consisted of a successive
stripping away of the illusions in which she lived cocooned. It
therefore images the procedure to which the cultivated, leisured
classes of Europe must be exposed. This interdependence
accounts for the structural vitality and integrity of *Heartbreak
House*. Both she and they must learn the nature of the world in
which they live. So Ellie Dunn begins, with everything to learn,
in a daydream woven around her by Hector's amorous lies; she
proceeds from that sweet dream to a nightmare of hardheaded
realism by deciding to marry Boss Mangan—a man whose
appearance of solidity is quite phoney—and finally gets closest to
reality—and to imaginative creation—by being able to imagine
a future after the slate is wiped clean. She chooses neither Hector's fairy tales nor Mangan's prose, but Shotover's and Shelley's
poetic vision. In later Shaw to cross all out and begin again is
more and more frequently the ultimate gesture of wisdom. Like
Shotover, she looks for 'hardship, danger, horror, and death',
for the return of the bombers, both as a way of having life more
intensely and as a way of destroying the false gods and mental
cobwebs that block the road to vision. Beyond her now lies
Shaw's lost country, Blake's England, and Bunyan's.

Where so much is conducted inside a metaphor (the house
that is a ship) and by means of a dialectic of metaphors, the
expected bombs are Yeatsian chiefly, as the great stage-curtain
prepares to drop:

Aeroplane and Zeppelin will come out,
Pitch like King Billy bomb-balls in
Until the town lie beaten flat.

It is appropriate to the air of shining apocalypse that Shaw for
once permits his Epigone to marry the Cheiron, again in metaphor:

Ellie. Only half an hour ago I became Captain Shotover's white wife.
Mrs Hushabye. Ellie! What nonsense! Where?
Ellie. In heaven, where all true marriages are made.
Lady Utterwood. Really, Miss Dunn! Really, papa!
Mangan. He told me *I* was too old! And him a mummy!
Hector [*quoting Shelley*]

'Their altar the grassy earth outspread,
And their priest the muttering wind.'

Ellie. Yes: I, Ellie Dunn, give my broken heart and my strong sound soul
to its natural captain, my spiritual husband and second father.
*She draws the Captain's arm through hers, and pats his hand. The Captain
remains fast asleep.* (p. 798)

This innocuous disposition of things is a metaphor for the whole
Cheiron/Epigone idea, as Shaw conceives it, at its most exemplary and successful. Yet one cannot help observing how deftly
the two individuals concerned in it keep each other at arm's
length; Shaw dramatizes this element in the greatest of their
scenes together, when the Captain's attempts to escape to the
rum ('... it's dangerous to keep me ...') are counterparted by
Ellie's willingness to let him lose his hold on reality through its
lack: 'You must never be in the real world when we talk together' (p. 790). The austerity and impersonality are far less
damaging in the case of this play than in that of *Pygmalion*. For
Heartbreak House is all of a piece; it would be as vain to complain
of Ellie's metaphorical marriage as to complain about cultivated
Europe being represented by an eccentric English family living
in a house built to resemble a ship. Yet in this last version of the
theme the same reluctances, though handled with greater art,
are as plain to see as they were in *Pygmalion*.

VI

The ending of all these plays lies with the future and not with
the marriage, which is each time postponed, qualified, or neutra-

lized. Mrs Langer has held that comedy is a symbolic representation of our happiness in feeling that we can master the changes and chances of life. Shaw does not reject some such view of comedy; but he pushes aside what has been its traditional symbol, the ending in marriage, a sign of the continuity and renewal of life. No doubt he does so partly because he thought that this sign had ceased to be effective, because it had become sentimentalized, institutionalized, complacent, or worse. But, like traditional comedies, his comedies do finish up with an attempt to represent and validate the renewal and affirmation of life. For Shaw, this takes the form of a paean to the future, a Shelleyan prophecy—Shelley *was* above all his poet; the decks are cleared, the gear is stowed, the pupil sees at last that there is a harder and more adventurous life ahead; the Professor of Greek chooses the 'way of life' although it runs through the factory of death, Major Barbara is transfigured, Liza is liberated from the past, Ellie from her illusions, there will be 'more life and more light' since all these people have become, not gods-like-animals, but, in Wells's phrase, 'men like gods'. They are ready in their own way to follow the guidance of Ra and the footsteps of Caesar. In *Heartbreak House* the metaphor of the ship-of-state insensibly transforms itself into the Shelleyan image of the soul voyaging like an enchanted boat.

The transfiguration and the paean are essentially the traditional comedy-ending in a somewhat disguised form; they underwrite Shaw's claim to be a writer of classic comedies. At this point in the plays Shaw wanted his characters to appear in a great symbolic attitude, images of those who have learnt that there is, after all, a road out to the way of life, and that, in Major Barbara's words, God's work can be done for its own sake. The learning process and its culmination in a kind of glory, or solitude, of understanding is what supplies the dialectic at least of *Major Barbara* and *Heartbreak House*. So that the image may exist in its self-dependent purity, the marriage is subordinated; and in choosing not to rely on that traditional source of strength, Shaw is consequently driven into dependence upon his own theatrical and rhetorical powers, and must make them carry conviction. One difficulty is that, even in *Major Barbara* and *Heartbreak House*, Shaw's 'poetry' is not quite good enough, although it is true that phrases such as 'Major Barbara will die with the colours' and Ellie's 'I hope so' are more tolerable in their theatrical context than they are out of it. In *Caesar and Cleopatra* and in *Pygmalion*, on the other hand, the considerable ironies that enliven the relationship between master and pupil contribute immensely to its vitality as it is enacted in the course of the plays and it is therefore the vigour of the plays themselves that they finally enhance. But those ironies will be seen to cluster about the phrase 'making a woman' (of somebody), and, in awakening expectations in that region, they will of themselves serve to raise doubts and questions about the reductive way in which Shaw uses the phrase and about whether he oughtn't to have been more generous and traditional in his definitions.

Although the learning process as conducted between Cheiron and Epigone supplies much of the drive of all four plays, it is enough, perhaps (if all the implications are taken into account), to say that in two of the plays the relationship is essentially that of father and daughter (*Major Barbara, Heartbreak House*); this is less subtle, if at times much odder, than what we find in *Caesar and Cleopatra* and *Pygmalion*. There, the ambiguities—which arise from the fact that Caesar *could* be Cleopatra's lover or Higgins Liza's—are enormously enriching, but do not always seem, especially in *Pygmalion*, to be under perfect control.

So at last the diapason breaks up, into smaller units. But what the four plays have in common might hang in the air. I wrote that *Heartbreak House* was a 'last version', but it is by no means the last version of all in Shaw's work as a whole. Indeed the pattern described by it repeatedly offers itself in his life and art and is the clue to some of their unexplored mysteries. The topic is part of a very much larger one: about Shaw as a great creative genius, much neglected by fashion.

Index of titles

The writings of William Butler Yeats

POEMS

COLLECTIONS

General index